"David Wexler adroitly addresses a central problem in male-female relationships, namely the male propensity for emotional withdrawal, sarcasm, humiliation, intimidation, emotional blow-ups, and infidelity. Wonderfully empathic with men's experiences, *When Good Men Behave Badly* helps men who do not wish to behave badly develop the needed emotional skills. This book will open men's minds and hearts to a very different way to approach male-female relationships."

> —Ronald F. Levant, Ed.D., ABPP, Co-Editor,
> *A New Psychology of Men*

when
good men
behave
badly

Change Your Behavior,
Change Your Relationship

DAVID B. WEXLER, PH.D.

New Harbinger Publications, Inc.

Publisher's Note

Excerpts from *Affliction* by Russell Banks, copyright © 1989 by Russell Banks. Reprinted by permission of HarperCollins Publishers Inc.

Excerpts from *Continental Drift* by Russell Banks, copyright © 1985 by Russell Banks. Reprinted by permission of HarperCollins Publishers Inc.

Excerpts from *High Fidelity* by Nick Hornby, copyright © 1995 by Nick Hornby. Used by permission of Riverhead Books, an imprint of Penguin Group (USA) Inc.

Excerpts from *I Know This Much Is True* by Wally Lamb, copyright © 1998 by Wally Lamb. Reprinted by permission of HarperCollins Publishers Inc.

Excerpts from *The Great Santini* by Pat Conroy, copyright © 1976 by Pat Conroy. Reprinted by permission of Houghton Mifflin Company. All rights reserved.

Distributed in Canada by Raincoast Books.

Copyright © 2004 by David B. Wexler
New Harbinger Publications, Inc.
5674 Shattuck Avenue
Oakland, CA 94609

Cover design by Amy Shoup
Edited by Jessica Beebe
Text design by Tracy Marie Carlson

ISBN 1-57224-346-5 Paperback

All Rights Reserved

Printed in the United States of America

New Harbinger Publications' Web site address: www.newharbinger.com

06   05   04

10   9   8   7   6   5   4   3   2   1

First printing

To the future: my daughter, Juliana, and my son, Joseph

Contents

Foreword   vii

Preface   xi

Acknowledgments   xv

1   Good Men and Broken Mirrors   1

2   The Power of Women   19

3   Fathers and Sons: Curses and Blessings   41

4   Midlife, Affairs, and Projections   67

5   Men's Brains   103

6   Odysseus, Relational Heroism, and Imaginary   127
    Crimes

7   Guy Talk   147

8   What Women Can Do   167

    References   191

Foreword

Real men, what David Wexler calls in this important new book "good men," are *not* self-sufficient, narcissistic lone rangers who care for nothing other than satisfying their own needs. Research, clinical study, and personal experience reveal that the vast majority of men are yearning for meaningful, mutual, and lasting connection, but, too often, their inner fears push them to lose these opportunities for genuine relationship or to go astray. If we want more men to become empathic to themselves and others, we must first become empathic to men's emotional pain, in a manner that neither excuses the responsibility for certain "bad" action, nor vilifies a man who is struggling to come out of the emotional cold—back into the fold of human connection and kindness—after he slips from grace.

When Good Men Behave Badly strikes exactly the correct balance between understanding men's issues with relationships in psychological depth and providing clear and pragmatic behavioral suggestions for improving their capacity for intimacy. It utilizes many men's proclivity for "action plans," rather than just words, in a positive and productive manner, by giving them and their loved ones creative strategies for how to improve how men think, feel, and behave in the midst of a relationship. The book neither excuses the common faults or "bad" acts that basically decent men may fall prey to, nor castigates men, many of whom are struggling with inner demons from their long forgotten pasts. Such struggles can lead to the hurtful behavior in intimate partnerships which, in turn, unwittingly causes "relational" pain—not only for these men's loved ones, but for the men themselves.

David Wexler takes us on a journey back to men's boyhood, when so many were forced into rigid models of masculine behavior that required stoic independence, the avoidance of showing the world their emotional pain, and the need to keep their normal human vulnerability a secret from both their closest loved ones and themselves; all this in order to create and maintain the false facade of a "real boy" or "real man." The emotional straitjackets into which many of today's "good" men were forced as boys were accompanied by a healthy dose of shame, directed toward those who dared to be different. Shame came through teasing and public humiliation; it was deeply embedded and threatened the heart of their self-esteem. Sadly, many boys today are still forced into those same emotional straitjackets. Can we be surprised then that these good men may often behave "badly" in the midst of an intimate relationship of genuine sharing? While such emotional connections are genuinely and deeply longed for, they remain, in the depths of many men's souls, a frightening threat to their false sense of bravado, their "masks of masculinity," which could at any moment break down, revealing their human vulnerability, and leaving them to feel shamefully "unmanly."

What a conundrum for the "good" men amongst us, and for the other men, women, and children who love them and whom they do their best to love. Yet have no fear, for Wexler's *When Good Men Behave Badly* provides practical solutions for men's relationship problems! Better than that, this book bases its action programs for behavior change on years of solid research and clinical experience that is brought to the reader in jargon-free, but intelligent, user-friendly nuggets that have been so sorely missing in the fields of relationship advice and understanding of men's development over the past decades.

Although this is a book meant to help men become all that they can be, written in male-affirmative, "guy-friendly" language, *it is also a volume respectful to women*, filled with numbers of useful suggestions to help them to better understand what really makes the men in their life tick, to recognize what is beneath the surface, and to offer opportunities to help the men in their lives make the relationship-enhancing changes they've been struggling to achieve for so long a time. Wexler's book works equally well when a man's intimate partner is another man, and helps all men who will read it and take it to heart to rediscover the validation that true connections bring, not only with the other intimate adults in their lives, but also with their sons and daughters—our next generation—with whose healthy development we, as adults, are entrusted.

When Good Men Behave Badly goes beyond fad and fashion to opportunities for meaningful behavioral change in relationships, encompasses state-of-the-art dynamic research while remaining a good read, and moves from poignant real-life stories to practical suggestions that will yield results. It's the closest thing to having a relationship expert by your side.

My only regret is that we didn't have this practical wisdom from Wexler earlier. Then, perhaps, we wouldn't have had to feel that men and women are doomed to live emotionally disconnected from each other on faraway planets and could have already realized that fulfilling relationships are possible today, right here on Earth!

I highly recommend this book to all men trying to understand themselves in the context of a loving relationship, to all of us who love these "good" men who may sometimes slip from grace, and to anyone who wishes to create a world of happier and healthier intimacy, beginning today. 'Tis a consummation devoutly to be wished, and *When Good Men Behave Badly* makes it a practical possibility from its first pages to its last.

—William S. Pollack, PH.D.
Author of *Real Boys, Real Boys Voices,* and *A New Psychology of Men.*
Director, Center for Men & Young Men, McLean Hospital
Assistant Clinical Professor, Department of Psychiatry, Harvard Medical School

Preface

I decided to write this book because it hadn't been written. As a therapist, I needed a user-friendly book for men (and for women trying to understand them) to help them recognize some of the ways they kept getting into trouble in relationships. And I needed it to be written in a way that both respected men and challenged them to do better. And it needed to be a book that didn't just give them a pep talk about good values, but also offered them specific insights about how their minds, emotions, and behavior sequences worked so they could anticipate trouble situations better. Plus it needed to be a book that did not alienate men by branding them as relationship criminals, but did not trivialize their mistakes either.

And, perhaps most importantly, it needed to be a book that men would actually read and find interesting. One that had lots of engaging examples, quotes from books and movies, discussion of research studies that had practical value, and plenty of specific action plans, guidelines, and exercises to accelerate the learning curve. And the language used in the book had to reflect "guy talk," framing new ideas about relationships in a way that was compatible with readers' views of masculinity.

So I wrote this because I needed it, and I thought many people would find it valuable.

The primary sources of material for this book have been the men who have trusted me with their personal stories and their relationships. (I have changed their names and details about their lives to protect their privacy.) Powerful and illustrative scenes from movies and books are also sprinkled throughout to help bring home the lessons of men who struggle and men who heroically succeed in the world of relationships. The latest research on male psychology, boys' development, couples' communication patterns, and neurochemistry will help you understand where all this comes from and bolster the case for both the importance and the possibility of change.

I am addressing good men who, at times, behave badly. A good man is a man with fundamentally positive values who cares about his kids and his partner. He seeks emotional attachment and connection. He feels empathy and concern for the people he is close to. And he sometimes acts badly because he has not been trained to identify and express his emotions, or because his capacity for shame is too easily activated, or because he expects too much from his relationships, or because he takes things too damn personally. Or simply because he is a little clueless about certain basic relationship skills that women often seem more adept at.

The bad behavior that this good man is sometimes capable of includes everything from a little sarcasm or criticism to nastiness, coldness, and intimidation. Bad behavior can mean infidelity, humiliation, put-downs, or just emotional withdrawal. It may just mean shutting down and giving up. The good man occasionally lapses into bad behavior when he feels threatened, stressed, anxious, powerless, or helpless.

And he is completely responsible for this behavior, regardless of what triggered it. That sense of personal responsibility is part of what defines a good man.

I do not want you to deny the *behaving badly* part, but I also want you to keep a vision in your head, a narrative in your brain, of the *good man* part. And this book is designed to help you celebrate what is truly good about masculinity. I have found that the narrative—the story you tell yourself about being a man in your relationship and the story you tell yourself about the others around you—either makes you or breaks you. Much of this book is about challenging the old story lines and finding new stories that are more accurate, more compassionate, and more productive for yourself and your relationships.

The theoretical constructs that dominate this book emerge from the field of self psychology. I have tried to generate user-friendly definitions of the terms from self psychology that are especially relevant in making sense of your life and relationships: *mirroring selfobject, broken mirror, twinship selfobject, and independent center of initiative.* These concepts have been enormously useful to me in my career helping men and couples and in my personal life as well. This approach generates a fundamentally humanistic perspective that gets to the heart of what we all seek in relationships. It gives us a map that shows us where we sometimes go wrong and ways to go right.

(Other psychological terms, like *normative male alexithymia, cognitive dissonance,* and *the golden fantasy,* may seem like Greek at first—some actually are Greek—but should make sense very quickly.)

The approach I use here is relentlessly optimistic about human nature and human potential, reflecting a belief that a better guy lies within. But some men are not good men behaving badly. Some men are actually bad men behaving badly, and they do not deserve the benefit of the doubt when their behavior is controlling, manipulative, threatening, or abusive. This book is not for them, and I warn women to avoid them. Chapter 8 is a special primer for women about identifying which men to avoid and which to believe in, how to bring out the best in men, and how to raise good boys and good men.

Throughout this book, I refer to wife, girlfriend, and partner interchangeably. Although the primary emphasis is on man-woman relationships (married or not), many of these issues are certainly relevant in gay relationships as well.

Also, let me say that I am making an array of generalizations about men throughout this book. There are a million exceptions. Perhaps you far exceed the woman in your life in the area of emotional intelligence, and perhaps you have long since silenced the demons of masculinity and repaired the bastardization of true masculinity.

But perhaps you, like many men, have not. To some degree, you may struggle with the central themes identified in this book. And since enough men do, it makes more sense to say "men do this" and "research about men indicates." My genuine apologies, in advance, if you feel offended or not clearly seen. As Carol Kane said sarcastically to Woody Allen in the 1977 classic *Annie Hall* when he rattled off a series of assumptions about who she was and where she had come from, "That's okay. I love being reduced to a cultural stereotype."

If you read this book and integrate the ideas, your way of operating in relationships will blossom. But it is even more likely to improve if you diligently follow through on the various exercises scattered throughout. I highly recommend getting a journal or spiral notebook before you start, and using this to record your responses to the exercises. The information you read here will be valuable to you, but the personal examples that you generate with the exercises will be even more valuable. If you are currently in a relationship, ask your partner to read this along with you and clue her in on your thoughts and feelings as you read the different sections. After all, that's one of the main points: including her in your inner life. And you should read her chapter, too, because there are sure to be a few nuggets in there that will be helpful to you as well.

The brilliant psychologist Carl Jung said, "One is always in the dark about one's own personality. One needs others to get to know oneself" (1977, 165). That's what it's all about. There is nothing like an emotionally intimate relationship (with an adult partner, with your kids, with your parents, or even with your closest friends) to help you really know yourself. Go for it.

Acknowledgments

The most important contributors to the development of this book have been the men I have worked with over the years, who have struggled and worked hard and let me into their lives.

I would also like to thank my editor, Spencer Smith, who passionately believed in this project and whose enthusiasm for my work spurred me on. He and Heather Mitchener challenged my work but always believed in it, and it is a much better book as a result. Many, many thanks to Jessica Beebe for her eagle eye and for pushing me to say exactly what I really intended to say. And thanks to my agent, Kimberly Valentini from Waterside Productions, who worked relentlessly to find this project the right home.

I also owe a tremendous debt of gratitude to other writers and clinicians who have blazed trails and inspired my own thinking and my work: Terry Real, Bill Pollack, Ron Levant, Joseph Pleck, John Sanford, Don Dutton, John Gottman, Amy Holtzworth-Munroe, Jackson Katz, and Steven Stosny. And to novelists (the greatest psychologists of all) like Russell Banks, Pat Conroy, Wally Lamb, and Nick Hornby, whose stories offer elegant descriptions of the inner workings of the male soul.

And the ultimate thanks to my family, my center: my father, for offering such a strong foundation for being a man, and my mother, for providing a mirror that helped me believe in myself. And to my daughter, Juliana, who is my greatest agent and idea person; my son, Joe, whose boyish delight, moral center, and gentle soul will make him a very, very good man; and to my wife, Connie, who brings out the best man I can muster and who makes this all worthwhile.

1

Good Men and Broken Mirrors

In Russell Banks's 1989 novel, *Affliction*, Wade Whitehouse plans a special Halloween weekend with his eleven-year-old daughter, Jill, who lives with her mother (Wade's ex-wife, Lillian). Wade tries hard to make sure Jill has a good time, but he fails; Jill feels out of place at a Halloween party and she pleads with her father to take her home.

Wade's feelings are hurt. What he sees reflected back to him through Jill's distress is an unbearable reminder of his failure as a father. He is shamed by the fact that Jill is unhappy.

> I need a drink, he thought. He had not believed he would tonight, but Jesus H. Christ, did he need a drink. That kid had made him all jumpy tonight. He did not know what the hell had gotten into Jill, but whatever it was, he had let it get into him too. It was only more of the same old stuff her mother had been putting out for years, he thought, and no matter where it came from, Jill or Lillian herself, it always had the same effect on Wade: it made him want to hang his head in shame and run. (25)

Feeling unsuccessful at making a child happy, or at making a partner happy, is hardly a unique experience. For Wade, however (and for many other men), this sense of incompetence elicits an unbearably painful feeling, and he desperately searches for some way to escape from the pain. Shame is at the center of his experience.

What does Wade do? Swimming in his own sense of incompetence, he turns on his daughter. He blames her for reflecting an image of himself that he cannot bear, treating her like the Greek messenger killed for bringing bad news. He becomes sarcastic. He blames her for ruining everything. When he discovers that she has called her mother to pick her up and take her home, Wade tells Jill that she can just sit and wait without him. She says, "Fine." She tries to explain to him, "Don't worry, I love you, Daddy, I do. But I want to go home" (29). She is a smart girl, trying to assuage her father's worst unspoken fear. But it's not enough.

As the scene unravels, Wade turns against his ex-wife and eventually pushes her husband. Why? What is the trigger? Only that his daughter wasn't comfortable at the Halloween party. And he could not bear how this made him feel about himself.

What we have here is a case of a good man behaving badly: a man who has good values and meaningful aspirations, but who is too easily derailed by the experience of shame. And when he is shamed, some of the worst behaviors emerge, behaviors that do not fit with his image of himself and which only rarely emerge in the absence of this shame.

One man in a men's group described it this way:

> *I can't stand it when my wife smokes. I see her smoking and I get sarcastic, tell her in front of our kids that she is a shitty mother. The big fight we had started over smoking. I tried to grab her cigarettes out of her hands and she started screaming at me. She never used to smoke. When we first got together, everything was so perfect. I know probably everybody feels that way, but it was so special to me. Now it's just not the same. And I think that every time I see her smoking, it reminds me of how she's changed, and how I don't have the same feeling any more that I used to have.*

When he saw his wife smoking, it signaled his own failure. He wasn't able to influence his wife in a positive way. He couldn't shape her into a better role model for their kids. And what he once envisioned as perfect was no longer so. It was unbearable.

You may view this perspective on men's behavior as unburdening us from responsibility for our own behavior, as if to say, *Oh, you poor guy, you never learned how to deal with emotions very well and you feel frustrated—what else can people expect from you?* Nothing could be further from the truth. When you learn about your internal triggers, you are in a much better position to truly take charge and take responsibility. You can be powerful—not over others, but over yourself.

Mirrors and Broken Mirrors

Glenn finds it hard to deal with the sense of loss over what once was.

> *The first four to six months we were together, I thought*
> *I was just walking on water. Everything I did was wonderful.*
> *Everything about me was cool. I felt great. It was almost like*
> *I looked at her and I would always feel great about myself.*
> *And then it all came crashing down. She doesn't look at me*
> *the same way anymore. The kids demand a lot of attention. It's*
> *like she doesn't think I'm that great anymore. So now, I don't*
> *even talk to her about a lot of things because they might upset*
> *her and mess up her picture of me even more—even when I*
> *know that she'll get even madder at me later for lying to her.*
> *And then I get mad at her, like it's her fault that I don't feel*
> *like I walk on water anymore!*

When a man comes home to his wife and children, he expects that something will take place between them that will offer him a state of emotional well-being, or what is referred to in self psychology as a state of *self-cohesion*. The need for self-cohesion is primary. It originates in the interaction between the young child and the most central attachment figure, usually the mother. The child has a compelling need to look into the face of his mother and see reflected back to him eyes that say *You are wonderful* and a smile that says *You make me happy.*

The Good Mirror

This is his magic mirror, and the figure in the mirror is known in self psychology theory as the *mirroring selfobject*. A selfobject is another person (or place, activity, or special object) that functions to keep us feeling cohesive. The self psychology theory of normal child development described by Shapiro (1995) states that all children, at regular points in their development, need validation and acknowledgment from parental figures; these figures serve as the mirroring selfobjects. Over time, if the child experiences these positive interactions, he develops the capacity to feel pride and take pleasure in his accomplishments—to feel competent, valuable, and worthy of appreciation.

When a child looks into the eyes of his parent and sees reflected back to him a loving and approving look, his basic sense of himself is deeply validated. He feels alive and worthy.

When you, as an adult male in a relationship, look into the eyes of your partner and see reflected back to you a look of love and delight and profound respect, you likewise feel alive and worthy.

This process is, of course, not fundamentally any different for women than it is for men. It's just that men are typically less aware of how powerful these needs are and more likely to withdraw or act out when the needs are not met. And men ascribe a special power to the women in their lives to validate their self-worth.

Broken Mirrors

Children who are deprived of these essential responses, or who are instead subjected to criticism and ridicule for their efforts to achieve, become arrested in their development of an internal sense of confidence and competence. As adults, they are always looking to some outside source of approval or recognition (mirroring). But no mother, no father, no teacher, no coach, and no therapist ever provides the perfect mirror. A child's mirroring figures, as we all know rather too well, may be quite fragmented themselves and have little capacity to offer the loving and confidence-enhancing reflection that the child desperately requires. Or, in some cases, there is a mismatch between child and mirror-figure such that the child eternally feels a lack of understanding, a dearth of genuine appreciation, and a fundamental gap in attunement. Even in the best of situations, the mirroring can be experienced as incomplete. The child thus develops gaps in his sense of self: he mistrusts and disrespects his own internal signals and states; he doubts his own self-worth and competence. He desperately turns elsewhere for validation and he becomes excessively sensitized to signals that might suggest that he is unappreciated, unneeded, or unsuccessful.

The reflection offered by women as a mirror in a man's life is especially powerful. You may find that you crave mirroring and that, as the relationship with your partner moves on, your wife and the life you have together have not sufficiently made up for what you have never quite fully received. Or at least what has never become a solid and reasonably resilient part of your personality. When your partner seems more interested in talking to her sister than to you, or when your sex life wanes, you may become fragmented. The mirroring selfobject—at least in its positive form—has disappeared from your experience. When these responses are not forthcoming, you may be unable to maintain your sense of self-worth, self-esteem, or personal value. Various behaviors reflecting this fragmentation may ensue: gambling, substance abuse, reckless sexual behavior, aggression, impulsive actions, or workaholism; or simply pouting, emotional shutdown, sarcasm, or passive-aggressive behavior. You have to *do* something to escape emotionally, discharge the tension, or regain a sense of control and importance.

Ernest Becker, in his 1973 book *The Denial of Death,* describes a broken mirror phenomenon. Here, it is not so much that the mirror reflects back a picture of us that is an injury; instead we see a broken mirror when our loved ones, and anyone else who seems to represent us in some way, turns out to be imperfect. If your wife or your kids (or, for that matter, your employees) are flawed, what does that say about you?

> When we look for the "perfect" human object we are looking for someone who allows us to express our will completely, without any frustration or false notes. We want an object that reflects a truly ideal image of ourselves. But no human object can do this; humans have wills and counter-wills of their own, in a thousand ways they can move against us, their very appetites offend us. . . . If a woman loses her beauty, or shows that she doesn't have the strength and dependability that we once thought she did, or loses her intellectual sharpness, or falls short of our own peculiar needs in any of a thousand ways, then all the investment we have made in her is undermined. . . . We get back a reflection from our loved objects that is less than the grandeur and perfection that we need to nourish ourselves. We feel diminished by their human shortcomings. . . . For this reason, too, we often attack loved ones and try to bring them down to size. (166–69)

Since the perfect mirroring inevitably wears off to some degree, even in the best of relationships, the man who especially needs self-object mirroring is doomed to a cracking of the mirror and a cracking of the self. It is this experience that you must identify and own if you have problems in your relationship with your partner or children. You need to understand the origin of this unrest and resentment so you can position yourself to take responsibility for it. As with most other psychological experiences, once you identify and make sense of your distress, a profound organizing effect takes place, which allows you to respond more maturely and appropriately to the genuine problem.

Broken Mirrors and Acting Out

A breakdown in the mirroring experience can be the trigger for desperate and often destructive acts. Try thinking of this emotional injury in terms of the experience of parents who behave badly toward their kids, which is parallel to the experience of the frustrated, verbally abusive husband (White and Weiner 1986). The parent experiences an emotional injury. He experiences his inability to make his child react as if she were part of him and really knew what he wanted as an assault to his sense of self. Here, the mirroring selfobject function is extremely important and quite fragile. So long as a child (or partner) provides the appreciation needed, the father's self-esteem is maintained. When the applause fails, his internal experience of the self begins to fragment and tremble. The father needs to be respected and obeyed and made to feel worthwhile; when he does not see that positive reflection in the interpersonal mirror, he is left feeling vulnerable, helpless, and outraged.

It happens to the best of us. One time my fifteen-year-old daughter sat through a lecture I gave in San Jose, California, in which I showed the film clip from *Affliction* where Wade Whitehouse turns against his daughter. Right after this presentation, my family headed off to the Santa Cruz boardwalk. I had been planning this for a long time as a special treat for my kids, and I knew they would really like it. My daughter, however, copped an attitude and complained that this was really kind of boring. I became defensive, and I said to her, "I planned this for *you,* and it's like nothing's going to make you happy!" She looked at me and calmly said, "Dad, you sound just like that dad in *Affliction.*" I was busted, and she was right.

Listen to what my client Casey says, describing how he blows up and puts his wife down:

> *I've been married ten years. The first six years were picture-perfect. We had little spats, but that was all. But then this thing called parenthood came along. She was more critical of me, plus the heat from my career got way turned up. And she just got more and more of an attitude. And I'm thinking, "You're not the only one entitled to have an attitude." I became the sole breadwinner, and instead of making her an equal partner in our lives, my father came out of me.*
>
> *I just became my dad! Instead of looking at the fact that she was stressed out, I just blew up. I never hit her or anything. I just put her down, blamed her for everything. Everything that I had said I would never do, I did anyway!*

Here's an example from my own experience to help expand our understanding of this broken mirror phenomenon from the more extreme to the daily and trivial. Despite the difference in severity, these examples are all fundamentally alike and reflect fundamentally similar psychological processes.

On a leisurely Saturday afternoon, I returned home from food shopping, put the groceries on the kitchen counter, and headed off to my daughter's room to say hello. She was sitting and reading a magazine. She looked up at me with one of her beaming smiles. This is a terrific mirror.

Then I looked around her room. World War III had descended: clothes everywhere, books and papers strewn—all parents know this story. I shook my head and smiled and said, "So when's the maid coming?" I knew better. My wife and I had made a firm pact to leave the issue of the damn room alone and, like all intelligent parents, keep our battles to the big ones. But I couldn't keep my mouth shut.

My daughter's smile turned to ice. She glazed over and gave me a dismissive wave. I left, feeling stupid. And injured. Her glazed and scornful look was the broken mirror, and it reflected back a picture of myself that I did not like.

So I walked into the kitchen, where my wife was putting away some of the groceries. She said casually, "Oh, I wanted those little yogurts. The ones you bought are too big." On the scale of nasty and critical comments, with 100 being horribly insulting, this was about an 11. But I exploded nevertheless. "Fine! You don't like the way I shop, I'll just do it all over again. Give me those yogurts! Give me the receipt! I'm going right back there and getting them exactly the way you want them!" My wife looked at me and said, "What the hell's wrong with you?"

I stormed out to the store. I came back in a huff, slamming the door, new yogurt in hand. My wife was sitting on the couch. She calmly repeated, "What the hell's wrong with you?"

We talked for a while, and it all fell into place. I was injured by the broken mirror experience with my daughter. And this catapulted me into an emotionally vulnerable state in which another injury, even if extremely minor, was likely to be overinterpreted, over-personalized, and overreacted to.

This is the process that most good men behaving badly go through. If you see yourself behaving badly in a relationship, try to go the source: Which mirror has broken? Where is the emotional injury that set the stage for this? Again, this does not absolve you of responsibility. Instead, it is a way for you to become even more emotionally intelligent and ultimately more responsible.

Disappointment and Dysphoria

Some disappointment like this is inevitable, given the limits of human relationships. The problem with the man who behaves badly with his partner or children is that he has mistaken the flood of good feelings that comes from a close relationship with a promise that the good mirror will always shine. So if, in your eyes, the mirror breaks, then your sense of self shatters, and you blame the mirror. It's like she had *promised* to keep up the positive mirror, and now she has broken the promise.

Wade Whitehouse reflects: "There was nothing wrong back then, nothing, or so it seemed then. . . . Those were wonderful times, he thought, truly wonderful times. After that, things all of a sudden started going wrong. They were only kids, he and Lillian, and they did not know how to repair anything, so when something in the marriage broke, they just went out and got divorced" (26).

Dysphoria is a depressed mood state, the opposite of *euphoria.* Some men, like Wade Whitehouse and my client Casey, plagued with the dysphoria of the broken mirror, turn overtly against the people closest to them. Others simply turn to whatever they can find to help them cope with the gnawing emptiness.

Eduardo, married with three young children, engaged in compulsive sexual behavior. He was drawn to secret, anonymous, and depressing encounters with gay men in porn store booths. Eduardo, a wonderful family man and great provider, was a *very* good man acting badly—toward his wife, his family, and himself. But it was essential for him to make sense of the fundamental needs that he was seeking to fulfill with his compulsive sexuality. "The guys there feed my ego. They are *very* complimentary—I don't get too much of that at home. And the ones I am drawn to are the guys who are married, like me. We're exactly alike, looking for the same thing in the same place."

Eduardo sounds like an addict. He hates what he is doing, but he feels compelled. It is the only way he has discovered to temporarily repair the effects of the broken mirror.

Exercise: Facing the Broken Mirror

The next time you notice yourself doing whatever it is you do that gets in the way of your relationship (pouting, becoming sarcastic, acting like a martyr, yelling, getting critical, withdrawing), try to figure out what kind of broken mirror experience preceded this.

- Did your partner say something that hurt your feelings?

- Did your kids act in a way that made you feel incompetent?

- Did your mother or father make some remark that made you feel unsuccessful?

- Did you notice that a friend of yours seemed to be more successful than you are, making you feel bad about yourself?

Perception and Reaction

If you behave badly in a relationship, it is typically the case that you have experienced a fundamental emotional injury or mirroring breakdown preceding this outbreak. Something has gone wrong. Your feelings have been hurt. Your self-esteem has been diminished. You feel unimportant, or devalued, or disregarded, or rejected, or powerless, or helpless. These emotional states challenge your sense of masculinity. You enter a mood which, unchecked, leads you unconsciously down a slippery slope of toxic self-talk, dysphoric emotions, and dysfunctional behaviors.

Misattributions

The research of Holtzworth-Munroe and Hutchinson (1993) is particularly illuminating here. They examined the *misattributions* (flawed descriptions of why behavior is occurring) of men who abuse their wives compared to nonabusive men. They found that violent husbands were much more likely to attribute the most negative intentions to their wives' behavior. When presented with vignettes of situations like a wife talking to another man at a party or a wife who was not interested in sex on a particular night, these men were much more likely to be convinced that she was *trying* to make him angry, hurt his feelings, put him down, get something for herself, or pick a fight. The researchers also found that when the men perceived a situation of abandonment or rejection, they were particularly likely to respond with bad behavior. These are emotional injuries to these men, and like all emotional injuries, they are strictly governed by the cognitive interpretation of the event. A nonabusive husband might interpret the same situation in a different, more benign way. If his wife were spending a lot of time talking to another man at a party, he might be a little irritated at her, or he might make nothing of it, or he might actually feel pleased that she was attractive and popular and having a good time.

Even among men who are not violent, misattributions can dominate. Devin, a man in one of my groups, described an argument he had with his wife. On Monday night (the night of the week especially significant because it was football season), he came home from work to find his wife exhausted and depressed. She told him she was really feeling down and just didn't have the energy to put dinner together. So, being a good guy, he told her not to worry and proceeded to fry up some chicken and bake a couple of potatoes. He cooked while trying to watch the football game, which was a sacrifice for him.

When he proudly presented her with dinner and sat down to watch the game, she sat and ate just a few bites. Then she pushed the food aside and said that she wasn't really all that hungry.

Devin did not blow up (a significant step forward for him), even though he was telling himself this story: *What the hell? I bust my ass to take care of her and then it turns out she wasn't really hungry in the first place! That woman is just yanking my chain!*

Independent Center of Initiative

In Devin's eyes, at that moment, his wife was allowed no *independent center of initiative*, the term used in self psychology to recognize that the other person has his or her own independent reasons for making a decision—reasons that have nothing to do with you! Although Devin couldn't see it at the time, his wife was making a decision based on other factors besides how her decision would affect him.

After his wife stopped eating, Devin just got very quiet and withdrawn. His wife knew he was upset. Later that night she tried to talk about it with him, and she explained (again!) that she was trying out some new birth control pills that were really messing up her appetite. She had cravings, then lost her appetite unpredictably.

Since this relationship had a fundamentally positive foundation, and since Devin fundamentally wished the best for his wife, and since he fundamentally believed that she was not someone whose primary motivation was to mess with his head, this new information was a relief to him. He no longer had to interpret her behavior as an act of disrespect or manipulation. His wife had her own independent reasons for behaving the way that she did.

We hear the same theme when listening to Paul. "My wife wanted to take this job where it takes her on the road for weeks at a time, sometimes a few months. This is not what she promised me when we got married! This is breaking her vows! And why would she do this when she knows how much this means to me and how much it affects me? What it means is that she just doesn't care!"

Paul was making a couple of mistakes in his thinking. He could not recognize Karla's independent center of initiative. All he could see was the way her decision was affecting him—and since it was affecting him, she must be intending for it to affect him. He was interpreting Karla's personal decision as a sign that she didn't care about him or respect him. And he was unable to recognize that he was getting what he had always said he wanted: for Karla to be more expressive and assertive about what she wanted and needed.

The night after I blew up at her and we had this big fight,
I decided that I really wanted to try and make things better.
I came home and I said to her, "C'mon, honey, let's both go
for a walk. Let's spend some time together." She said, "Okay,
I'll go for a walk, but I don't want to talk about our relation-
ship. You get too upset when we try to do that and I don't
want to go there." So I'm thinking that I don't need this shit,
these restrictions on what I can talk about and what I can't.
I just said "fuck it" and we never even went for the walk.

So what happened when Karla put this restriction on the walk? She simply made it clear what her needs and boundaries were, based on what she had just experienced from Paul the day before. And all he could recognize was that he was being "victimized" by her: another misattribution.

Men's Powerlessness

Researchers like John Gottman (1994) have described the experience of powerlessness that men have in difficult interpersonal relationships. Many men—especially those who withdraw, escape, become critical, or become abusive—have very low tolerance for difficult or aversive feelings. When they experience some emotional injury or discomfort, they feel overwhelmed. A mistake may lead to shame, frustration to helplessness, emotional distance to loneliness. In this model, men do whatever it takes to defend against these extremely dysphoric states. They may behave with passivity, placating or apologizing excessively just to keep the peace. Or they may take a more active approach, as men in our culture tend to do: lashing out at the person who seems to be causing this pain, engaging in controlling behavior to eliminate the sources of discomfort, abusing substances as an escape from the feelings, acting out recklessly through sexual escapades or dangerous driving, or taking bold but impulsive action to provide some relief. The problem behaviors run the gamut from sarcasm, emotional withdrawal, and passive-aggressive behavior all the way to substance abuse and domestic violence.

In another novel by Russell Banks, *Continental Drift* (1994), Bob Dubois's story reflects this kind of male experience. At a time when his family's financial situation is unraveling, Bob heads off to get some shrimp nets to catch shrimp for family meals. In the tackle store, he runs into the legendary baseball star Ted Williams. Since Bob grew up in Boston, this is equivalent to meeting the pope.

When he comes home, he is in a daze from this experience and he has completely forgotten about the shrimp nets. He tries to explain to his wife, Elaine, about how magical this experience has been. Bob's speech is very moving, reminiscing about days spent with his father as a youth. Elaine is politely uninterested and is more concerned about dinner, the kids, and her impending announcement that she has taken on a part-time job to help out with the finances.

"Bob," Elaine says, interrupting him. "We have to talk."

"Yeah?" He whips out his cigarettes and lights one, and his hands are trembling. "Everybody seems to want to have a fucking talk with me these days. . . . I can't even come in here and get a little excited about seeing my goddamned childhood hero, a man who's a fucking god to me, without you bringing me down for it!"

"All I said was . . ."

"All you said was, 'I want to have a talk with you,' in that damned accusing way of yours, as if I was a fucking little kid, like you're going to tell me what's what and how it's all my fault! I know already what you got to say to me! . . . You want to tell me what I already know. You want to tell me what shit this all is. *Shit.* This . . . whole damned life." (269–70)

Bob hears nothing but potential shame in what Elaine apparently wants to talk about. Elaine is a broken mirror to him, despite whatever it is she is trying to do or really wants to talk about. She is stunned by his description of their life together.

"Is it? You feel that way about it?"

He remains silent for a second. "Yeah. It's shit. All of it, shit, shit, shit. And now you want to tell me how it's all my fault," he says in a low, cold voice. "You like doing that, telling me how it's all my fault. . . . Well, you didn't want me to go on shrimping anyhow. All you do is bring me down about things I get excited about. You, you never get excited about anything anymore. All you do is mope around here with a long face." He crosses to the television set and snaps it off. "I hate that fucking thing!" (270–71)

Although it may not appear so from this scene, Bob is a man with strong family values, emotional sensitivity, and a vision of a good life that he desperately wants to provide for himself and his family. But, as this scene illustrates, he is very vulnerable to careening off course when he feels dismayed about his own self-worth.

This is a classic broken mirror story. Bob sees reflected back an image of himself that is not appealing: his bank account is nonexistent, his wife is forced to take a job, the TV set is blaring, his daughter sucks her thumb, and his wife doesn't show enough damned interest in an experience that was so precious to him. She is not mirroring the positive, worthy-of-appreciation self that she once did.

And thus, in Bob's mind, it becomes her fault.

In this state, under these circumstances, Bob perceives his wife *only* as a potential mirror figure, without an independent center of initiative. This means that, at that moment, all that matters to him is what she can offer him to make him feel better. Elaine's behavior, feelings, and independent center of initiative are peripheral to his need for self-cohesion: he will do anything it takes to avoid the dysphoria and regain some measure of well-being. For some men, this means gaining control over someone else. And, for some men, this means emotional, verbal, or even physical abuse.

Searching for Twinship

The *twinship selfobject* is parallel to the mirroring selfobject, referring to the need we all have to be members of the same club or clan, to feel that we are all in this together. Like the experience of mirroring, the twinship experience can be deeply emotionally fulfilling. In moderate doses—like moderate doses of mirroring—this is one of the most human and enriching experiences of all. It helps provide self-cohesion. But the longing for this, if you're feeling deprived of it, can catapult you into destructive behavior patterns. Consider Eduardo, whose inner emptiness led him to a desperate and shameful search for twinship. It is especially interesting to pay attention to his description of one of the key positive ingredients of this experience: "We're exactly alike, looking for the same thing in the same place."

The healthy awareness of the need for twinship would allow you to say to your wife or partner, *You know, I feel really lost sometimes without all the special times we used to have together. It just seems like having kids and getting used to each other and money problems have really taken their toll. I guess you must feel the same way.* Here you, as a man, shift from needing your partner to be a mirror reflecting you to recognizing the ways in which the two of you are profoundly alike. She is no longer the enemy, but rather a comrade along the difficult road of life. A comrade who is inevitably flawed, but no more fundamentally flawed than you.

Elaine has an intuitive sense about the power of twinship experiences. She tries to defuse Bob and engage him from this point of view. "Bob, you can't hear yourself, or you'd shut up. Can you listen to me for a minute? . . . Now, you listen to me for a few minutes. I know you're working hard, as hard as anyone can. And I know you're worried and scared. Like I am. And you're right, it's true, this life is *shit,*" she says (271–72).

She proceeds to tell Bob about some of the plans she has developed to help them get out of this bad situation: her job and counseling for one of their daughters. Unfortunately, Elaine is too late. Her attempts to get them involved in solving these problems together, as "twins," fails because of Bob's emotional disarray. He hears and sees only failure and self-blame, and he unravels even more.

Exercise: We're in This Together

Here are some examples of blaming statements converted into twinship statements. As you review these, think of situations when you have made blaming statements to your wife or partner and consider how you might have been able to convert them into twinship statements instead.

Blaming Statements

1. You're ruining everything in this relationship.

2. It's like you're never happy to see me when I come home! You have become such a bitch!

3. I never get to have the free time I used to have before our kids were born!

4. I am busting my ass working hard, and there's never any money for me to have the stuff I want!

Twinship Statements

1. We are both screwing up a lot, and I really want us to work on it.

2. It's like you're never happy to see me when I come home. I want to figure out what's going wrong so we can try to make this work better.

3. I guess we both don't have the free time we used to have before our kids were born.

4. Wow, it's tough for both of us to be living on such a tight budget!

When you think about your relationship as a twinship experience, you are less likely to feel resentful and victimized. Remember that our universal longing for twinship also means that twinship statements are much less likely to lead to defensive responses from your partner.

Shame, Shame, Shame

According to psychologist Donald Dutton (1995), male shame comes from public exposure of one's vulnerability. The whole self feels bad. If you were a boy whose father engaged in a pattern of shaming you, you can probably figure that your father was desperately attempting to bolster or reassure his own shaky sense of self. Or maybe it was just force of habit, based on what was modeled for him. Regardless, for the boy, who needs to feel loved by this main source of his male identity, it is a series of crushing blows.

Shame-o-phobia

Men who have been exposed to shame will do anything to avoid it in the future. If you were shamed as a boy, your radar is probably hypersensitive to the possibility of humiliation, and you may be almost phobic in your reactions. You may tend to project blame and perceive the worst in others. Tragically, you are especially desperate for affection and approval, but you cannot ask for it. Sometimes the smallest signs of withdrawal of affection will activate your old wounds, and you lash out at the perceived source of this new wound. You can describe none of these feelings; you don't even know where they have come from.

A number of different researchers, clinicians, and writers have developed paradigms to understand this pattern in male psychology. Terrence Real (1997) describes the "silent epidemic" of male depression, in which men who have been repeatedly shamed about their emotional states and genuine needs turn to various forms of "addictive" behavioral patterns to escape the intolerable negative emotions. He identifies the source of this condition as "the loss of the relational . . . that wound in boys' lives that sets up their vulnerability to depression as men" (137). This relational impoverishment creates the base for the feelings of shame, worthlessness, and emptiness that haunt many men.

Shame and Acting Out

In the 1997 movie *Good Will Hunting*, Will (played by Matt Damon) is a young man deeply shamed by the abuse in his past. He struggles to form a relationship with an intelligent, emotionally mature young woman, Skylar (played by Minnie Driver), who falls deeply in love with him. But his shame keeps him hidden and holds him back. When she suggests to him that he move out to California with her, he withdraws and refuses. She challenges him to tell her why and to let her know more about himself. What could have been, and should have been, a very positive mirroring experience (*It feels so good to have this great woman confirm her love for me and her belief in me!*) instead becomes a trigger for shame.

Will tells her he can't go. Why? Because he has a job here. Because he lives here. When Skylar, hurt and confused, asks him to tell her what he is so scared of, Will starts to unravel. He wildly, defensively, recklessly accuses her of using him for a "fling" before she marries "some rich prick your parents'll approve of!" Skylar dishes it back, demanding he be truthful with her. Will opens the faucet and it all comes gushing out: He doesn't really have twelve brothers. He's an orphan. He had cigarettes put out on him when he was a kid. His scar was not from surgery—the "motherfuckers" stabbed him!

And Will, in his shame and his fear of dealing with traumatic memories and his terror that nobody like Skylar could possibly love him with all that he has been through and all that he has done, loses it. He pushes her against the door, slams his hand against the wall, screams in her face. He yells at her that he doesn't need her help and demands that she never "bullshit" him.

And then, the unkindest cut of all. After she challenges him to tell her that he doesn't love her, he does just that. His face, enraged a moment ago, goes cold. He tells Skylar, "I don't love you," leaving Skylar collapsed in tears.

Will cannot bear to do what seems like such an obvious solution to his pain and alienation: Talk to her. Tell her about his inner world and what he has experienced. Trust that she will be brought closer to him rather than pushed further away. He cannot bring himself to do it. The immediate pain is too great, and it drives him to acting badly. The greatest injury he inflicts is not the defensiveness or the yelling or even slamming his hand right next to her face. It is the emotional shutdown and the emotional cruelty of *I don't love you*. Will is a good man acting badly.

Will and other men like him—men who are terrified of taking emotional risks—can and often do find a way to take a chance and rise above their troubled past. Even when faced with the possibility of experiencing shame, you can choose to relate rather than withdraw, to offer your heart rather than shut it down.

Michael, a man who felt profoundly injured when his wife turned him down for sex, yelled at his wife and became mercilessly sarcastic with her. He told me about his propensity for shame.

I never knew my father. He left when I was one, then occasionally reappeared but never followed through on anything. My mother remarried a jerk. My older brother, a half-brother, he always made me feel worthless. He was a put-down artist. Now it's so easy for me to feel put down by my wife. And now I feel even more shamed for what I have done to her. I can't look her in the eye sometimes. I go to church and can't walk in the building because I have done so many things so wrong.

Like victims of post-traumatic stress disorder, men like Will Hunting and Michael experience waves of shame when a current situation even remotely resembles the shame-producing experiences of the past. But that was then, and this is now, and it is your job to learn the difference.

Men's Patterns, Men's Futures

All of these themes coalesce into a complex yet clear description of the ways that so many of us malfunction in relationships: The intolerable "nonmasculine" emotions put such unbearable psychological pressure on us that we feel compelled to do something immediate and powerful to escape from the pain. We drink, we criticize, we seek ungratifying sex, we gamble, we fight, we emotionally withdraw, we avoid. And we often turn our negativity on the perceived source of the bad feelings: the women and children in our lives.

This book is designed to help you identify and respect the emotional states that trigger your relationship problems and then to lead you into new ways of responding. This approach employs a self psychological perspective in helping you recognize the fundamental—and valid—emotional needs that you were experiencing when you made the behavioral decision which turned out to have destructive or self-destructive consequences. You can become less defensive by recognizing and validating your tender spots and by celebrating what is good and strong and heroic about being male.

The implications of this are profound. Your ability to genuinely understand your own unmet needs for mirroring and affirmation is potentially of tremendous value. The selfobject needs of good men behaving badly are valid. By recognizing that your choices about behavior are guided by your need for self-cohesion and control over your sense of self (not necessarily over another person), you can gain a new, deeply respectful perspective and learn to express your needs in more acceptable and effective ways.

As you read through this book, you will learn about the particular power that men ascribe to women, and the ways in which the modeling of masculinity generates a powerful legacy from father to son and again from father to son—and ways to break the cycle. We'll take a look at the corollary issue of the male peer culture influence. You will learn to appreciate the soft underbellies of even the most emotionally guarded men. You'll learn about the male brain and male neuropsychological functioning, which in some ways is not well adapted to the demands of modern relationships. You will also learn the latest research about issues particular to midlife that affect men and often lead us into emotional disarray and to acting badly.

Perhaps most significantly, this book will offer example after example of men's success stories. The story of Odysseus will show the paths with heart that men are capable of choosing. A series of structured exercises will help you transfer the concepts from this book into your everyday life and the everyday lives of the men around you.

Those of you who are not men (otherwise known as women) will learn to recognize men who are dangerous and not likely to have a tender heart within. You will also learn ways to help bring out the good man and even tips on how to raise boys to be the best possible good men they can be.

Your job as a man, or as someone affected by men, or as someone trying to help men, is to understand the patterns of response to emotional pain and to develop a new narrative of yourself and a new set of tools for coping with these very human experiences. The perspectives from clinicians like Terrence Real, from novelists like Russell Banks, and from self psychology—all of which emphasize the breakdowns in self-cohesion leading to damaging behavior—offer us a map.

2

The Power of Women

The look of love that men rely upon from women is one of the most potent forces in male psychology. Men crave the look. The look serves as a powerful mirror that reflects back to men an image of themselves as being important, valuable, honorable, wanted, smart, or sexy. Rob, the narrator in Nick Hornby's 1995 novel, *High Fidelity*, complains about his girlfriend: "You hear that? She's not very good at slushy stuff? That, to me, is a problem, as it would be to any male who heard Dusty Springfield singing 'The Look of Love' at an impressionable age. That was what I thought it was all going to be like when I was married."

The need for this look of love is not, by itself, a problem. It is oh-so-commonly human. As with other emotional needs, your goal for personal growth and development is not to transcend the need. Instead, the realistic goal is for you to become more resilient and flexible about the quantities and qualities you need in order to feel reasonably fulfilled. In other words, to learn to focus on the half-full glass of what you do have rather than on the half-empty glass of what she was supposed to offer all the time but doesn't. And to be reasonably centered within—and reasonably respectful without—when these needs are not quite fulfilled.

> I thought there was going to be this sexy woman with a sexy voice and lots of sexy eye makeup whose devotion to me shone from every pore. And there is such a thing as the look of love—Dusty didn't lead us up the garden path entirely—it's just that the look of love isn't what I expected it to be. It's not huge eyes almost bursting with longing

situated somewhere in the middle of a double bed with the covers turned down invitingly; it's just as likely to be the look of benevolent indulgence that a mother gives a toddler, or a look of amused exasperation, even a look of pained concern. But the Dusty Springfield look of love? Forget it. As mythical as the exotic underwear.

I'm beginning to get used to the idea that Laura might be the person I spend my life with. . . . But it's much harder to get used to the idea that my little-boy notion of romance, of negligees and candlelit dinners at home and long, smoldering glances, had no basis in reality at all. That's what women ought to get all steamed up about; that's why we can't function properly in a relationship. It's not the cellulite or the crow's feet. It's the . . . the . . . the disrespect. (274)

Listen to Rob, the narrator in *High Fidelity*. He is in the process of discovering that the little looks, in the everyday context of ordinary interpersonal transactions, are plenty. What guy would ever dismiss the thrill of "huge eyes almost bursting with longing?" Very few. Would you? But those huge-eyes moments are few and far between in even the most successful relationships (after the honeymoon stage), and you may find yourself struggling to appreciate the more ordinary looks of "benevolent indulgence," "amused exasperation," or "pained concern."

Often, in hearing the stories of men who have become embittered toward their partners, I listen for the story behind the story. And when I get past the resentment, and the frustration, and the emotional withdrawal, what I often find is just plain hurt: *I guess I'm no longer the great guy you thought I was when you married me!* or *I just want to have her look at me like she's happy to see me!* Do these sound familiar?

It's enough to make a good man behave badly.

Garry told me about the rawest of feelings that generated his destructive behavior in his relationship with his wife. "What's the emotional trigger? I think it's being taken for granted, feeling 'less than.' I've never actually physically abused Linda or the kids, but I threaten and intimidate them. I know it. I put them down and curse them."

After a long time bitterly reporting to me all of his wife's faults—her moodiness, her disorganization at home, her coddling of the kids—another man, Luis, finally got down to the core of it all: "I just want a woman who runs up to me when I come home and it's all 'on.'" I took that to mean that he desperately craved the look of love. All the rest of his complaints were ultimately superficial, if he only could get the look. The particularly painful part of Luis's story was that his wife, Deborah, reported—and I believed her—that *she* was the one to initiate an affectionate response when Luis walked in the door, and that he always seemed cool and withdrawn. For Luis, it was never quite enough. He needed a constant stream of mirroring from Deborah. Because he had grown up with deficits in mirroring, he was especially vulnerable to the moments when there was even a slight breakdown in the mirroring he now received from the one person whom he granted the special power to give it. When he felt injured and deprived, he shut himself down emotionally. Once he got on that track, he perceived his wife's intermittent lapses in attention as signs that she was cold and ungiving.

Once this narrative of her took hold for Luis, his wife's new behaviors became data that only served to confirm this hypothesis. As Deborah put it, "He has 'named' me as an unaffectionate person, and there doesn't seem to be anything I can do about it!"

Here's an example of how sweet and meaningful the response from the most important woman can be. Kent, a good guy if I ever met one, also had a history of intermittent drinking episodes and occasional verbal outbursts toward his wife and kids. He lived with a lifelong burden of feeling that he was inadequate, a message he had regularly received from his father. Now, as an adult, Kent heard this message coming from his very successful, domineering father-in-law, who had brought Kent into the family business.

After one explosive episode in which Kent had yelled at his daughter and hurled insults at his wife, she moved the kids out briefly and then insisted he leave. She refused to even consider a reconciliation until he joined AA, entered therapy, apologized to her and the kids, and showed her a consistently different pattern of behavior. This was rock bottom for him, and he realized that if he didn't change, he would lose everything he cared about. After several months, Kent's wife invited him back into the house and into her bed.

Several weeks later, Kent broke down crying as he told me,

I know that I have tried so hard to change and become more of the man that Jackie wants me to be and that I know I can be. I have stopped drinking, and I am sucking it up and making amends—"fourth step" stuff. And, very gradually, she is letting me back into her life. Last night, we were lying in bed, just both reading, and she reached over and just lightly touched my shoulder. "I'm proud of you," she whispered. Out of nowhere. That meant so much.

Another story, told by Benny, a man in a painfully distant and cold marriage, illustrates even further how the response from a particular woman can offer you psychological life or psychological death. For Benny, his wife's sexual interest could determine whether he felt alive or dead.

> *My wife and I are being shitty to each other. She blames me for all sorts of shit. It tells me that she doesn't love me. I got rejected from the time that I moved in with my grandmother for the rest of my life growing up. Now I walk in the house and I feel like such a shithead. I don't believe I'm such a terrible guy, but my wife makes me feel that way. She says, "You're persecuting me, you're taking shots at me!" To her, I just don't exist.*
>
> *So what do I do? I make myself feel dead inside. Just dead. If I don't feel dead, then I'm all over the place with my emotions. And I act dead with her too.*

You can almost scrape the emotional pain off these pages. Benny has given his wife unbearable power over his emotional well-being, and it is killing his relationship. He allows her to make him feel like he "just doesn't exist." His oppressive need, and subsequent emotional coldness and aggression when it is not fully met, serves as a self-fulfilling prophecy of rejection.

In his desperate attempt to bolster himself and find a more satisfying mirroring experience, Benny turns to prostitutes. These are his hired mirrors. "Those twenty-five-year-old models, they just make it seem so okay! They make you feel so right. And that's not what it's like when I walk in the door at home. I don't hate my wife—it's just so painful to me that she's lost interest in sex, that I never get a hug, that I never feel very special."

If you are a woman reading this and thinking about your relationship with a man, ask yourself if you desire this power to govern his sense of well-being. The women I talk to say that it is only a little bit appealing; of course it feels good to be needed. But the rest of it is pure burden, often forcing women to spend more time than they want to worrying about how their partner will be affected. With only some exceptions, this power is not a power that women have signed up for in the relationship contract.

The Experience of Powerlessness

This reliance on women for validation can lead you to feel that you're not in control of your own emotional well-being. Emotional dependency on women can be touching at times, but it can also result in emotional withdrawal or resentment. It is not a big series of leaps to go from feeling dependent on someone, to feeling a certain degree of powerlessness or helplessness as a result, to resenting that same person for the power that you perceive her to have over you.

The Fear of Women

Theo gives us a raw glimpse into the psyche of a man who fits this profile. The setting here was a group for men who were having trouble in their relationships. Theo intermittently became verbally abusive and emotionally withdrawn with his wife. Theo knew that he was handling things wrong. And he knew that this behavior violated his own personal code of ethics about how you treat others, and how you treat women, and how, in particular, you treat women you love. But his vulnerability to women, and his rage at feeling so affected by them, kept getting the best of him.

In one of our group sessions, one of the other men made a crack about women along the lines of *You know how it is, guys. You can't trust a woman with a credit card!* It was blatantly sexist, but he was clowning around, making fun of his own sexist attitudes as much as he was making fun of women. We all knew that, and he pretended to duck for cover from my female cotherapist. She gave him a mock I'm-gonna-get-you-for-this look, all part of the give-and-take in establishing an atmosphere where it is safe for these men to reveal their truest attitudes. And he pretended to cower some more. The group members laughed. So did I.

Theo did not. He was doing a slow—actually very fast—burn. Seconds later, Theo exploded. He sat up straight in his chair. His veins bulged. He turned red. "You see? That's it! That's the look! You see how she controlled him with the look! Look at how he suddenly got quiet. Because she controlled him! Women do that all the time!"

The group sat in stunned silence. I gently pointed out to Theo that people of both genders could disagree on some points and express their opinions. That didn't mean they were being controlling. In fact, *feeling* controlled is not always a reliable indicator that someone is actually controlling you. Besides, I pointed out, this interchange was lighthearted, and they were only playing.

I think Theo felt a little foolish as he saw his behavior reflected back to him in the mirror of the group's reaction to him. But he stood firm and insisted that this was a classic example of how women control men. He had a hard time calming down. I thanked him for letting us know how he felt and how he truly thought. Secretly, I felt a new wave of empathy for his wife, who lived with this volcano ready to explode if she made a wrong move.

Theo showed us, in living color, the reaction of a man who feels oppressed by the power of women. Every look, every little remark, determines how he feels about himself. He looks in this mirror all the time.

Later, in another group, Theo told us about an argument he had with his wife in which she accused him of being possessive and jealous. The group members shifted in their chairs uncomfortably, unable to immediately come to his support, knowing that Theo was more than capable of being possessive and jealous. He went on to describe how he sat down in his chair in the living room while she "verbally harassed" him for six hours. But he found a way to turn off his feelings and let her rant and rave. He finally felt like he was no longer vulnerable to her. "The most beautiful moment of my life—next to the birth of my son—was those six hours when I was *not* being controlled by a woman. I just didn't care. I could turn her off. It was such a relief."

He didn't care any more. Emotionally, she didn't matter. He had deadened himself to her, and to his own feelings. Like Benny, Theo was desperately attempting to survive emotionally, doing the only thing he could think of to protect himself. This was a perfect example of a man giving power to a woman in a way that had no appeal or interest to her whatsoever.

Feeling Left Out

I will never forget the story I heard from one couple in my office. Danielle and Jeffrey's baby was about four months old. When the baby cried in the night, Danielle was in the habit of going to her and nursing her, thus soothing her so they all could go back to sleep. Jeffrey had a different philosophy about nursing schedules, and they argued about whether it was the best thing to continue to breast-feed in the middle of the night. So far, this sounded like a normal, healthy child-rearing disagreement between two intelligent and informed but disagreeing adults.

But then the story turned weird. One night, when they heard the baby's cries, Danielle started to get up. Jeffrey tried to talk her out of it. She insisted. He blocked her path. She tried to push him aside and get to the now louder baby. He wouldn't let her. One thing led to another, and he finally found himself screaming at his wife, in the middle of the night, with the baby's screams piercing the house.

To Jeffrey's credit, he woke up from this possessed state and shut up. He slumped down in a chair and wondered aloud, "What is wrong with me? How did we get to this point?" Jeffrey got to this absurd and destructive point because of his overwhelming (yet not consciously recognized) sense of powerlessness. His life, with a demanding infant and a distracted wife, was spinning out of control. He had ideas that he believed (perhaps correctly) would help them and would actually be the best thing for their child. He wanted to be a good and responsible father. Perhaps he was also feeling left out of the private bond between mother and daughter and could not tolerate the perceived loss.

Again, the ultimate behavior of this man—screaming at his wife over the screams of their baby in the middle of the night—only tells us that he has behaved badly. To help him change, we needed to dig deeper and help him understand why. In this book, I am operating on the good-man assumption: that you, like Jeffrey, are a good man with good values who will make good choices when you understand more of your emotional life and when you are equipped with other behavioral options.

You should be able to recognize some part of yourself in these stories. Accurate or not, fair or not, paranoid or not, you have to first recognize how these defining moments in your relationship look and feel to you. Then, and only then, does a window open for your defenses to soften and for new perspectives to become possible.

What Men Need from Women

Ask most men if they are affected by how women respond to them and, if they are honest, they will tell you that it means the world to them. As men, we offer women immense power to govern our state of self-cohesion and well-being. Joseph Pleck (1980) outlines two very important dimensions of men's reliance on validation from women: expressing emotions and reinforcing masculinity.

The Power to Express Emotions

We often perceive women as having *expressive power*, the power to express emotions and particularly the power to help us discover and express emotions. Many of us have learned to depend on women to help us feel; in fact, their richer emotional life and capacity for emotional expression provides an essential life spark for many of us. Whether we can identify this or not, we may feel lost without the fundamental connection to this spark.

Perhaps you know men like this, and perhaps you recognize at least some of your own experience in these stories. You may live your life with limited emotions; you love your buddies and you need them, but you may not show them the full range of your more vulnerable or tender feelings. Then you meet a girl (or later, a woman) and, for the first time, you can let your hair down. You tell her your deepest secrets and fears. You reveal experiences that have scared you or shaken you. You are playful and silly in ways that would never fit in the guy world or anywhere else. She—or rather the relationship with her—is the ticket to this hidden and wonderful reservoir. She—or rather the relationship with her—is the catalyst.

Perhaps most significant is the refuge that women offer you, or at least that you perceive only women as having the power to offer. Women offer a port in the storm from the dangers and stresses of relating to other men. They offer the sanctuary where you can express your needs without fearing that these needs will be used against you.

Listen to this dialogue from the 1971 movie *Carnal Knowledge*, written by Jules Feiffer and directed by Mike Nichols. Sandy (Art Garfunkel) and Jonathan (Jack Nicholson) are college roommates. Sandy is dating a woman named Susan (Candace Bergen) and developing a very sweet and loving relationship. Jonathan, however, is secretly having sex with her, and neither has told this to Sandy.

The two young men have an argument. Sandy tells Jonathan that Susan "tells me thoughts I didn't even know I had until she tells them to me." This drives Jonathan nuts. Jonathan thought he had the upper hand in the traditional world of men. He is "scoring" and Sandy is not. But now it appears that Sandy is winning. Jonathan is now threatened that Sandy seems to have something even more valuable than the affirmation of sexual conquest: expressive power. When Sandy tells Jonathan that "she thinks I'm sensitive," it becomes too much for Jonathan to bear.

In a comical scene moments later, he confronts Susan in the maniacal way that Nicholson the actor brilliantly portrays. He accuses her of knowing every private thought of Sandy's but withholding this gift when it comes to him. He insists that she "do it" with him like she "does it" with Sandy: "Look at me, Susan, now tell me my goddamn thoughts!"

"I Could Only Do It with Her"

Jared sat in my office one day and told me the whole story of his sometimes tragic, sometimes picaresque childhood. Jared's father was an abusive alcoholic who frequently beat Jared's mother, finally abandoning the family when Jared was twelve. What did this young kid do? He ran away and, believe it or not, joined the circus. He traveled with the circus until he was eighteen, developing charming social skills and a highly refined sense of how to get along by taking care of other people's needs. Jared was a master at reading people and adapting himself to the situation in front of him. He was introduced to sex at the age of thirteen by some of the older women in the circus and, true to form, became very successful with women because he knew what they needed and found ways to shape himself accordingly.

For a kid who grew up in a such a violent and dysfunctional home, Jared was a roaring success. He was astonishingly self-sufficient, charming and engaging, and successful with women. But he was always plagued by the gap between his outward persona and his inner feelings. He was a master at presenting a false self, but he never felt really known by anyone.

Until he met Jeanie. "With Jeanie, it was like I opened up for the first time. I could really talk about feelings with her. Men don't know how to do this; I could only do it with her. And then, it hasn't been that long, everything started going downhill. We haven't even been married a year." He started to tear up. "I can't do it again. I just don't think I can do it again. It just turns out badly." He paused. "I've always found a way to be successful at everything I do, but this is really a failure."

Jeanie served as the catalyst for Jared's emotional awakening: *I could only do it with her.* But it turned out that Jared did not have much experience with the demands of a mature relationship, and Jeanie herself (although effective at helping Jared feel nurtured and safe) was likewise immature in her relationship skills. It all unraveled quickly, and for Jared this meant not only the loss of the relationship but also the loss of possibility. Getting a taste of a truer emotional life—and then losing it—felt unbearable to him, to the point where he was telling himself that he could never do it again.

I heard echoes of this same theme from Kevin's dad, Robert. Kevin was a college student who came to see me after getting suspended for alcohol and drug problems his first year away at college. Kevin had become estranged from his father since his parents' divorce when he was eight. Now Kevin felt an intense wave of determination to develop some rapprochement with his father.

Robert was a domineering and emotionally closed man: very successful in business, very limited in his emotional relationships. He and his wife divorced because she grew weary of his emotional coldness and his workaholism. His kids, including Kevin, had marginal relationships with him in which they maintained a veneer of attachment, but actually felt very little for him.

When Robert became ill with cancer, he finally confided in his girlfriend, Barbara. He broke down in a way that he never had before. "I've never had a real conversation in my life with my son!" Robert burst into tears. But he could only say this to Barbara; she was the only person he would show his emotional soft underbelly.

Even though Barbara secretly told this story to Kevin, and Robert knew that she had, he couldn't bring himself to reveal to Kevin what he had finally, privately, revealed to Barbara. Kevin was deeply moved by this story and desperately wanted to be allowed into his father's heart in the way that Barbara had been. But, at first, Robert relied on Barbara to help him express his emotions and wasn't ready to share that part of himself with anyone else. Kevin persisted, however, and he was eventually successful at getting his dad to communicate on an emotional level. Robert was able to learn from the experience with the woman in his life and gradually develop an emotional life of his own.

Masculinity-Validating Power

The second way that men rely excessively on women is by depending on them to remind men of their fundamental masculinity and masculine self-worth. In this way, men give women what Pleck describes as *masculinity-validating power*. When a woman refuses to offer this validation, or when a man's unrealistic expectations and subsequent distortions convince him that she is withholding this, the man may feel lost. He desperately demands the restoration of his virility, masculinity, self-worth, and ultimately self-cohesion by the powerful confirming source.

Again, remember that we men wrapped up in these interpersonal dynamics have made an unconscious decision to offer this power to women. These are not, for the most part, powers that women wish to hold. These are powers that we have handed over to women.

Defining Real Men

Miguel, a twenty-four-year-old Latino, sat in my office one day and described how confused he was about how to handle some difficult situations with his wife. I had never met her, but Miguel described his wife as very attractive and consistently drawing attention from men in public

My wife has always complained I have this big temper and I'm such a hothead. So we are out at the mall, walking together, and we walk past these two guys who really check her out and start laughing. I know exactly what's up, because I've done so much of it myself. I want to do something, but then

I remember that she wants me to chill out, so I just pretend like nothing's happening.

Then, when we get home, she starts laying into me: "You're such a pussy! How can you let those guys treat me like that? Why don't you stand up to them like a real man?"

So what is it? Does a real man chill? Or does he pick a fight to defend his honor and the honor of his woman? I know that next time, I'm gonna go after one of those guys if that's what she wants!

Miguel's story captures the masculinity-validating power. Who has the power here to determine his belief in himself as a man? She does. Because he has given it away. Do you recognize yourself in this story? For every man who says that he alone determines what a real man is, there are thousands more who recognize the emotional truth in this man-woman transaction. What she says, and how she treats you or looks at you, means so much.

Feeling Powerful

Joseph Pleck (1980) describes another scene from *Carnal Knowledge* that gives us an over-the-top illustration of how men give away this power and how vulnerable men can be when women do not follow the script. At the end of this movie, after countless busted relationships and years of engaging in a dance of prodigious sexuality and emotional shallowness, Jonathan cultivates a relationship with a prostitute. We watch as she offers him obviously scripted lines designed to bolster his shaky virility—and he collapses in distress and rage when she varies from the exact words necessary for him to have an erection.

When she finally gets it right, her script has her praising him for being a powerful and strong man with an "inner power so strong that every act no matter what is more proof of that power." She seductively tells him that he is strong, and masculine, and robust, and virile, and domineering, and irresistible. And finally, with all of this mirroring, he gets hard. At this point in his life, there's no other way for him to get it up.

The ways that men turn to women for masculinity validation vary, of course, in as many ways as men interpret masculinity. In *Carnal Knowledge*, Jonathan equates masculinity with sexual prowess, and this is what he needs validated in order to feel like a real man.

Men's Value and Self-Worth

My client Gene, however, responded most profoundly to validation of his ability to communicate. Seeing the mirror of approval in the eyes of his wife, Jeanette, made it all seem so real and so "masculine."

> *All my life, I have been sure that I was weak, a coward.*
> *Because I never stood up to my abusive old man, like Ben*
> *finally did in the* Great Santini *movie that you told me to*
> *watch. I am so sure that any woman I get involved with will*
> *finally see what I am missing. And I assume that I will pass*
> *on this abusive parenting to my kids.*
>
> *But when I start to tell Jeanette about these feelings, and*
> *she looks into my eyes and starts tearing up, and she tells me*
> *how much closer she feels to me, it's like she believes in me.*
> *If she sees me as being okay as man, then maybe I am.*

Carlo's intense reliance on his wife for validation of his masculinity revolved around his need to be important and valuable to her. Carlo, a handsome, balding man in his fifties, sat quietly in my office while he listened to his wife's complaints about their marriage. He stared her down without saying anything. He idly inspected his fingernails while she tried to get through to him. Finally, he decided to air his grievances and feelings toward her. The following example may seem almost comical, but it reflects a desperate man. Two facts you need to know to understand this outburst from Carlo: Carlo's wife was very attached to her pet parrot, and she had been trimming Carlo's hair throughout their marriage. Carlo began, "You offered to trim my hair, but you always forget to trim my ear hairs. What underlying psychological message are you trying to express? You groom that frigging bird much better than you groom me. It's almost like you are mated to him. You're right—at first when we thought the parrot was a female, it didn't bother me so much. Then we find out it's a male, and it's like you have more of a bond with this male than with me!"

Carlo actually felt threatened and displaced by his wife's attachment to her parrot, especially because it was male!

Dr. Alfredo Mirande (2003), professor at University of California Riverside, tells a personal story about the power of women to shape men's view of themselves.

> *It is women who teach us to be men. They play a defining*
> *role in our development as men. When I was a child, I watched*
> *one time as my uncle was pushing around and threatening his*
> *wife. My mother, his sister, said to him, "How can you call*
> *yourself a man if you beat up defenseless women?" My uncle*
> *was completely humiliated—she was calling him on his*
> *manhood. Women have this power. This had a profound effect*
> *on my masculine development. I learned that it is despicable*
> *for a man to hit a woman.*

Exercise: I Feel More Like a Man When She . . .

Think about the impact of your partner's responses and actions on how you feel about yourself as a man. Be honest! Mark any of the items below that you think could complete the sentence "I feel more like a man when she . . ."

_____ tells me she loves me

_____ has the wildest damn orgasm you could possibly imagine!

_____ laughs at my jokes

_____ lets me know that she respects something I have done

_____ does things that I approve of, making me feel proud

_____ is someone I know I can really trust—it means she must love me!

_____ is happy to see me

_____ touches me

_____ says cool stuff about me to other people

_____ pays more attention to me than to her male parrot

On a separate sheet of paper or in your journal, add as many items as you can to this list.

There is no sin in having the woman you love affect how you feel about yourself. But it is important for you to know yourself better—and to be careful about blaming her too much if you start to feel your positive feelings about yourself slipping away.

Misattributions and Misperceptions

When you tell yourself the narrative that explains yourself and your relationship, you are like the stationmaster at Grand Central Station. You send the train—your emotions and behavior—on the track to Pittsburgh, Boston, or St. Louis, and once the train is headed that way, it takes quite an effort to stop it, switch tracks, and send the train in a different direction.

"It Was an Assault!
A Goddamn Assault!"

Daniel stood in my office peering out at me through his horn-rimmed glasses. He waited nervously for me to sit in my chair, then sat down in his, across from his wife, Elise. She looked at me with eyes that said, *Please help me out here! I don't know how to get through to him!* They proceeded to relate the most recent conflict, an argument about how much time to spend reading a bedtime story to their little girl. Daniel wanted to read to her longer, but Elise protested that their daughter's bedtime kept getting pushed back later and later, and it became a problem in the mornings when it was time to wake her up for preschool. The argument was going nowhere. So, according to both of them, Elise got up from her chair and started to walk out of the room. Daniel, standing in the doorway, blocked her path and made no effort to get out of the way. She paused at the doorway, looked at him briefly, and brushed against him as she went through the door.

Sitting calmly in my office, both of them agreed on these facts. But as soon as I asked Daniel how this affected him, the quieter, meeker exterior suddenly disappeared. "How did that make me feel? How did that make me feel? I'll tell you how that made me feel! It was an assault! A goddamn assault! I felt physically threatened by her!"

I doubted that. Both agreed that she had barely brushed against him. She had no history of violence in their relationship. Instead, what Daniel was reacting to was the pain of her disapproval and perceived rejection of him. "What do you think it's like when she criticizes me like that? Telling me I'm doing something wrong when I like to read a story to my own daughter! It's like a knife going right into my heart. Do you know what that's like? Do you have any idea what that's like?"

The core problem here lay in Daniel's interpretation of the events. When Elise complained to him and asked him to change something, he heard that he was worthless. When she brushed past him, upset and frustrated, he read that she found him disgusting. Daniel experienced these events as extremely painful, rejecting, offensive, and shaming. And when he felt this bad inside, he concluded that Elise *intended* to make him feel this way. She was the very powerful mirror, and the picture of himself that was reflected back to him was devastating and unbearable. He blamed the mirror, but he had been looking at the mirror through the foggy lens of a lifetime of self-doubt, rejection, and fear of abandonment.

And once the conclusion was locked in place, once the mirror was viewed in this way and given this enormous unwanted power,

Daniel's train was launched on an emotional and behavioral track that was almost always destructive. (Daniel went on, in this state of self-justified resentment, to turn to me and calmly say, "She's an idiot! She has rocks in her head! How do you ever get through to a woman who has rocks in her head like that? She's a complete idiot!")

If you recognize a little bit of yourself in Daniel, your essential task is to develop a greater tolerance of these distressing moments. Once you develop this, you have at least the opportunity to entertain alternative narratives about what is taking place. If you think your wife is in a bad mood, you will react differently than if you think she is trying to humiliate you. If you tell yourself that there is room for healthy disagreement in the best of relationships, you will react differently than if you believe this is an indicator of her hatred and your worthlessness. As psychologist Ross Greene tells parents about dealing with their kids, "your interpretation will guide your intervention" (1998, 14).

The same self psychology perspective that helped you understand the broken mirror can help you recognize the fundamental injury to the sense of self (or selfobject breakdown) that usually precedes emotional withdrawal, pouting, accusations, or abusive behavior. If you can recognize this vulnerability—and if you can develop the ability to communicate your needs—you will be more self-directed. You will have more power to turn away from the desperate or self-protective reactions that often emerge at these moments.

The Secret, Silent Decision

John Gottman (1999) has identified an array of toxic indicators that predict, according to his research, almost certain deterioration of relationships. By examining the interaction of a wide variety of couples—including successful, happy couples—he and his team have uncovered what they refer to as the Four Horsemen of the Apocalypse: criticism (or accusations), defensiveness, contempt, and stonewalling. When couples engage in these behaviors frequently, the relationship is much more likely to be dysfunctional and volatile. The researchers have found that couples who regularly use these styles with each other are almost certainly headed for unhappiness, affairs, verbal or physical abuse, or divorce. (Gottman claims that his research team can predict this with 90 percent accuracy!)

The problem arising from the Four Horsemen is not only how emotionally beat up each person feels. The Horsemen also represent a painful and destructive decision that one or both partners has made about the other: *He (or she) is not a good-hearted person, is not truly on my side, and is a threat to me. I have given up.*

In dysfunctional couples, negative mind reading runs rampant. It is as if each partner has made what Gottman calls a "secret, silent decision" that the other is an adversary and not worth respecting. Each assumes the worst about the other.

An ally's narrative goes something like this: *Oh well, he is in a bad mood. He has been under a lot of stress lately and needs more sleep.* An ally views negativity as unstable (highly alterable, fluctuating) and the cause as situational (external).

On the other hand, in an unhappy marriage, the same behavior is likely to be interpreted as stable (enduring, unchanging) and internal to the partner. The accompanying narrative might be something like *He is inconsiderate and selfish. That's the way he is. That's why he did that.*

Here's another example that illustrates the immense power of misperceptions. Namir and his wife, Ellen, came to see me because of the tensions in their marriage. Namir was a very emotionally intense and extremely intellectually gifted man in his forties. He had a history of gambling problems and emotionally abusive outbursts— and he was extremely attached to his wife. Ellen's views and responses to him provided an unbearably powerful mirror for his sense of well-being.

Several months before coming to see me, they were taking a shower together. Namir made a sexual overture to Ellen; she (according to Ellen) politely indicated that she wasn't interested. Namir went ballistic. He became enraged and started screaming at her, hurling nasty insults about her frigid sexuality. The emotional injury, and her fear of his rages, was impossible for her to live with.

Ellen became colder and emotionally withdrawn over the next several weeks. She finally told him that she wanted to separate for a while. At first he graciously agreed, trying to show his respect for her feelings. But he could not tolerate this for long, and soon he began showing up at her workplace uninvited and calling her repeatedly.

Although they were still separated and Ellen was still somewhat afraid, she agreed to his request to come in for counseling. When I asked Namir what it had meant to him—what his perception was—when Ellen turned him down sexually in the shower, he spewed out a flurry of passionate feelings: "It means everything! I don't even know who I am without her! If she doesn't want me, it means I am not a man! I only want to have that look from her that tells me I am loved and valuable." This was Namir expressing his raw need and vulnerability. Much of what he describes is painfully human, but his intensity and lack of coping resources are what lead him astray. "So I just had to do something! I want to just force her to make me feel the way I know she alone can make me feel! And sometimes I just want her to feel as scared and powerless as I feel! I know I need help. It isn't fair to her, and I know I just keep driving her away." Namir paused, then became tearful. "I'll do anything you tell me to do."

All of Namir's emotional despair and destructive behavior began with his misperceptions of Ellen's motivation and misinterpretation of her response to him. He was unable to just say to himself, *I guess she's not in the mood.* Or any of a thousand variations on this statement. Instead, all he could say to himself was this: *She and she alone can make me feel good about myself, and she is purposely withholding this from me!*

It is clear from Gottman's research that the secret, silent decision is hardly the exclusive domain of men. Rather, it is right at the core of the decisions any of us makes in a relationship: male, female, gay, straight, adult, child. But especially for men like Namir—and perhaps for you—there may be no more powerful intervention than developing a more flexible, generous, and realistic view of your partner.

Exercise: What's Your Story?

1. Pick out a situation when you got into an argument with your partner, or even one of your children.

2. Identify the story (narrative) you were telling yourself at the time.

3. If your narrative included her not being a decent person who cares about you, you probably felt totally justified in retaliating. You may have felt tempted to give up and to forsake the relationship rules you usually believe in.

4. When this happens again, try substituting a new story line.

To help you do this, I've included some negative narratives and some corresponding, more hopeful stories. As you read these examples, pay attention to any that sound familiar. Then, on a separate sheet of paper or in your journal, create as many of your own examples as you can.

The Story of Doom

1. What a bitch!

2. She doesn't care about anybody but herself!

3. I can never get through to her!

4. She always wants it her way!

5. I just don't trust her!

6. She's always trying to control me.

The Story of Hope

1. She gets really bitchy sometimes!

2. Right now I feel like she doesn't have a clue about what I need.

3. I feel so frustrated trying to get through to her right now.

4. Damn, I thought *I* was stubborn, but she really is!

5. Most of the time, I know she's with me, but it doesn't feel like it right now!

6. I can tell she's freaked out about something when she gets this controlling.

Notice that the stories of hope are not all that pretty—they are just more temporary, limited, and realistic. It's impossible to be in an intimate relationship without feeling critical or unhappy with your partner. The stories of doom, however, create a narrative that justifies destructive behavior in response. With a few exceptions, this narrative—and the emotions and behaviors that inevitably trail behind—is something you can do something about!

"Mommy and I Are One"

The research of Silverman, Lachman, and Milich (1982) helps explain some of the unquenchable passion for deep attachment that so many of us experience. While their research was not exclusively based on men seeking attachment to women, it sheds some more light on the attachment phenomena often described as "the urge to merge."

The authors lay out their belief that under particular circumstances, even the fantasy of experiencing a merger or deep connection can enhance self-cohesion. They employed an unusual method of testing this. Research subjects watched, for brief exposures not long enough to register consciously, slides containing the subliminal message "Mommy and I are one." The researchers hypothesized that the subjects' universal longing for oneness would be satisfied in some way as they received this message.

After multiple studies (and many variations of the message and type of subjects studied), the conclusions were usually positive. Smokers who were exposed to the message maintained abstinence from smoking longer. Male schizophrenics showed some reduction in pathological symptoms. Depressed women reported less depressive symptoms and depressive thinking after exposure to the subliminal message. Obese women who were exposed to the message lost more weight than women who were not.

The Special Connection

Why would an intervention like this make any difference at all? First of all, I should point out that this didn't always work, and the use of subliminal messages as a treatment may or may not be valuable in the long run. And the research was not just based on male longing for merger experiences with women. But the research helps illuminate some important issues that often underlie the longing that men have for a special connection.

This search for oneness originates from the primary, symbiotic relationship between mother and child: first within the womb, and then, to a lesser extent, outside. This is the oceanic state of complete well-being, when you were never really called upon to face the ultimately lonely state of being human. There is no way to return to the womb, but you can seek approximations of this experience through a wide array of events, interpersonal and otherwise, in your adult life.

Most men, when I try to explain this, think this yearning is reserved for the deeply pathological or emotionally immature among us. Certainly, if your longings to merge dominate your relationships, you are in trouble. You are likely to be stuck in a regressed, disturbed, and ultimately hopeless life. But when these yearnings coexist with your other needs (such as autonomy and independence), they suggest no such disturbance. In fact, your recognition of these longings and your search for situations which help satisfy them can be viewed as an indicator of your emotional health.

The opportunities are everywhere—not to return to the womb, perhaps, but to find something good enough. Think for a moment about the many events in life that can arouse these merger feelings. Interpersonal oneness experiences always involve a direct connection with a single person or with a group of people. The most obvious is perhaps the most potent: romantic union. The blissful merging that takes place in sexual and romantic love—both during peak moments of sexual union and during the little romantic moments of lovers who feel as if the world exists only for them— revives the original moments of union from infancy. Anybody who has been in love knows the golden experience of not knowing where your own body stops and your lover's starts.

None of us can bear to stay in this boundaryless state because of our need for an independent sense of self. The classic fear of commitment usually stems directly from our fears that we will lose all boundaries and become trapped in the world of another. Still, as with so many aspects of emotional and psychological life, we are drawn to go back to the well again and again to experience it once more.

This merger experience does not require romantic or sexual love. You have probably had moments with close friends or family members—with nothing sexual at stake—when you felt as if you were at one with another. College friends locked in conversation deep into the night will often say afterward, "I just felt like we were reading each other's minds. I knew exactly what you were going to say!" One element that often makes the psychotherapist-patient relationship so significant is the experience (for the patient, and often even for the therapist) of being very deeply connected. Patients often report, "I just felt like she understood me so completely, like she knew everything about me. It's like she was psychic." This is the exhilaration of being deeply seen and known.

Men and Special Connections

So what does all this have to do with the frustration of marriage, the dark moods, and the power that men project onto women?

We all live, to some degree, with the psychic wound of losing the blissful umbilical connection. And we all, to one degree or another, turn somewhere in an attempt to restore this feeling of wholeness. This is normal and healthy.

But these intense longings—conscious or unconscious—for the oneness experience can be a fragmenting experience for you if you are desperately hungry for this powerful connection. Your perception and judgment can become warped with misattributions whenever you feel the oneness experience slipping away from you.

The problem lies in the unrealistic expectation that many of us have. Buried deep inside, men and women both often unconsciously believe that their partner will fill the empty space inside: *As long as we are together, I will never feel empty or alone.* When a woman fails to provide this magic restoration of our original feelings of wholeness, we men are often deluged with disappointment. It is usually not conscious, and you usually do not have words to describe the experience. You may have waves of resentment toward her for bursting the bubble. It's as if she has promised you something all along and is now brutally failing to deliver.

When she fails to live up to this vision of how things were supposed to be—either because she changes or simply because the relationship evolves to a more individuated level or because reality catches up to the projected fantasy—you come to believe that she is letting you down. A new fantasy may begin to creep in: *There is someone else out there who can do it better!*

There may be, in reality, someone out there who can do it better, and this possibility must always be considered. Yet, unless you recognize that no romantic love—no love of any kind—can truly heal you or restore your wholeness, you may be doomed to keep searching in disappointment. The dilemma keeps recurring throughout these complex situations. We know how enriching interpersonal connections can be, and how impossible it is to develop personally except in the context of relationships with others. On the other hand, since we left the womb, no other can truly make us whole, fill the empty spaces, and take away our pain. We are entitled to, and can reasonably expect, a partner who knows us, cares about us, and excites us. We cannot expect her to be all-knowing, all-caring, and all-exciting. The early losses that we have all suffered cannot, in the end, be undone.

In his article "The Golden Fantasy" (1977), Sydney Smith describes the wish to have all of one's needs met in a perfect relationship. This fantasy, like "Mommy and I are one," is embedded to some degree in all of us. Even if the fantasy is never realized, just knowing that it might be possible somewhere and someday can be a source of vitality and reassurance for many people. "This fantasy touches on the deepest issues of one's life and . . . indeed one's very survival may depend upon its preservation. . . . To give up the fantasy is to give up everything, to lose the primary source of comfort . . . , even one's sense of meaning. It is as if the fantasy provided a self-definition: without it there is no existence and the world becomes a place without hope" (311).

Perhaps you are one of those men for whom this fantasy takes on extraordinary prominence. When you fear that the fantasy won't be realized, you can become threatened and fragmented. Most importantly, your attachment to the golden fantasy may sabotage your ability to find meaning and fulfillment in real relationships. "While they are on an endless search for a fulfilling experience, they seem unable to make use of the loving relationships around them. . . . To decide to work at a particular relationship is to confirm that the fantasy is dead (or that Paradise is lost) or that what was once within one's grasp is forever gone" (318).

The golden fantasy, while so alluring and sustaining in many ways, can erode any chances for you to become truly fulfilled by the actual, imperfect relationships that are available to you. She is never quite good enough. The legitimate longing for a richer and deeper relationship becomes blurred with the insatiable search for someone who can fulfill the golden fantasy.

Once you understand your need for connection and mirroring with the women in your life, you become empowered. You can take responsibility for your moods: just because you feel injured or self-doubting does not necessarily mean that your partner has tried to make you feel that way. You can begin to learn how to validate yourself instead of needing a woman to validate you. Or you can try to find other sources of validation that neither lead you to withdraw emotionally from your partner nor threaten your primary relationship. In other words, remember that it is healthy to need, unhealthy to need excessively, and essential to do nothing that is fundamentally disrespectful to someone you love and care about.

3

Fathers and Sons:
Curses and Blessings

Every time a father berates his wife, he is cursing his son. Every time a man models entitlement, he is cursing his kids. Because we know that boys who observe abusive behavior—from patterns of sarcasm and put-downs and emotional withdrawal all the way up to physical intimidation and violence—are much more likely to engage in these behaviors in their own adult relationships. And we know that boys who grow up experiencing excessive put-downs and rejections from their fathers are much more sensitized to perceived rejection and humiliation in their future relationships—another curse!

My client Marco told me,

> *My father used to put me down. He slapped me around, called me "shit for brains," told me he should have never had me. Now, when my wife says something that sounds even a little bit critical, I hear the same damn thing in my head: "shit for brains, shit for brains . . ."*
>
> *If I stacked something wrong in the store, he'd slap me upside the head in front of other people. He would call me stupid. I was always nervous about the type of job I was doing. He would slap me if I screwed up until I got it right.*
>
> *I was a good enough athlete to play college ball in three sports, but he would always criticize me. I once got a whipping*

for not winning a race—he thought I hadn't put out full effort.
The way my father brought me up caused me more problems.
I'm not satisfied with who I am, and I never will be.

Conversely, fathers have the power to inspire. By modeling the best traits of masculinity rather than a caricature of machismo or emotional illiteracy, fathers have enormous influence over the template of their sons' manhood. A father's belief in his son is one of the most powerful mirrors that a boy will ever experience.

I have learned to never underestimate the power of a father's approval of his son. I have witnessed even some of the most defended teen boys, who carry themselves with attitudes communicating disinterest and even disgust for what their fathers think of them and their tattoos and music and attitude, well up in tears when their fathers communicated sincere love and appreciation.

When I was in my late twenties, I became engaged to a woman whom I had been dating for several years. To make a long story short, we experienced a major crisis several weeks before the wedding and decided to call it off three weeks before the set date. We canceled caterers, bands, and photographers. Family scheduled to fly in from out of town canceled their trips. We returned some presents that had already arrived.

My most intense anxiety, barely second to the pain of this crashing relationship, involved informing my parents, and particularly my father, of this "failure." With the help of a couples therapist who was guiding us, I managed to handle this with some dignity and success. And, although both my parents behaved themselves with grace and came through, I always worried that my father was secretly disappointed in me.

Actually, I didn't even realize that I was still carrying around this worry and shame. But several months later, out of nowhere in the middle of another conversation, my father (not known for being particularly emotionally articulate) turned to me and said, "You know, I don't think I would have had the courage to do what you did when you called off your wedding."

I thanked him. And I remember that moment now, more than twenty years later, like it was yesterday. My father had given me his blessing. He had reframed the decision I had made as one requiring courage rather than one worthy of shame and indicating failure. I probably shouldn't have needed him to tell me that, but we are all human. We never shed the need and longing for positive mirroring, the need to look in the mirror of an important person and see a reflection of ourselves as fundamentally good and valuable.

Good Fathers Behaving Badly

John Sanford and George Lough, in their book *What Men Are Like* (1988), identify origins of typical patterns in problematic father-son relationships. One of the key factors they identify is the father's unresolved hurt feelings from his own childhood. This type of father lives with a hurt little boy within himself, one who is always ready to be rejected, and this makes the father oversensitive to what he perceives as rejection.

Emotional Withholding

Here we have another chapter to the broken mirror story: the man, previously wounded, turns to another person—this time his son—as a mirror to confirm his self-worth and to offer him a sense of well-being. Sanford points out that we fathers who are laboring with these personal issues tend to either avoid relating to our sons or go out of our way to be good fathers, but then feel hurt when we don't feel properly appreciated or rewarded. We experience the child's rejection of our help or our values as a fundamental rejection of our self. And, in our own overt or covert way, we blame the son. We blame the mirror for breaking on us.

Rick weighed over three-hundred pounds and had long ago stopped counting. He told me his story about his ongoing war with his seventeen-year-old son. Rick grew up with an emotionally abusive father. He was called a quitter. His birthdays were ignored. When Rick was in a boating accident at sixteen and suffered some mild cognitive deterioration, both parents gave up on him and stopped encouraging him in school. His younger brother, who had previously been receiving even less attention than Rick, became the family star.

Now, as a father, Rick had spent years humiliating his own son. Stephen could never do well enough. Rick humiliated him in front of his friends, calling him stupid, calling his friends scum. Although Rick had a vague sense of how corrosive his fathering skills were, he defended his treatment of his son in the ways that fathers have been justifying this sort of treatment for many generations: *I need to do this to make a man out of him.*

One day Rick told me about the rage and resentment he felt about simple acts of generosity toward Stephen. "Stephen has this job working at a gas station. And my wife makes him lunch and asks me to bring it over to him. I'm thinking, *There's taco stands right near there, let him get his own lunch. Nobody ever brought me fucking lunch when I was a kid!*"

Nobody ever brought me fucking lunch when I was a kid! was the mantra that kept repeating itself inside his head whenever his son called upon him to drive him somewhere, help him with his homework, go to a teacher conference, or buy him something he really wanted. And when Stephen's pickup truck—the most important thing in his life—had the wheels squealing from rubbing against metal, and Stephen needed Rick to drop off the key one morning at the tire shop, Rick copped an attitude. He refused to vary his schedule and try to accommodate Stephen. *Nobody ever did that for me!* kept ringing in his head.

Rick, at this moment, was paralyzed by the wounds of his past. He didn't know why he turned so cold toward his son, and he spent a lot of time creating justifications for his behavior. As humans, we all need to create order and to form patterns. So Rick, unable to identify his hurt and resentment toward his own father, created order by convincing himself that his actions were right—thus perpetuating the legacy.

None of this changed until he became more conscious of the way his emotional pain drove his behavior. This is the essential building block for changing the pattern. You'll hear the story of how Rick found a way out in chapter 6 when we celebrate men who change.

Holding Back

Another manifestation of emotional shackles is the pattern of being emotionally restricted. Do you ever experience a poignant moment with deep feelings when your only expression is a tiny teardrop, a little joke, a change of subject, a distancing analysis of the situation?

Luke and his father sat in my office. Luke had finally summoned up the courage to confront his old man. Luke, nineteen and recently expelled from school for his marijuana and alcohol abuse, revealed to me in our first session together that he had lived his whole young life as a "politician." He had always managed to put on a show, showing others what he knew they wanted to see from him. And nowhere was this more true than with his father, with whom Luke had not had a "real conversation" since he divorced Luke's mother when he was eight.

Through Luke's impassioned breakthrough, his father sat quietly and took it. His face was frozen, but his eyes were watery. Luke cried. He screamed. He told his father how much he meant to him, and how hard he had tried for such a long time to please him. All he could get in response was the wooden face.

Luke turned to me and said, "You see? You see what I mean? He just sits there. I can't ever reach him!" And I looked over at his dad and saw the pain in his face. This was a man who desperately wanted to show more but simply did not know how. Showing more was a skill that he had lost many years ago, probably in his own childhood. Even though his mind knew what he should do and his heart called out to him to show his son even a little of how touched he was by his son's desperate reaching out, he couldn't. The best he could offer was a little moisture in his eyes and the words "Yes, these are important feelings."

I pointed out to Luke that his father was really doing the best he could right now. And that even though Luke felt shortchanged, his best shot was to read between the lines and see that slight moisture in the eyes of this man as if it were another man pouring his heart out.

Not every boy with an emotionally abusive father becomes overtly abusive himself, which is a rather mysterious blessing. But they are affected nevertheless. Sandy was a seventeen-year-old boy who was sent to me for treatment because of his mediocre grades in school and his pattern of lying and deception with his parents. Sandy described his father's pattern of expressing anger like this:

> *My dad just tunes out my mother when he doesn't want to talk to her. He will keep watching TV. When she asks to get his attention, he will slowly, very slowly, start turning the volume up louder with the remote control. Then she'll get upset and he'll say, "What? What? I can't hear you over the TV!" Then when I have done something he disapproves of, he will shun me. I will get up to give him a hug when he walks in the door and he will remain wooden, not hugging me back, like I don't exist. We'll pass in the hallway, and—you know how people each move out of the way a little bit to let the other person pass? He won't move at all. It's like I'm invisible. He just bumps into me like I'm not there.*

Sandy's father employed a style of expressing anger and controlling others that Gottman calls *stonewalling* (1994). But Sandy, at least so far in his life, was as gentle a soul as you will ever find. He was, despite his intelligence and skills at being a "nice guy," clueless about how his family issues were affecting his school performance, and he was in denial about the chronic lying and deception.

Sandy was gentle, but he could not feel very much. He was a nice person, but rather passionless. He was understanding, but pathologically unassertive. His father had left his mark.

Wounded Fathers, Wounded Sons

When I think of men who have become hardened by the wounds of childhood, I remember listening to a radio talk show caller several years ago. It was December, and the focus of the show was the state of the Christmas spirit in our society. The caller went off on a rant. He complained that the problem with our entitled, narcissistic society begins in childhood when kids receive Christmas presents without having done anything to earn them! All I could think was, *Who wounded him growing up?* What deprivation must this man have experienced to generate a social philosophy blaming unearned Christmas presents? And how sad that he has developed a life philosophy to justify the pain he had experienced, rather than recognizing the pain and building a philosophy based on something more than trying to deny trauma.

Another time I was in a public restroom. A young man was already in there, behind a divider, and I could overhear him saying to his child, "There was no reason for you to be throwing that tantrum in there! There was no reason for you to behave like that in public! You can probably get away with that now, but when you're a little older, that kind of behavior will get you a good whipping! I'm really mad at you!" I sneaked a peek at this man. The child he was addressing was an infant, no more than four months old—and he was changing his diaper! I had been sure that he was talking to an older child, who would be at least somewhat able to cognitively integrate these corrections and instructions. If it hadn't been so sad, it would have been hilarious, this father trying to talk sense into his four-month-old and threatening him with future consequences. I didn't know this man, but I suspected that he was like many other young fathers I have come to know: wanting desperately to be a good and responsible father, but needing education both in skills and capacity for empathy; not knowing yet how to do it differently than it had been done to them.

Broken Mirrors: Overattachment and Overidentification

The world of fatherhood is filled with good fathers sometimes behaving badly. (This is not to exempt motherhood, but simply to focus on the particular issues that challenge men.) Most of the fathers I know who have made tragic mistakes, or simply subtle, everyday blunders, have been operating out of a well-intended but unattuned effort to be a good dad.

The breakdown between your intentions and the effect of your actions can sometimes be attributed to bad timing, like when you try to have an important conversation with your son when he's concentrating on PlayStation; or your lack of awareness about a certain subject, like why your seven-year-old boy wets his bed or why your twelve-year-old girl has to rush home to get on instant messaging with her friends; or the fact that your child may be constitutionally very difficult to parent.

Taking It Personally

But the most profound problem that directly and painfully sabotages our positive impact on our kids lies within our own personalities and personal histories. As fathers, we tend to over-personalize situations because of our own unresolved emotional issues and perceive our children's behavior as if it is a direct—and very negative—reflection of us as men and as fathers.

The problem here is the inability to appreciate the child's independent center of initiative. Like Wade Whitehouse in *Affliction*, who can only make sense of his daughter's unhappiness as a personal reflection on him, you may be very quick to make judgments that are clouded by your own insecurity. The child loses big here, but so do you.

When a perceived broken mirror reflects a dark light back on you, you are likely to lose access to your wiser judgment about what is happening with your child and what to do about it. Suddenly—and worst of all, unconsciously—the issue becomes your own sense of self. At those junctures, you may be quite capable of rationalizing the response to your child as being justified, deserved, or for the kid's own good, when it is really only to make you feel temporarily better or less powerless.

"One time my son, when he was nine, was trying to do this bike stunt where he would have to make his bike jump in the air and then come down over some boards. He couldn't do it. He was scared. I really got on him: 'You're a baby, you're chicken, you're weak. I'm going to take your bike away from you!' I kept thinking he was letting *me* down! It was like he was disrespecting *me*." Tom told me this story as his marriage was unraveling. He had become a lot smarter by the time he told me this story; back then, he had actually been able to convince himself that boys needed to be pushed by their fathers or else they would remain permanently stuck in the clutches of over-protective mothers. He was determined not to let his son become "feminized." "But it was all bullshit. It was really just about me! My kid was timid; so that meant I was a loser as a dad. All I could think of is what my old man would have said to me, and what he would have thought if he saw me 'letting' my son get away with backing down from a challenge. You see? It was all about me! I couldn't see past my own shit and see that the kid was just scared. And he really needed me to be understanding more than anything else."

I remember the story of another man, a second grade teacher who felt chronically ineffective in his work. His five-year-old daughter was clearly a handful, as five-year-old daughters tend to be. One day he came home and her toys were scattered throughout the house. He told her to pick them up, and she ignored him. He raised his voice and told her again, and she had a five-year-old smartass answer. Then he picked her up and sat her on her bed, screaming at her that she had better listen to him, *now!*

His next words have always stuck with me: "I let these second grade kids run all over me all day long, but I'll be damned if I'll let that happen in my own home!" It was all about him. When he heard himself say these words out loud, in front of me and his concerned wife, he started to cry. He told us that it just sounded so pathetic.

Stuart, another man who came to see me, felt powerless. Not only in managing his two kids, thirteen and eleven, but throughout his life. He came by these feelings honestly. Injured in Vietnam, he lost a leg. And he had spent many of the subsequent thirty years fighting with various VA clinics about problems with his prosthetic leg. He felt frustrated and helpless. In his job, he felt insignificant: he was low on the totem pole, not earning the respect that a man of his age and experience should have.

One day he came home from work to the wailing of his thirteen-year-old daughter. Apparently, his daughter's "best friend" had been spreading rumors accusing her of promiscuous sexuality. Stuart listened to his wife as she told him what had triggered all this. And he came up with a plan, in the spirit of being a good father who feels the pain of his kids and wants to do everything he can to come through for them when they are hurting.

Stuart announced his plan: "Okay, here's what we're going to do. We're going to call your friend's mother and insist that she get her daughter to apologize. And especially to go back to the kids that she told this to and tell them that she made it up and that she is sorry!"

His daughter's response to this plan was to wail "Noooooooo!" even louder than before, the way only a thirteen-year-old girl can wail. Stuart's wife turned to him and quietly stated the obvious. "I don't think she wants us to do that."

Stuart's response was to stand up and lay down the law: "I know what I'm doing here. It's time that you all listened to me for once! If you don't go along with my plan, it's a sign that you don't respect me—and I'm outta here!"

Neither wife nor daughter said anything. Stuart stormed out of the house and actually spent the night in a hotel. He came back the next morning rather sheepishly, realizing that he had thrown an adult version of a temper tantrum.

To his credit, Stuart—a good man behaving badly if there ever was one—understood what had happened. He had simply become unbearably overwhelmed with feelings of powerlessness. At the time he didn't know how to recognize it, name it, or express it. He just felt compelled to escape it through a grandiose attempt to feel powerful. He lost his perspective; suddenly the unfolding drama had turned into a drama only about himself.

His daughter's distress had become a broken mirror, and her drama had become merely a reflection on him. He had not been capable of recognizing that this was actually a potential twinship and bonding experience. They all felt powerless together.

Rob, an introspective doctor in his forties, came in to see me distressed by his frustrations and his excessive criticism of his fourteen-year-old son. First, he wanted his son to see me, then he decided he wanted me to see the two of them together. He finally settled on the core of the problem: himself. We compared notes and war stories about the frustrations of fatherhood. It was a twinship experience and helped him normalize what he was going through. The centerpiece of the challenge for Rob was to recognize how hurt and resentful he felt because his son was not playing his part in Rob's vision of the father-son relationship and, as with a marriage crisis, to learn to take care of these emotional needs elsewhere—or at least recognize that it was not his son's responsibility to meet them.

Rob came to see himself as a very good parent tripped up by his own emotional needs, occasionally behaving badly.

"Why'd You Make Me Play Second Base?"

In the 1990 movie *Parenthood,* starring Steve Martin, this pattern of men overidentifying with the fate of their own children is dramatically and hilariously portrayed. Martin plays the role of Gil Buckman, a concerned, well-meaning, and slightly neurotic father with a nine-year-old son. Kevin is a sweet but very anxious kid who does not exactly meet his father's idealized image of a bold, adventurous, and confident boy. But Gil, a good guy, does his best to put aside these expectations and love his son just as he is.

Gil is the coach of Kevin's Little League team. At a crucial point in the ninth inning of a game, he encourages Kevin to fill in at second base. The movie then veers off into Gil's fantasy of Kevin's college graduation. Kevin, of course, is handsome, confident, and the chosen class speaker. In his speech, he informs the audience of the key to his past. "When I was nine years old, I had kind of a rough time. A lot of people thought I was pretty mixed up. But there was one person who got me through it. He did everything right. And thanks to him, today I am the happiest, most confident, and most well-adjusted person in this world. Dad, I love you. You're the greatest!" The camera focuses in on his father, standing up in the crowd to the wild admiration of all.

After this fantasy dissolves, reality sets in. Kevin muffs a pop-up that allows the other team to win. He storms off in tears, screaming at his father, "Why'd you make me play second base?"

Now the dark fantasy takes over. Gil imagines a future with Kevin in a university clock tower, randomly picking off students. Someone cries out, "It's Kevin Buckman! His father totally screwed him up!" Kevin screams out to his father in the crowd, "You made me play second base!"

The moral of the story: Your kid is who he is. Your role is to be the best father you can be, which means deeply appreciating him as he is. If his behavior does not match your standards, adjust your standards. If your own issues about proving yourself as a man take over when it is time to offer yourself to your kid, think first and act second. Parenting is not about you.

Setting the Stage for Adult Relationships

No matter how much emotional armor they eventually develop, boys have sensitive souls. Boys are especially sensitive to experiences of rejection, humiliation, and shame in their relationships with their fathers.

Damaged Radar Mechanisms

This sensitivity predisposes them to be men whose radar is very finely tuned to the nuances of humiliation. It's a kind of post-traumatic stress disorder, where stimuli that somewhat resemble the original traumatic situation trigger intense—and distorted— reactions that resemble the original emotional response to the original trauma.

This experience of early rejection and humiliation is like a curse that haunts men as they enter the emotionally raw and demanding world of adult relationships. It haunts them, typically, in only the most intimate of relationships: with lovers and children.

Donald Dutton (1998) has studied boys who experience this kind of paternal humiliation and how this eventually affects them in adult relationships. It turns out that it's not just any old punishment that generates this predisposition. Every father punishes, sometimes excessively or unfairly, and every boy usually feels bad. Dutton's research suggests that there are three particular styles of punishment that are especially shaming or rejecting, setting the stage for these personality patterns: punishment in public, random punishment (in which the child or teen truly does not see the relationship between the alleged misdeed and the punishing response), and responses that come across as global criticism rather than specific correction of specific offenses.

One of Dutton's studies found that men who experienced this kind of parental rejection were much more likely to be abusive in their adult relationships with women, and paternal treatment came out as an even more important predictor than maternal treatment. It seemed that the emotional aspect of paternal treatment was paramount. Being punished in a rejecting way by your father was the worst thing that could happen, far worse than simply being punished.

To their surprise, the researchers found that the biggest childhood contributors to adult abusiveness were (in order of descending importance) feeling rejected by one's father, feeling a lack of warmth from one's father, being physically abused by one's father, being verbally abused by one's father, and—in fifth place!—feeling rejected by one's mother.

In Pat Conroy's 1976 novel, *The Great Santini,* Bull Meecham is a demanding and charismatic Marine colonel pilot who runs his family the way he runs his squadron. Bull Meecham (aka the Great Santini) plays against his eldest son, Ben, in an annual one-on-one basketball game in their backyard in front of the whole family. Ben, now seventeen and the star of his high school basketball team, has finally reached his father's level and actually beats him in this game. But this leads to very disturbing consequences. Bull has never been able to bear to lose to any of his children. When he senses that his son is besting him in this game, Bull cheats and plays dirty, but to no avail. Desperate to regain some sliver of self-esteem after his defeat, he insults his daughter, strikes his wife, and launches a relentless attack of verbal humiliation on his own son. He calls him a mama's boy. He keeps taunting him, telling him to go ahead and cry.

He starts to bounce the basketball repeatedly off his son's head. "You're my favorite daughter, Ben. I swear to God, you're my sweetest little girl!"

Ben, to his enormous credit, stands his ground and refuses to lower himself to his father's pathetic level. He walks calmly away, withstands the blows to his head, and finally yells at him, "Yeah, Dad, and this little girl just whipped you good."

Bull's response to his son hits the jackpot for humiliating punishment. It is random and irrational. It is public. It is global. And it is highly shaming.

There is a direct correlation between boys who are treated like this and grown men who are especially sensitized to experiences of rejection and humiliation. If you are one of these men, when your wife makes a comment about how she wishes you lived in a bigger house, you may hear *You are an inadequate loser!* Your son ignores you when he sees you at Back-to-School Night, and you read this as *You don't matter much to me!*

This hypersensitivity is especially destructive because there are so many situations in which we actually are rejected or in which we are put down. These are painful enough! Boys who experience especially high levels of paternal rejection or humiliation grow up to be men who perceive put-downs or rejection in even more situations.

Exercise: Put-Downs from Parents

For each statement below, consider how often the experience happened to you with your father (or stepfather or important male figure) and mother (or stepmother or important female figure) when you were growing up. Write in *never, occasionally, often,* or *always.* If you had more than one mother figure or father figure, answer for the person who you feel played the most important role in your upbringing.

After you have answered these questions (adapted from Dutton's research on shame, 1998) and paid attention to your feelings, go through and answer the way you think your son or daughter would answer these same questions about you.

	Father	Mother	Me
I think that my parent wished I had been a different kind of child.			
My parent criticized me or told me I was useless in front of others.			
I was treated as the scapegoat of the family.			
I felt my parent thought it was my fault when he or she was unhappy.			
I think my parent was mean and held grudges toward me.			
I was punished by my parents without having done anything.			
My parent was absent or not around very much and it made me feel like there was something wrong with me.			
My parent made fun of things I would say or do and I felt stupid or foolish.			
My parent would be angry with me without letting me know why.			

Projecting the Blame

Rejection and humiliation not only cause you pain but often lead you to turn into a good man behaving badly. You externalize the source of your dysphoric feelings, not only taking your child's behavior personally but also blaming your partner.

Barry's story helps us see this correlation between the father-son relationship and adult partner relations even more clearly. His father's humiliations of him were excessive, irrational, and random. They communicated disgust. And Barry evolved into a man crippled in his intimate relationships, blaming his wife when he felt bad.

I was two when my parents were divorced. I went with my father, and he remarried a "not nice" woman. That didn't work out, and it was my aunt, my father's sister, who really raised me. I hardly ever saw my mother growing up. I kept asking myself, Why doesn't my mother want to be with me?

When you get right down to it, I really raised myself.

I saw my father on weekends—sometimes. He would give me these brutal, random beatings. One time (we had some farm animals, but it wasn't really a farm), his duck got out from its pen. We were all trying to get it back. The duck kind of hopped onto me, and I couldn't grab it before it slipped away again. My father started smashing me. He broke my nose by pounding me so hard in the face. All because he couldn't get control over his duck.

He would get me to work on his acreage. He had me drive around a lawn mower, and he would stay within a few feet of me. Whenever I would mow the lawn incorrectly, like in the wrong pattern, he would smash me with this six-foot broomstick that he kept with him all the time.

When it was raining on the weekend, he would call up and tell me not to come: "I won't pick you up this weekend because I can't get any work out of you."

I wet the bed till I was about ten or twelve, but nobody paid any attention to the possibility that something was really wrong.

As an adult, I became a junkie. Not a real junkie, but I drank a lot and got hooked on achieving things and on exercise. I kept feeling like I had to do something to kill the pain.

And now I've been married for ten years. I blamed her for all of my problems. There was something bugging me every day. Every day I felt like I had to get out of this bad feeling, this big malaise. I knew something was wrong, and I just made her feel like it was her fault.

Raoul is another man whose adult emotional and interpersonal life has been directly shaped by emotional abuse from his father. Raoul speaks with painful clarity of having watched himself self-destruct in his family relationships. Pay attention to Raoul's confusion about being both the "golden boy" and the verbally abused kid. This difficulty in integrating different aspects of the parent-child relationship is quite typical in emotionally abusive families. The child is left, among other things, profoundly confused.

I was the middle child of three. I could do no wrong; I was the favorite, the golden boy. But there were still a lot of

expectations, especially from my father. He was very critical.
If I hit three home runs and then popped up, he wanted to
know, Why not four? He always was telling me I was
screwing up. At work they called him "The Bear." He was evil.
He would yell at me when he was mad at someone else. I've
seen him make a grown man cry. The guy told him he couldn't
work any more under these conditions, and my dad just said,
"Go pick up your check—nobody's waiting on you."

When I got married, I expected her to be "wifely" like
my dad expected my mom: dinner on the table when I got
home, the kids all behaved, the paper waiting for me. All that
chauvinistic stuff. I was really jealous and controlling, I would
get critical. I told her, "You're gaining weight!" I was really
moody. I thought her family was against me and I didn't want
anything to do with them. One time when she was thinking
of leaving me, she left in her car. I wasn't done talking to
her. My kids were in my car, but I just took off after her.
I demanded she talk to me. I didn't care about anything
except getting my way.

Then when she was so nasty in court, I was really hurt.
I thought, What did I do to deserve this? I was bad, but I
could have been worse!

I never wanted to have this kind of temper or to treat
anyone like this. I know how I felt and I never wanted anyone
to feel this way! My kids are scared of me. I've degraded them.

Raoul, by his own description, is profoundly fragile and
vulnerable, and he has allowed these qualities to develop into defensiveness and victimization. When you feel emotionally beat up—
more beat up than the rest of us—it doesn't take much more data to
confirm the hypothesis that the whole world is treating you this
way.

Boys Who Can't Grow Up

Sometimes the patterns from childhood that trouble us as
adults are less obviously negative. Vincent was a sensitive, deep-
thinking man in his thirties who was deeply attached to his aging
(now dying) father. He had always sensed his father's need for him,
and Vincent had shaped his whole life around ensuring his ongoing
attachment to his father. One time Vincent's girlfriend spent the
night at his condo. His father called him at 8:00 A.M., and Vincent felt
he had to lie and pretend that he was alone to avoid disappointing
his father or risking his disapproval. And he couldn't bear the

possibility that his father's feelings would be hurt by Vincent's attentions and attachment elsewhere. The relationship with his girlfriend, not surprisingly, did not last.

> *My father is such a sweet, wonderful guy. He means every-*
> *thing to me. And it is the most important thing in the world*
> *for me to make him happy. As a kid, I awoke all the time in*
> *the middle of the night, terrified, thinking "You won't continue*
> *to exist after Dad dies!" It was never anything he said to me.*
> *I just knew it was true. Now that he* **is** *dying, I can't*
> *concentrate on anything. What will become of me? It's*
> *ridiculous. I'm thirty-four years old, I am quite competent,*
> *I have my own business, people like me. I'm a good citizen.*
>
> *But my father is all sorts of things at once. He's really*
> *critical and demanding. He can't handle feelings and gets into*
> *this I-don't-want-to-talk-about-it shutdown mode. He doesn't like*
> *people. He thinks everybody out there is a son of a bitch.*
>
> *He's always told me, "You don't need anyone else but*
> *your family!" And I've lived like that. Now he's dying, and*
> *I have nobody else. I enter every relationship playing a role, like*
> *I need to keep this woman from getting information about how*
> *insecure I am. I sure may look like a man to the world, but*
> *inside I don't feel like one at all. I'm afraid all the time. The*
> *only thing that keeps me going is running off to my parents'*
> *house, faking a good mood, and getting the love and affection*
> *I need. And I never want it to change.*

Vincent's patterns in relationships are unlikely to make it into most books about men's issues and certainly unlikely to attract attention to Vincent as having relationship problems. He is such a nice guy and appears to be such a good catch, that it takes a while before the women he gets involved with really comprehend how limited he is because of his relationship with his father.

Vincent is a really good guy. Some of the very traits that derail his relationships—his attachment to his family, his generosity to a loved one, his attempts to avoid conflict—would be welcomed with open arms by many women. But Vincent has not truly grown up, and he is overwhelmed by the challenge of balancing an adult intimate relationship and his intense attachment to his father. Vincent claims that his father has given him his blessing to find a relationship, but the message is still an ambivalent one.

In Wally Lamb's 1998 novel, *I Know This Much Is True*, Dominick's dysfunctional and abusive childhood has sealed his heart. He grew up in a house of fear dominated by Ray, a bully who abuses his power over his stepsons. Dominick learns to defend himself internally against the unpredictable emotional abuse of his stepfather. He tells how he watched his stepfather punish weakness. Out of self-preservation, Dominick learned to hide his fear. Dominick is a classic survivor of a crummy childhood: basically intact, but haunted by what Terrence Real (1997) calls "the secret legacy of male depression" sabotaging his deeper relationships.

The twist in this novel is that Dominick has a schizophrenic twin brother, Thomas, who is emotionally vulnerable and poorly equipped to erect the defensive structure that his twin has been so successful at building.

But Dominick's talent for survival comes at an enormous cost, including the breakup of his marriage to the warm, beautiful Dessa, whom he loves, loses, and still loves. He turns away from her at key moments throughout their relationship. He struggles with his cold heart, watching himself as if in slow motion on a screen, screwing it up, yet feeling impotent at changing the course. He is trapped by his sealed heart. His pain lies as much in watching impotently as it does in the actual loss of the riches that a mature, loving relationship can bring.

Reframing Manhood: "Real Men"

From our fathers, and from the father figures in our lives, we learn lessons about being a "real man." And some of them are not so hot.

Cognitive Dissonance

Growing up in the Philippines, Mai attended religious schools with strict behavioral codes. Whenever he or his schoolmates would misbehave, the offending boy was forced to stand in front of the class, strip down to his underwear, and bend over. The instructor would ceremonially whip the boy with a long cane about a half inch in diameter. The usual caning was twenty strokes.

Mai learned not to cry or whimper when he was caned. He learned not to become distressed at the blood seeping through his underwear onto his pants after he got dressed.

He even told me that the caning was not so bad. When he was tempted to ditch school for a day, he told himself that the caning was only about fifteen bad minutes of pain. He knew he could take it, and it was worth it for a day of doing something he really liked. He shocked me when he told me that the caning hurt a lot less than the look of disapproval he would get from his father when he was unhappy with his behavior. That was real pain!

What stood out the most, however, after hearing his ugly description of the public caning, was his editorial comment about how this had affected his life. I expected to hear him talk about how he would never want to repeat this, or to have his own son go through this. Instead, his narrative about this piece of history was "It was a good thing that the teachers at the school beat me with a cane. Otherwise, I would probably be a drug addict by now."

I hear this all the time. Men try to make sense of the abusive treatment they have experienced growing up. Many of these men claim that if they hadn't been hit with a belt or felt intimidated by their fathers (or in Mai's case, his teachers, with the knowledge and approval of his father), they would have been out of control. Unable to face the fundamental nature of the abuse, they are forced, psychologically, to turn it into something else: *It made a man out of me. Or It was good for me. Or It sure kept me in line, and that's good.*

The irony, of course, is that I hear this from men who are ruining their closest relationships with their angry, destructive behaviors. I feel like saying (but have learned not to, for purely pragmatic reasons), *Look where this legacy has gotten you!*

This is not true for all men, but perhaps you are one of the men who cannot bear to see the trauma you have experienced in relation to your father or father figure. Sometimes the trauma is overt and intense, like Mai's. Other times it is much more subtle, like the son who recalls being humiliated by his father in a kitchen table debate and insists that it made him intellectually stronger.

This is a case of *cognitive dissonance*. Cognitive dissonance is the conflict created when your self-image conflicts with the reality you find yourself in. Cognitive dissonance is uncomfortable and threatens your sense of well-being, so you adjust your narrative to explain the conflict. If you have an image of yourself as a good father, and you yell at your kids, you are stuck with a disturbing dissonance. Psychologically, you are left with two choices:

1. Tell yourself that the yelling behavior is actually a good thing so you don't have to live with behaving badly as a father.

2. Consciously experience the humiliation and shame, and acknowledge that even good fathers sometimes act badly and that you need to work on this.

If you are a son, and your father threatens you or puts you down, you are left with similar choices:

1. Tell yourself that the yelling behavior is actually a good thing so you don't have to live with the idea that your father is a destructive person in your life.

2. Acknowledge how much this has wounded you, consciously experience disappointment in your view of your father, and acknowledge that even good fathers sometimes act badly and that he needs to work on this—and decide that you do not want to repeat this pattern when you are a father.

The first choice is the more popular. It is so much easier to go this route because it maintains a fundamental identification between father and son, which is crucial to children and emotionally seductive to adults. The second choice requires more psychological maturity—certainly far more maturity than most children can be expected to have. It requires the capacity to tolerate ambivalent feelings toward a person whom you have idealized. And it requires the ego strength to integrate the different aspects of your personality and behavioral patterns.

Children are usually not developmentally capable of taking the second route; they almost invariably assume that they deserve the abuse or tell themselves that it is somehow a good thing. Terrence Real (1997) calls this *empathic reversal:* the boy who has been traumatized adopts a relationship to himself that mirrors and replicates the dynamics of his early abuse. This is the link between trauma and depression. Instead of challenging the narrative of the trauma, he justifies it and turn it against himself. He becomes, at the core, depressed. And, equally if not more disturbing, he rationalizes these values and repeats these abusive behaviors in his own interactions with those closest to him and most vulnerable to him.

Masculinity Traps

The narrative that you develop about the behavior of your father or other formative male figures is crucial in generating your working definition of masculinity. Like most men, you probably developed some narratives that were powerful and positive. As a boy, you learned lessons about men who are responsible, who are confident, who are respectful, who treat women well. Other narratives are not positive at all. Many men, to varying degrees, are plagued with narratives that are caricatures of true masculinity.

I distinctly remember lessons I learned from my Uncle Morrie. Morrie, I knew, loved me very much and would never consciously wish any harm to me. He was intellectually brilliant but often emotionally unintelligent. He was ignorant of how powerful his competitive instincts were. He had been shaped by the credo of toughening boys up, physically and mentally. For me, at times, he was a loving uncle behaving badly.

We were in the living room of my grandparents' house, known as the front room. I was eight or nine or ten (I seem to remember this incident happening again and again). Our whole family was there: my parents, grandparents, several aunts, uncles, and cousins. And Uncle Morrie called me out to the center of the room with a big smile on his face: "David, come here, let me shake your hand. Give me a good shake." This seemed like fun. Except that this burly man gripped my hand in a powerful and painful squeeze, crushing my small paw. He was laughing, looking around at his audience, and they were all laughing too. "What's the matter? We're just shaking hands!"

And I struggled. I was in intense pain. I wanted to yank my hand away and cry and kick him in the shins. But then it occurred to me: *I am supposed to act like a man here and not show any feelings or pain. I will be doing something wrong if I show how I feel. Look, even my parents are joining in on the joke, so it must be okay.*

These lessons do not die easily.

Remember *The Great Santini*? Bull Meecham has been relentlessly pressuring Ben all his life to live up to Marine Corps standards of masculinity, where a man establishes honor by never giving an inch and gaining revenge whenever he feels challenged.

It is the night of the big basketball game between Ben's high school and the rival high school. Ben is dueling with the star player of the rival team, who manages to get in several cheap shots. Bull watches this from the stands and becomes more and more irate, yelling at the referees to call fouls. Finally, the rival player knocks Ben down while he's in the air on a layup. Ben is shaken up, but still okay to play.

The volcano erupts. Bull comes storming out onto the court. He stands over his son as he is getting up and points at him. "You better get that little bastard or you don't come home tonight! I'll beat your ass if you don't get that little bastard. . . . You'd better get him, goddammit, or don't come home" (342–43).

Ben is left with a terrible dilemma. He has two competing visions of masculinity: On the one hand is his father, insisting that Ben demonstrate that he is powerful and absolutely unyielding. On the other is his own emerging set of values, which tell him that the demand for power and revenge is a doomed and destructive course.

He chooses his father's path. He sets up a confrontation on the basketball court with his rival, goes after him, and breaks his arm. A brawl ensues, and Ben is kicked out of the game and kicked off the team for the season. His team loses the big basketball game. But he has obeyed his father.

Why? Partly out of pure fear: "I'll beat your ass if you don't get that little bastard." But also out of loyalty and respect. Ben wants to believe in his father and his father's values, and he is experimenting to determine whether these values fit for him. They don't.

Exercise: Man Lessons

As a man, you have been shaped by the important people and the important experiences of your past. Think and identify three times in your life when you learned some important lesson about being a man.

This lesson may have been very positive and valuable—or it may have been negative and crippling. Here are some examples:

When I watched my father criticize my mother and she would try harder to please him, I learned that this was a way a man could get things to be his way.

When my girlfriend told me that I was being selfish by getting into a fight with some other guy who liked her, I learned that only an insecure man would go off like that—and I didn't want to be like that.

Write down three examples like this that helped shape your male identity, positive or negative. You may want to talk to your partner or to other family members who remember key incidents that you may have forgotten.

Sometimes adult men are painfully aware of the legacy that has shaped them, and likewise painfully aware of how they are perpetuating this same legacy. Andrew came to see me after his relationship with his girlfriend broke up. She told him that he scared her, even though he had never been physically abusive at all. He had some idea of what she was talking about, though, and he continued to get more clued in as he talked about his memories of his father.

I remember watching my father as he walked past the two Dalmatians barking at him from the house next door. I go into the house and then I hear the hose running and more dogs barking. I look outside and see my old man power spraying the frigging Dalmatians! Just hosing them down, like in the South in the sixties! I say to my mom, "What's he doing out there?" And she just looks away and says, "I don't know." Just like

*she always did and always does. "I don't know." Afterward
I say to him, "What were you doin' out there?" and he tells
me that this was how he gets them to stop. "Yeah, but they
kept barking." "I know, but eventually they stop!" "Yeah, well,
eventually they would stop if you just let them alone too!"*

*Then I go off driving with him and I remember why I am
such a tense driver. A car comes along that is trying to switch
lanes, with plenty of time ahead, to make a turn up ahead.
And my old man just drives the exact same speed as the other
driver, never letting him get ahead or drop behind to make his
move. I knew that he knew exactly what he was doing!*

Andrew paused and put his head down. "Maybe I am doing a
lot of the same things."

And the legacy continues. Andrew's light at the end of the
tunnel is his growing self-awareness and growing commitment to
being a different kind of man than his father.

Exercise: Men Are Supposed to . . .

In your journal or on any sheet of paper, complete these sentences.
Your answers should provide a profile of the messages you received
growing up about the male role and identity. Then describe what
happens to men when they step outside the box and do not conform
to these rules.

Men are supposed to be . . .

Men are supposed to have . . .

Men are *not* supposed to . . .

When men do not conform to these rules and expectations, . . .

Breaking the Chain: Fathers Who Talk to Their Sons

Some sons are never released from the burden of their fathers'
messages. These boys grow into men who are always swimming
upstream, always trying to reinvent themselves. Some men get stuck.
They perpetuate the legacy. Sometimes they see themselves doing it
but feel powerless to stop it. Some men resolve the cognitive

dissonance that comes from abuse by convincing themselves that their attitudes and behaviors make sense and are actually the cornerstones of being good and responsible men. Other men—through hard work, new and powerful influences, marriage and fatherhood, or pure luck—are successful. If anything, they are better men for having faced some tough challenges on their own paths. They have embarked on a path with heart.

Stories of Twinship

The key to breaking the cycle is recognizing and taking advantage of opportunities to share twinship experiences with your son. My own father was able to do this for me, although it didn't come naturally. I was a couple of years out of graduate school, just starting my career, and I felt like a failure. I looked at my appointment book and saw huge empty spaces, which meant that not very many people wanted to come see, and come pay me, as their psychotherapist. The white spaces were a broken mirror.

My wife and I went to visit my parents, and I decided to take the plunge and discuss my worries with my father. I told him what was happening, and I told him how worried I was that nothing was falling into place professionally the way I had always envisioned it.

I asked him what it had been like when he and his brother started their own law business. "Did you have days when you just waited for the phone to ring? Did you have big empty spaces in your calendar? Was it hard for you go face potential referral sources when you actually felt like you were begging?"

My father misread the situation and misunderstood what I needed from him. I was looking for a twinship experience. But he thought I needed a pep talk. "Oh no, we never had days like that! We were busy right from the start. And we always knew we were going to be successful. Never a doubt in our minds!"

I slumped visibly. My mother, overhearing the conversation, stepped in and firmly corrected my father about his historical description. "Don't you remember the days when the two of you just waited for the phone to ring? And all the time you put in doing work practically for free for family members? All the hours volunteering your services so you could develop some connections and name recognition?"

He picked up the cue from her and corrected himself. He started telling me, in more credible detail, about all the things that did not go well at the beginning. About how they couldn't even afford a secretary. About spending a lot of time sitting in his office, reading books, waiting for the phone to ring with some business.

When I heard this, I had what I wanted. Although it had taken some prodding from my mother, who read between the lines more accurately, he eventually came through. I got my twinship experience, and was able to develop the narrative that my experience of failure and worry could be framed as transitional, inevitable, normal, and likely to pass.

This experience helped me redefine masculinity to include more than uninterrupted success. My sense was confirmed: you try things, you take some chances, you have hard times, you feel stupid a lot, you hang in there, and things usually work out.

Fathers who know—or learn—how to read the emotional needs of their sons are in a position to offer the most wonderful gifts. How can you do this?

Chill on the lectures. Act, don't yak.

Be an anthropologist. It is your job to really find out about the world your kids live in and get down to their level. This might mean playing Chutes and Ladders with your four-year-old or watching MTV with your teen daughter. Turn off being a parent who editorializes, teaches, evaluates—just join in.

Ask real questions. When you ask your son how everything went at school today, you are likely to get an equally vague answer. Ask questions that indicate that you know something about his day and his life: *Which of those essay questions did your English teacher spring on you? What movie did you guys finally pick to show at Movie Night?*

Listen, don't fix. Most men are oriented toward problem solving and are uncomfortable with emotions. See if you can listen to the story and just let your child know that you are paying attention. Ask questions that generate exploration of thoughts and feelings: *Wow, when she said that to you right there in the cafeteria, your knees must have been shaking! I know mine would have been!*

Get physical. The universal language of affection is touch: soft touches, bear hugs, shoulder squeezes, kisses on the forehead.

Be real. Offer personal stories (within reason). Share doubts and fears. Create twinship experiences whenever possible.

Recognize how powerful you are. Your kids are acutely sensitive to your approval and are powerfully shaped by the modeling you provide. Even teenagers who seem defensive and bored report that the two most powerful forces that impact them are losing access to their social world and engendering the disapproval of their parents.

Sometimes it's hard to believe, because they don't show it, but it's true. Use this power respectfully and sparingly.

Apologize when appropriate, but don't overdo it.

Pay attention to your mixed feelings about your kids. In addition to the usual feelings of pride and happiness, a man may also feel resentment, jealousy, and competitiveness in his relationships with his kids, especially with his sons. These are not fatal flaws as long as they are made fully conscious.

Try to see your children just as they are: sometimes loving, sometimes rejecting or rebellious, always just being themselves. If you experienced emotional wounding from your own father, you are more at risk to feel hypersensitive to rejection or failure in your relationships with your children.

Remember that it is not your children's (or anyone else's) job to make you feel better about yourself as a man. Your children may be a different psychological type from you, and it is your job to adapt yourself, not try to change them.

Parenting is not about you.

A Father's Blessing

Terrence Real (1997) tells the story of his lifelong struggle with his father and talks about his sense of being cursed by his father's warped values about masculinity. Finally, as his father was dying—with rigid defenses softening, emotions and regrets flowing, a reordered sense of priorities emerging—he sent his son this message: "May you and your brother reach your fullest potential in every regard. My blessing to you is this: May nothing in my past, or in the family's past, hold you back or weigh you down. If there are any encumbrances on you, I release you from them. You hear me? I release you. I want you to be free. Happy, strong, and free. That is my blessing to you, son" (333).

He goes on to tell his son, "It's no small thing." And it's not.

You may never get this blessing from your father. Perhaps he is no longer living, or perhaps he just isn't capable of taking the emotional risk of saying this to you. But if you can begin to see your father as a real person with flaws and limitations, rather than seeing his disapproval or emotional withholding as indicators of your inadequacy, you can begin to break free.

4

Midlife, Affairs, and Projections

You hear two different stories about midlife. Midlife is the worst of times, and it is the best of times.

The first story that you hear so often is of midlife despair, the midlife crisis, the sense of loss. You hear about physical aging, increasing illness, menopause, aging parents, dying parents (sometimes even dying peers), job loss, the empty nest, the awareness of mortality and vulnerability. You hear of feeling burdened by responsibilities of mortgages, college tuition, and child support payments. You hear about increasing boredom and dissatisfaction with relationships. You hear about hopelessness.

Taking over as the patriarch and watching your parents' power recede is a sobering experience. It can feel lonely and overwhelming, plunging you into desperate attempts to deny that this shift is taking place. You may retreat from this emerging responsibility with bouts of immaturity. You may feel more vulnerable and have no one to talk to about it. Or you may not know how to.

You hear the story of what men have not done. And of what men have done, but have done wrong. Sins of omission, sins of commission.

Yet, in some ways, these are the best of times. This second story that you hear about midlife tells you about a new awakening. You hear about the possibilities of transformation. Life begins at forty. You really become your own person at fifty. You are established in your career. Your children are growing up. You are learning more about yourself as you raise them. You hear about feeling free of the demands and expectations of young adulthood; now you can do whatever you want. You don't feel as much pressure to prove that you are smart, successful, competent, or sexy. You begin to value wisdom and good judgment over physical power or attractiveness. Anything's possible. You are still in pretty good health. And you have figured out who you are. You know yourself and your partner in more intimate and honest ways than ever before. Sex is richer and even more fun (although less frequent and perhaps less acrobatic).

You release yourself from some of your unrealistic goals, and you feel more determined to do some of the things that you have never done. As your sense of time becomes more finite, you develop a new urgency.

You hear, if you listen carefully, the story of a richer spiritual awareness. You feel more deeply connected to your community and even to the universe. You are wiser, and you have less need to prove something to the world. You are entering a life stage when your ability to manage stress and multiple tasks equips you to handle the roles of parent, lover, businessman, mentor, friend, and community leader.

Instead of the sins of omission and commission, you hear about learning from your mistakes and having the opportunity to do what you could never do before.

Which story is the truth? In fact, they are both true, and they run a parallel course as you pass through this period of life. The transitions are inevitable, but the crises are not. Many so-called midlife crises are actually bad events that could have happened at any time in the life span. Contrary to popular opinion, very few men or women enter a genuine clinical depression or breakdown in functioning at midlife.

Midlife Defined

The different stories of midlife transitions and midlife relationships could fill a much larger book than this one. No one can even decide exactly when midlife starts and when it stops. It used to start at thirty-five, then forty, now many say fifty. But does age forty-five stir up similar issues for the woman whose children are grown and off to college and the woman who has two toddlers at home? Is the fifty-year-old man in a happy second marriage faced with the same inner conflicts as his counterpart who is unhappy in his first? Does the professional woman who has made a mark in her world go through the same midlife issues as the mother who stays at home and itches to be out in the world more? Do single men and women have anything in common with those who are married? How different are the experiences of straight and gay couples? How does the experience of the man whose parents are dying compare with that of the woman whose parents are fit and active? Do women whose menopause is only mildly disruptive have anything like the experience of women who become depressed, emotionally stormy, sexually uninterested, and fatigued?

Some people develop a classic midlife crisis, while others barely notice any ripple.

Here's what we do know about midlife. For the purposes of this book, I'll define it as the period of life beginning around age forty and ending around sixty-five. Why sixty-five? Because that is when most careers end.

What makes this midlife transition challenging and often threatening? You are aging. Gravity is having a profound effect on the condition of your body. Both men and women are rounding. Wrinkles and stretch marks and varicose veins appear. You can't run as fast, lift as much, or develop an erection as quickly. Women lose the firmness and shapeliness of their youthful bodies. Hair grays or disappears completely.

Mortality strikes. You realize that you have been alive longer than you will continue to live in the future. Perhaps one of your peers or someone only slightly older than you dies, etching a brutal image in your mind: this could happen to you at any time.

In the terms of developmental psychologist Erik Erickson (1950), you struggle with the issues of *generativity* versus *stagnation*. Stagnation makes you feel like your life is over and your hopes dead. Generativity reawakens your hopes and possibilities, and you become more deeply connected to your inner self, to others around you, and to the world at large. You may become more spiritual. In stagnation, the drive for generativity stalls. You feel doomed, bored, and restless. You may take desperate actions to kill these feelings, or simply retreat and give up.

Midlife Relationships

The fundamental issues of midlife—both positive and negative—play themselves out in our relationships. Many men and women enter a state of despair over all the hopes they have not yet achieved and may never achieve. Yet, just a few years later, many men and women uncover a layer of self-confidence, self-direction, and personal freedom that they have never found before. And they often discover themselves to be in a richer, more emotionally honest relationship than they were in before. Under the best of circumstances, this new relationship is with the same partner, but, as we all know, not always.

A strange convergence is taking place. Our needs, as men and women, are changing. Just at the stage when men are turning more to the relationships in their lives, women are likely to be turning toward the development of their independent sense of self.

Both men and women often project the blame for their unhappiness and lack of fulfillment on their most intimate partner, even when these feelings are triggered by other pressures like raising children, caring for aging and dying parents, work stresses and disappointments, aging bodies and the loss of self-esteem, fears of mortality, or the tediousness of family life. They can become lost in dark moods, enveloped in an impenetrable fog of blame that distorts the view of the other.

You say: I feel lost, undernourished—you should pay better attention to me! I feel empty, and you should fill me up!

She says: I can't really be myself around you. You don't understand me! You don't give me what I need! You are threatened by my independence and assertiveness. You don't accept my feelings. You demand too much from me. If you changed, I could come into my own! I could finally feel fulfilled!

Do these sound familiar? How about these:

I can never get what I need from him.

In her eyes, I'm not the great guy I used to be—and I guess I never will be.

It's impossible to satisfy her.

Plenty of women would be very happy to pay more attention and give me more love than you do!

Why won't he ever listen?

Sex just isn't what it used to be.

We're just coexisting.

Sometimes these accusations are true. Sometimes the marriage really has died, or it was never alive in the first place. But, much more frequently, both men and women at midlife become frustrated too easily. You are hungry for something new, and you see no way to break out of the frustrated, trapped feeling. You feel desperate and stuck.

Often the answers can be found within: within yourself or within the relationship that may seem dull, dead, and doomed.

Couples often feel bored and stagnant because both partners have hidden key aspects of themselves from each other and even from themselves. Your assignment is to take responsibility for your own needs and feelings, avoid projecting blame onto your partner, and find the hidden parts of the personality within each of you, finding something new in yourself and in her. Each of you, at midlife, longs to emerge into a new and less restricted self. You can build a new relationship—within your current marriage or, if your marriage is truly dead, elsewhere—that offers a structure for personal growth and happiness that was never truly available to you before.

If not now, when?

Using the Power of Midlife to Build a Better Relationship

To take advantage of this opportunity, you need to know yourself. Self-knowledge is power.

Moods and Feelings

You need to understand the powerful pull from moods, and the difference between moods and feelings. Moods are not feelings. A mood happens when you are having powerful feelings but are not attending to them. You know something is wrong, but you don't know how to make sense of it. Given the tendency of men to act on their feelings rather than discover them, moods can be dangerous and destructive. You become itchy and action oriented, and you tend to project blame. You feel like you have to do something, but you don't know which direction to turn.

Moods, with their dark clouds, projection of blame, and emotional withdrawal, are signs of stagnation. When you are in a mood, you can have no real relationship with your partner. *She can't understand, she doesn't care, she's a bitch, it's all her fault anyway.* In a mood, you can't move forward.

Feelings are not always pretty, but they are signs of vitality and generativity. Feelings open the door to new energy within yourself and new energy in your relationship. Most women can relate to honest expression of feelings, but they are alienated by moods.

Triggers

Moods are triggered by events and the feelings that these events evoke in you. Any of the following could be a trigger:

- feeling injured or upset by something

- feeling embarrassed or humiliated by something your partner, or someone else, said

- feeling unhappy with your work

- feeling frustrated and ineffective as a parent

Indicators

Moods come with their own characteristic thoughts, feelings, and behaviors. Any of the following is an indicator of a mood:

- believing that there is no point in talking to anybody about how you feel

- thinking that everyone is just out for themselves and no one really cares about what you are going through

- telling yourself that you just have to work this out on your own

- believing that your partner is determined to make you feel bad about yourself or to deprive you of things you really need

- acting cool toward your partner, finding fault with her, or putting her down

- feeling sorry for yourself

- noticing that other people seem to be very cautious about approaching you

- exaggerating and overreacting to slights from others

- trying to make others feel guilty for depriving or hurting you

Dissolving the Mood

The cure for moods is ridiculously simple and hopelessly hard. Moods dissolve into good old-fashioned complicated feelings when you find the words and talk about them.

First you need to identify the feelings. Develop a language to describe exactly what is bothering you and how it makes you feel. Think about it, write about it, meditate or pray to get clarity about it.

Then express your feelings in a respectful way. Share this with someone who cares. Ideally, this would be your partner, but if that seems impossible or unwise, talk with someone else who gets it: a family member, friend, therapist, clergyperson, coworker, support group, or chat room pal. Just make sure that the person you turn to does not represent a threat to your primary relationship.

The Call of the Wild

In midlife, you may want more emotionally but not know exactly how to reach out for it; you may have limited resources to turn to, and you may blame your partner for not giving you what you need. Unfortunately, you may start hearing the "call" of another woman as the quickest ticket out of your dissatisfaction. Some men don't even know what has hit them until they have had an affair.

You may find yourself looking at your relationship as the source of your discontent: *If only I could get* _____ *from her, then everything would be all right again!* You may love your wife dearly and not want to give up your family life. However, since we know that many men are only marginally aware of their feelings, it may be that your close emotional connections with others are underdeveloped. So you may not know how else to calm these internal storms except by turning to another sexual relationship. Men tend to eroticize emotional connections: *I know I can feel close if we have sex!*

At these moments, what you think you want may not be what you truly need. The unconscious man (unconscious of his deepest needs and feelings) needs to develop into the conscious man so he can think clearly and discriminate between true signals and illusions.

Your task, as a man at midlife, is to develop more of what author Daniel Goleman (1995) refers to as *emotional intelligence:* more sensitivity, relational abilities, access to emotional life, introspection. Men are often looking for something deeper, yet only a minority of men know how to put those longings into words and pursue courses of action that are likely to lead them there. Instead, they blame, drink, withdraw into moods, seek revitalization through affairs, or give up.

Why are you hungrier for a deeper experience in your relationship life at midlife? This hunger doesn't always express itself as direct longing and reaching out, although when it does, everybody's job is a lot easier. You often just become more frustrated and resentful that your emotional needs aren't getting met. Midlife is a time of male awakening to deeper connections with the inner self, with others, and with the world at large, but many men don't have access to other relationships in the same way that women tend to. And it is the world of relationships that provides the most potent trigger for a man's leap forward in the midst of midlife issues.

The Unconscious Man

When Trent first came to see me in my office, I wasn't quite sure what to make of him. He was a forty-three-year-old air traffic controller, bright and creative, but also very rigid emotionally. I could see it in the way he held his body very stiff and erect, as if even his body had to think before it did anything. His life was organized and scheduled from morning to night. He exercised obsessively, never missing a morning or evening workout. Although friendly and humorous, he told me that he had no close friends— except for his wife.

His relationship with his wife sounded very positive. This was the second marriage for both of them, and they had both learned much from the mistakes in their first marriages. I met her in the second counseling session, and she seemed lively, bright, and emotionally sensitive—much more so than Trent. She was worried about her husband because he seemed to be withdrawing more, even more than he typically did. I got the distinct impression that they, as a couple, were very self-enclosed. They both seemed cut off from most friends and practically all family, although Trent's wife had at least a few female friends that she could talk to. She seemed like a very good partner for him.

When Trent's back went out the year before and he could no longer exercise, he became deeply depressed, although he was too proud to describe this as anything but "feeling moody." To admit more would be too much a sign of weakness.

Trent told me that he had always had an intense and conflicted relationship with his father. Trent blamed his father for his own difficulties in social relationships and for his limited career success.

> *My thoughts and feelings all seem to lead back to my father. I hate the way he was, so domineering and cold. He was perfectionistic and demanding, always looking for what was wrong. Now I'm so demanding with myself. I have doubts about my IQ. I don't make enough money.*
>
> *I'm always afraid that I'll get put down or yelled at by someone. I can't take compliments—I "spoil" them—and I'm not very good at giving them. Just ask my wife.*
>
> *In my first marriage, I always felt like a failure. She was always critical of my body. I had a problem with premature ejaculation and she always humiliated me.*
>
> *Right now, everything looks so dark. It's like there's nothing I can see. Nothing fulfills me. There's really something missing.*

*Something is wrong with my marriage. My wife and I
aren't on the same wavelength anymore. If she were really right
for me, I wouldn't be feeling so sullen and cut off, would I?*

Trent, like many other good men, was emotionally isolated
from everyone but his wife, and he was increasingly cutting her off,
too, from what was taking place in his inner world. Women generally build multiple emotionally close relationships and therefore
have more options for meeting their needs. When Trent needed more
than his marriage could provide, he had nobody he could turn to.
Support, attention, affection, and emotional closeness had only come
from his wife. His sexual relationship was his primary means of
satisfying emotional needs.

In the session with his wife, Trent calmly announced that he
had quite suddenly become attracted to a young woman who
worked at the airline ticket counter. She made him feel "loved and
appreciated." Although he and his wife had always gotten along
very well and had been compatible, he announced to her right then
that this marriage was holding him back from getting what he
needed in life. He said he was thinking of leaving.

In my own mind, I began to call Trent the unconscious man
because he was caught in a whirlwind of emotional conflicts with
very little awareness of what was happening to him. What Trent
really needed was an emotional connection. His crush on his young
coworker was simply a misguided attempt to satisfy this need.
Trent's wife tolerated this phase, and Trent quickly came back to
earth and felt a little stupid. He never became a poster child for
emotional intelligence, but he found ways to communicate better and
to value what he had.

Something's Missing

Is that all there is?

This is the mantra of the man in midlife crisis. I hear some men
(and women) say that they feel overwhelmed with sadness immediately after sex, after a big birthday celebration, after a promotion at
work. These events are all supposed to be fulfilling and sustaining,
yet they can leave you with a painful gap between your expectations
and reality. It seems like it's never quite enough. You may desperately try to preserve the rare moments when you find yourself free of
boundaries, when you experience deep pleasure or deep connection
with others. You want to hold on tight to these moments—and when
they pass, then something's missing. It may not have a name or label,
but it is missing.

Levinson's research (1978) identifies a crucial aspect of male adult development called *the Dream*. If you are a man who has lived through young adulthood with a vision of how your life should be, then you have been guided by the Dream. This stage of adult life is dominated by a push toward productivity.

This sense of purpose, while very challenging and often difficult to fulfill, is very organizing. You are guided by clear goals and themes. The obstacles are tangible, the achievements (for the most part) measurable.

The increasing awareness of your ticking clock at midlife, however, often causes the values which governed this Dream stage to lose their hold over the order of things. Two types of disorientation and disillusionment can occur.

The Dream Unfulfilled

The first type of crisis strikes you when you wake up one day and realize that the Dream is not going to happen. You face the often sobering realization that what you see is what you get. You will probably not achieve significantly higher levels of career success than you already have. If you haven't yet written the great American novel or become vice president of your company, you probably never will. The rock band that you have been trying to put together for years may never quite make it in the way you dreamed, and you may need to settle for producing music rather than performing it. Your idealized visions of your family life—how successful or wonderful your kids would be, how loving and appreciative your relationship with your partner would be, how nice a home and lifestyle you would be able to create—may not have quite materialized. In some cases, they may be very painfully unmet. You may fear that there is nothing to look forward to except for a slow deterioration and narrowed possibilities.

In an episode of *The Sopranos* (2000), mob boss Tony Soprano is disturbed by hearing his teenage son embracing existentialism and arguing that there are no absolutes. This makes no sense to Tony—until his psychiatrist, Dr. Melfi, tells him that many people become overwhelmed with intense dread when they realize that they are solely responsible for their own decisions, actions, and beliefs. They can only see death at the end of every road; it is the only absolute truth. Tony, plagued with depression and panic attacks, despondent over the ducks who fly away from his swimming pool, and a mother who arranged for a hit on him, takes this in and replies, "I think the kid's on to something."

Crisis in Meaning

The second type of crisis affects you if you *have* achieved your dream—but suddenly find it meaningless. It does not fulfill you: *So what? Now I am successful. I don't feel any happier. I don't have the approval of my father. I still can't relate to my kids the way I want to. I feel alone. The fundamental struggles never really change!* You may be a man who has the luxury of knowing that he is capable of following through on a vision of how things should be. You may not be plagued so much by doubts about your success as by doubts about your values. In some ways this is easier; in other ways it can be worse, simply because it is less tangible and more elusive.

Both of these men ask similar questions. *What's the point? What does it all mean? Can I expect any more? Should I insist on more? Do I change myself? Do I try to change my surroundings or the others in my life? Is that all there is?*

There is nothing pathological or disturbed about a longing for stimulation or a need to experience a new sense of self, a need to develop an intense attachment, or a need to be understood. The potential problem lies with the route that you take to satisfy these needs—not with the needs themselves. This is a crucial distinction. It leads each of us to a level of self-respect and self-awareness that makes discovery of the path with heart a more manageable task.

You need to be able to distinguish between the signals for this true path with heart and the false alarms. You need to understand the forces that, if frustrated, can drive you into dark moods, destructive behaviors, or the arms of another woman. I can't say that this is easy to do, but remember that self-knowledge gives you the power to choose more informed, and wiser, actions.

Regaining Vitality

Perhaps no fear threatens the man dealing with midlife issues more than the fear of getting old and stuck. Regardless of his chronological age, when a man fears that his possibilities and potential are slipping away, an old-and-stuck panic often ensues.

Thinking in self psychology terms, this old-and-stuck panic can drive you to do something—anything—which will help restore the self-cohesive state of feeling young and vital. When the only apparent future is dominated by deterioration and decay, your choices become driven. You may act desperately, often losing good judgment and even forsaking values that you would normally honor. If you are a hungry man, you will be tempted to steal, which you would never consider doing if you weren't feeling so desperate. And many men who feel that they are irrevocably losing their vitality will be tempted to have an affair, even if their values and judgment normally would never allow this.

Missing, at these crisis moments in midlife, are two key components in self-awareness and self-direction.

The Alarm Signal of Distress: Looking Within

The first component is a deeper understanding of the experience. The unconscious man only knows that he is suddenly fearful, unhappy, and threatened. Anyone who felt this way and could make no other sense of it would at least consider radical action to escape this. The conscious man can read these distressing states as signals that an internal crisis is brewing. Focusing on this as internal crisis is more difficult, but ultimately more rewarding. It requires a reframing of these events, recognizing that you are not so unique. You may be very special in many ways, but you are not unique. You have to at least consider the possibility that these moods are governed as much by classic, universal midlife issues as they are by your wife, your kids, your job, the state of the economy, global warming, or another woman. Although it doesn't automatically preclude bold actions or changes, this point of view most fundamentally points you first inward in the search for resolution.

In every conversation with men who are struggling with midlife distress, I remind them that thinking differently changes the experience.

Getting Smart and Making Choices

The second key component, of which the unconscious man is unaware, centers around the wide range of options for dealing with this crisis. Perhaps you feel the pressure of this distress and feel doomed. You retreat into dark moods. You doubt yourself. You pursue destructive behaviors—like drinking or overeating—in a desperate attempt to escape the distress. You become short-tempered and more controlling of others as your sense of control over your own life erodes. You may believe that there is only one way to relieve this: by turning to a new relationship, often with a younger woman, who will jump-start your sense of feeling young and vital.

Of course, it does not always have to be a woman. It can be a new material possession like a car, which psychologically represents much of the same sense of freedom and fulfillment. It can be a bold new career or hobby, or a new attempt at the perfectly sculpted body. Any of these *could* provide something truly valuable for you, especially if they were chosen with informed consciousness. But they also can lead nowhere.

Crucial to our understanding at this point, however, is recognizing the powerful impact these fears of losing vitality can have. Although you may analyze this process and identify ways in which you might act foolishly or impulsively, there is no mistaking the fundamental truth: it makes sense to feel scared when you are losing (or fear losing) something very important. These feelings are worthy of respect and compassion, although the choices that you make to cope with these feelings may not be. Just be aware, however, that the darker side of becoming psychologically old (loss of vitality, withering creativity, narrowing possibilities) is treacherous. If you let these dominate, they are sure to mess you up.

Affairs as Battery Chargers

If you struggle with the lure of an affair, and you are conscious enough to put words to the feelings, you may hear yourself talk about how damn boring your life is. This spurs you toward intense attempts at revitalization. This sense of boredom strikes right at the heart of the fear of becoming old and stuck.

Billy, a thirty-seven-year-old landscape architect, had been married to Karen for eleven years. He explained some of this to me as he looked back on his affair.

> *It's not so much that I wanted to get away from Karen. Karen herself was okay—when she could stop thinking about the kids. It drove me nuts, and always hurt my feelings whenever we tried to spend some time away from the kids. We went away for four days skiing, just the two of us—except she could never really be there with me. Every night she had to call them. She cried every night, too, because she missed them and because she was worried about whether they were okay. I could sort of understand that, but enough was enough. I needed some attention directly for me!*
>
> *Our whole life together had become so routine, so regular. We got up, made breakfast, got the kids off, went to work, talked at night about the kids or the house or paying bills, watched a little TV, and went to bed. Usually without sex.*
>
> *But, like I said, I really didn't hate Karen. I hated what we had become. Everything used to be so unpredictable and full of possibilities, and that seemed all gone. I felt like the life juices had just been sapped right out of me. Everything felt dull and colorless. My wife was a fine person, my kids were fine*

*kids, we had a nice life together, and I thought I would die if
I had to live like this, with this mood I had gotten into, forever.*

*So, when I met Laurie, it was like someone breathed a
big new gust of life into me. I could breathe again! The world
looked colorful! Then it got all mixed up in my head. I started
blaming Karen for the routine life we had. I saw her as the
problem. Why not? If I could feel something with Laurie that
I couldn't feel with Karen, it must have been her. Right?*

Laurie, of course, was the new mirror that reflected back a
wonderful and revitalized picture.

When the domesticity of your married life threatens your sense
of vitality at midlife and when you feel so smothered under the
weight of it all, the intoxicating appeal of another woman (or more
fundamentally, a new sense of feeling young and vital) can sweep
you off your feet. And you may not be able to explain what the hell
is going on until much later.

This is often the fuel for the passion of an affair. The unconscious man tells himself he needs this to become whole again. He
feels some restlessness inside, identifies it only superficially if at all,
then acts. But the conscious man insists on looking at a larger
perspective before acting.

If you are thinking clearly, you will probably recognize that
there are many ways to cope with and even learn from these threatening emotional states. Once you know what you are truly dealing
with, you have the option of trying to revitalize your life through
work, through your children, through your spiritual life, through
your marriage, through myriad activities and relationships. Most
importantly, perhaps, you have the option of thinking differently—
developing a new narrative—about your situation. Sometimes, the
new narrative leads to an internal acceptance or resolution of the
crisis that requires no obvious external action at all. Men are not
usually comfortable with this strategy, but sometimes deciding not
to act is the boldest plan of all.

Exercise: The Affair Inventory

If you are a man who is tempted to have an affair, think before you
act. If you are a man who is already having an affair, try to figure out
what needs you are truly looking to fulfill by pursuing this other
woman.

As you do this, keep asking yourself

- Will I really get what I need from doing this? Will it last?

- Is it worth the potential damage to my marriage, my children, my health, and my long-term self-respect?

- Are there other ways to find what I am really looking for?

For each question below that you answer yes to, write on a separate sheet of paper or in your journal at least three alternate ways that this need could be met. Writing anything about these feelings may feel like way too high of a security risk, but at least think through your answers to these questions!

Do I feel like I am getting old and hope that this will help make me feel young, alive, and vital again?

Do I have low self-esteem and need a boost to my ego?

Do I feel trapped in my life roles and want the freedom to act in a different way?

Am I tired of the routine life I have? Do I need some excitement?

Do I feel like I have always been deprived of what I need and this is my chance to get something for me?

Do I feel lonely, not knowing how else to feel close to someone?

Do I feel like my wife doesn't understand me and I need to find someone who really does?

Do I have doubts about my sexuality and need to remind myself that I am attractive and potent?

Do I miss having someone really appreciate me, compliment my looks, laugh at my jokes, and respect my work?

Do I need to find a way to prove that I can still have adventure in my life?

Do I need a jump start to feel deep emotions and not know any other way to do it?

Am I simply looking for variety in sexual experience?

And the ultimate question: Am I married to the wrong person? Do I really want to change relationships and develop a different life?

You may go through this exercise and still decide that it is worth it to have an affair. At least you'll be more conscious of why you're doing what you're doing.

Distress Tolerance

Marsha Linehan (1993) uses the term *distress tolerance* in her work with people who act impulsively and destructively. She defines distress tolerance as the ability to "bear pain skillfully" and to "perceive one's environment without putting demands on it to be different, to experience your current emotional state without trying to change it, and to observe your own thoughts and action patterns without attempting to stop or control them" (96). Borrowing from the wisdom of Zen Buddhism, she advocates using mindfulness skills, including the nonjudgmental observation of one's present emotional state, however distressing it may be. You might say to yourself, *I can't do anything right now to change how I feel or to change the situation, so it is better to accept this for the moment.* This is not an act of passivity or resignation. This is a conscious, bold, well-informed choice.

In their work in the field of relapse prevention, Marlatt and Gordon (1985) use the acronym *PIG,* or *problems of immediate gratification,* to help clients understand urges and learn to tolerate them. The illusion for people with intense urges is that the urge must be gratified, and gratified immediately. The feared alternative is some sort of unbearable pain or deprivation. What we know, however, is that most urges pass. An alcoholic who craves a drink usually discovers, if he can wait it out, that twenty minutes later the urge has passed. People on diets are trained to wait twenty minutes after the urge to eat the forbidden ice cream or chocolate chip cookies; if they still really want it after this time, then—and only then—does it make sense to go for it. Usually, the intensity has passed, not because of a satiation experience but simply because the mood changes and because most urges are transitory.

Even an urge as powerful and of such enormous consequences as suicide is usually fleeting. The special tragedy with most suicide attempts is that the intensity of this desperate urge to escape from life would have receded all by itself if the person could have just waited it out a little longer. We see this happening time after time. What seems unbearable at the moment often changes even without the person taking any direct action. The capacity to wait is not a sign of passivity or weakness but rather an active choice showing personal strength.

The same is usually true for the urge to act out based on internal distress at midlife. Sometimes if you wait it out and examine it and don't do anything stupid, it just passes.

Robert is an example of a man who was tempted to take some action but benefited from simply waiting patiently and observing his own emotions and self-talk. He came to see me, very discouraged by the state of his marriage. As far as he was concerned, it was just about over. The thrill was gone. He had become emotionally distant from his wife, with a long list of wounds from perceived injustices. He was not behaving particularly badly (no affairs, no violence, no public scenes of humiliation, no substance abuse), but his closed heart and emotional shutdown had become unbearable for all. He was living out in the guest house.

In his therapy sessions, sometimes with his wife and sometimes without, he spent a lot of time simply telling his story. I empathized with what it is like to feel emotionally wounded and attacked, especially when you perceive yourself as being a good guy.

We also hammered away at Robert's expectations of his wife. Her long history of anxiety and panic disorder had earned her the label of "my wife, who has this illness." I told him to knock it off and to pay attention to what he was getting out of having an "ill" wife. When he told me stories about his wife's complaints about his verbally aggressive behavior, I often told him that it sounded like she was exactly on target. I also pointed out that men who feel wounded often act like this without even realizing it.

After several months of this, Robert missed a few weeks because of business travel. In the next session he told me,

> It looks like Sarah and I are reconciling. I'm still living in the guest house, but we're often sleeping together in the main house too. We're actually talking and having fun together. We are even saying "I love you"!
>
> Remember all those complaints I had about how she was keeping the house, and how disrespectful it was to me? Well, I don't know how to explain this, but it just doesn't seem like such a big deal anymore.

And then came the line I always love to hear: "I have a hard time remembering what I was so unhappy about!"

I pointed out to Robert and his wife that they had maintained at least the possibility of a reconciliation, even though through much of their marital discord the Las Vegas odds would have been even at best. Neither of them had done anything impulsive, self-indulgent, or stupid. Nobody had an affair or threatened one. Outside of one nasty yelling incident, there had been no violence. Nobody made wild threats to leave forever. Neither made any irreparably wounding statement to the other. And they had managed to conduct themselves reasonably civilly in front of their kids. They may have felt tempted to do any or all of these things, but they did not. So when the relationship dynamics and the emotional climate began to shift for the better, there was enough positive foundation to rebuild.

Creating the New Self

Another primary reason for the lure of another relationship—or career, or lifestyle—is the potential for finding a "new self."

We all become defined (and often confined) by the group of which we are a member. Most families have someone who they make fun of, someone who is taken seriously, someone who always keeps things together, and someone else who stirs the pot. No matter what the person does, the group conspires to still view them the same way. The group maintains its balance this way, yet the individual can be stifled.

Couples can easily get stuck in their roles. So if you feel that something's missing, one strategy is to ask yourself what role you want that you don't think you can have. Sometimes, if you are a reasonably conscious man, the answer turns out to be not so complicated. One man whom I worked with said that he wanted to take some time off from his business and do more adventurous activities like skiing and flying planes. But he was afraid that his wife would be angry with him for working less and making less. When he spelled out his needs so clearly, he found out that she could easily live with this.

If you are in the throes of midlife issues and sensing the lure of a new life as a way to resolve them, you may feel like nobody knows who you really are. You desperately need a new mirror to reflect back a new picture of yourself.

Andy explained to me how impossible it seemed for him to become a new person while he was still in his marriage.

> *My wife cut me down so many times. I used to feel like a very successful, effective, and attractive guy. But she just laughed at me and made smart-ass remarks about my career. I never felt like she understood how respected I was at work and how many people really looked up to me.*
>
> *My role in the family was sort of like the clown. It was always "Daddy doesn't know how to do anything right, does he?" and "Men always think they're the greatest." And when I would try to show everyone that I was good at something, I felt foolish, like I was a little kid who had to have his mother tell him what a great dive he just took off the diving board.*
>
> *I could never really say this to my wife, but it seemed almost like she hated me, and it would come out in these little ways. It got to the point where it was like she had no idea who I really was. And I got scared that if things didn't change, I wouldn't know who I really was either.*

Men often develop a nagging sense that aspects of their personality that they once had have faded away, or that aspects that they might have had will never flower. Marlon Brando, speaking the famous line from *On the Waterfront* (1954), laments "I coulda been a contender!" Although he is hardly in midlife, he is speaking for all men who realize that a golden opportunity has passed them by, never to return. Or so it seems.

Entering another romantic relationship seems to offer a chance at a new life, or at least a new psychological and emotional life. Another woman can allow a man to feel attractive and special, or smart and sensitive, or valuable and needed, in a way that he hasn't felt for a long time or maybe never felt at all. Donald described the appeal of his lover.

> *It was like she offered me a whole new life. With her, I felt like I would have the chance to have children again and this time to do it right, to correct all the mistakes I made the first time around. I could feel alive. All the leftover hurts between me and my wife would be gone and I could start all over again. I've never really fancied myself as much of a lover, but she made me feel like I was such a magnetic man. Could I ever feel that way about myself with my wife? I don't think so. Too much baggage.*

Discovering this new self is not only about virility, passion, and excitement. It can also center around the yearning to develop a different side of the personality that has been held back. Billy talked about the lure of Laurie.

> *She was someone I could talk to on such a deep level. It was really a soul connection. One night I went to see the movie* Damage *with my wife. I was so moved by the man's passions and his obsession with this young girl. My wife thought it was stupid and I felt very alone and cut off. I thought there was something wrong with me for feeling like this. The next day, at work, Laurie called me out of the blue to tell me about this great movie she had seen and how much it had touched her. She said she understood these passions so well. She asked me if I had seen it yet. You guessed it:* Damage. *I felt reborn, like it was okay to be the real me.*

In the company of Laurie, his new mirror, Billy felt like he was someone new.

The pressure of maintaining the false self builds as the years go by and as other goals are reached. Without much conscious awareness, you may develop an urgent longing for the true self to emerge. It is as if there is a hidden man inside, the man who you were really meant to be, ready and waiting for you to find a way to liberate him.

When you try to make sense of the powerful draw of another relationship at midlife, keep in mind the power of this yearning for a new self. Again, from the self psychological perspective, you have to deeply respect the yearnings and drive toward self-cohesion. The decision about how to satisfy this yearning is a matter of judgment. Some men behave well and others badly. Some paths may make sense in the long run, others may not. But, no matter what the actions, the drive toward developing a new self is an honorable one.

Your emotional, psychological, and even spiritual needs can propel you outside your marriage in your quest. The tragedy is that many men think that only an eroticized relationship will meet these needs.

The Need That Can't Be Met

The classic bar pickup line *My wife, she doesn't understand me* captures another crucial motivation for the midlife affair. Here we are dealing with broken mirrors.

Billy described how misunderstood he felt:

I wish it were different, but I just have these very important needs that my wife will never be able to understand or fulfill. She just doesn't appreciate the same things I do about art, culture, or ideas. She doesn't have the same spiritual depth.

She doesn't understand how much I need to wind down at the end of the day and not be bombarded with the kids and responsibilities.

If she really understood my true needs and if she really cared, she would be more interested in sex, too. I need this so much to rejuvenate myself. But she doesn't seem to be on the same wavelength. It's just such an important part of my life— if she really understood, she wouldn't deprive me like this!

Who among us has not known this aching feeling of being mis-understood? It is at these moments that you are acutely aware of something that you don't have in your life, and you are drawn to any source or any path that promises to offer what is missing.

This flood of needs can seem so heartfelt and easy to identify with at times, and so immature and self-centered at others. When do you trust your impulses, and when do you see through them to a new level of self-awareness? What needs can you legitimately expect to be met through your relationship? When are these expectations an abrogation of your own responsibility in your marriage? When are your needs unrealistic, bound to overburden any partner, leading you to feel perpetually embittered about wives who don't understand?

Many of these dilemmas will never be clearly resolvable. But we do have some ways of looking at them that may shed some light. One need which is almost certainly doomed to be unmet over the long haul is the narcissistic need for admiration. This is an excessive need for mirroring, the mirror that never is enough. The ordinary supply of mirroring responses that most of us manage to get in our lives will not satisfy the narcissistic need for admiration, at least until we get more conscious and more resourceful.

Taking Responsibility for Moods

One way out of the noose of the narcissistic reliance on women for personal validation is by taking responsibility for moods.

Julian's wife was feeling relentlessly burdened by subtle pressure to admire him. He turned to her to acknowledge his career success. He turned to her to find his jokes funny and his stories really interesting. And, of course, he turned to her to make him feel sexy and attractive. And it just got to be too much. She felt this creeping obligation to be his cheerleader, a mommy who tells her son what a big boy he is. This was not what she had signed up for. She did not want to be his mommy, and the natural appreciation of Julian that had drawn her to him in the first place was getting smothered by this need, this need, this need.

So she told him, in so many words, to diversify his portfolio. "Don't plan and cook some great meal and then look at me expectantly, waiting for me to say what a great husband you are! That's not me! If you want admiration, cook for other people! You know they will always say wonderful things, and that's fine. But don't hang around waiting for it from me."

This felt so cold, but Julian knew somewhere deeper within that she was right. He was relying on her, as a mirror, to make him feel great—not just occasionally, but all the time. And he had worked himself into such a state that no other confirmation really mattered if he did not consistently have hers. So he started planning elaborate meals for his friends and giving more public presentations where his audience rewarded him. And he was forced, in a way that deep relationships with women often force men to do, to learn to tolerate the distress and appreciate the bounty of intermittent and plenty-good-enough mirroring.

Men and women who thrive on admiration or adoration are likely to run into a wall of intense disappointment. Some thrive in the early stages of relationships because they feel completely appreciated and admired. Who wouldn't enjoy this? But few relationships can sustain this level as the center of the relationship shifts from romantic attachment to raising a family, building a structured life, and seeing the partner in the full light of consciousness.

The narcissistic need for admiration sets the stage for an otherwise good man to behave badly in his midlife relationship. Recognizing these needs for what they are and developing a repertoire of ways to fulfill them empowers you to make choices with integrity.

The Meaning of Sex

In the 1977 movie *Saturday Night Fever*, Tony (John Travolta) is nineteen and not quite a candidate for midlife issues. But, in a somewhat comic fashion, he laments that he is feeling kind of old for the disco life in which he has achieved stardom. He is rethinking his values and his future.

He and the girl with whom he is falling in love, Stephanie, win a dance contest, but Tony is angry because he sees that the contest was rigged: the Puerto Rican couple really should have won. The whole scene makes him sick. He is sick of his trapped life and his stupid friends. He drags Stephanie out to the car where he and his friends usually take girls for sex in the backseat. She tries to calm him down. He starts kissing her and forcing himself on her. She protests, finally giving him a hard knee to the gonads. She storms off and he sits staring into space, despondent, confused, and ashamed.

Tony is a good man behaving very badly. Stephanie, savvy and no pushover, soon welcomes him back into her life because she truly believes in him. Tony was seeking sex as stress reduction, escape from dysphoria, and a reaffirmation that he was masculine and successful. It was his antidote to despair. There are probably better ways of approaching despair than this.

Each man brings different needs and different narratives into the bedroom (or the backseat). It is not just some purely animalistic, hormone-driven urge that leads you to adopting the goofy positions which accompany sexual ecstasy. The narrative, or the story you tell yourself about the meaning of sex, plays a crucial role in determining the emotions, the perceptions, and ultimately the behaviors that emerge. And the narratives at midlife about sex are especially likely to either liberate or imprison.

Hidden Bedroom Partners

Hajcak and Garwood, in their 1995 book *Hidden Bedroom Partners,* outline the multiple emotional and psychological needs that both men and women often bring into the bedroom. We can use sex to affirm our self-worth. To mask anger. To escape boredom. To gain control or power. To cope with depression or anxiety. To avoid loneliness. To gain revenge. To atone for misdeeds. To express pity. To express rebellion against social mores or restrictions. Even, surprisingly, to avoid intimacy, such as when we choose sex rather than meaningful conversation. Prostitutes usually have firm rules against kissing because it feels so much more intimate than intercourse!

On the other hand, sexual play and sexual union with someone you love is hard to match. The intensity and passion, the powerful sense of connection, is unparalleled. But it would not be credible to advise you that all of the rewards of good sex can be found elsewhere. (I made the mistake once of trying to convince a group of substance-abusing teenagers that there were other ways they could match the intensity of taking crystal methamphetamine. They stared at me for a moment and—almost in unison—said, "Yeah? Like what?")

But perhaps you can tolerate your disappointment about less frequent sex or sex that is not quite as adventurous or acrobatic as it once was. How? By finding other ways to meet most of the needs that you have so far met only through sex. By not depending on sex or on the responses of your sexual partner or partners to provide an inordinate amount of mirroring to bolster your shaky sense of self.

If you discover that one of your "hidden bedroom partners" is the need for self-worth, for example, you have a lot of other options. You can tell your partner, at a quiet moment, how you are feeling and that you just need some more reassurance from her. What you most need, and may actually be able to get, can be verbal (*I love watching you with the kids!*) or physical (cuddling in bed, a kiss when you walk in the door) or behavioral (an affectionate wink, a random love note, telling others about some way she is proud of you).

That's the most direct route, and in reasonably healthy relationships, it is often enough. I have been delightfully shocked watching how much mileage some men can get out of asking for and receiving these relatively simple gestures which fill the gap. There are a lot of you guys out there who are actually pretty easy to please—once you figure out exactly what it is that you need!

Even when this would take care of many of your unmet needs, your partner may not be able to offer it. She may be distracted or emotionally withholding. She may be sitting on a powder keg of resentment, feeling mistreated by you. She may simply be unskilled at offering this kind of affirmation or affection, even if she thinks your requests are halfway reasonable and she has the best of intentions of trying to offer you what you need.

If you think about it, there aren't too many aspects of the sexual experience that cannot be found elsewhere. When you recognize this, sex resumes its rightful role of a glorious way of feeling passionate and experiencing intense pleasure—Hajcak and Garwood call this "sexual sex"—as well as a means for experiencing something deeper and making contact.

Again, this is only possible if you are a conscious man. Otherwise, you may fall into the old familiar male cycle: Something happens. You interpret it in a way that makes you feel bad. The bad feelings flood you. You don't know what to call them or how to express them. Because you are a guy and you are oriented toward action, you feel like you have to do something to make these bad feelings go away. And, if you have traditionally used sex as a way to feel better about yourself, you will—out of force of habit—turn to this. And you will become quite demanding if you are denied this opportunity. Like Tony from *Saturday Night Fever*, you will be looking for sex in all the wrong places at all the wrong moments for all the wrong reasons.

Now is the time to diversify your portfolio. It is your responsibility—no one else's—to try and get your needs met in some other fashion in a way that is not threatening to your primary relationship or destructive to yourself. This proviso cannot be overemphasized. It is a natural inclination for a man wounded by having his emotional needs unmet by his partner to generate a very convincing set of justifications for self-indulgent behavior. These rationalizations are usually something along the lines of *My wife, she doesn't understand me* or *It's so unfair that I am not getting what I need from her*. And these rationalizations can easily seduce the otherwise good man into behavior which is not only self-indulgent but threatening to his relationship: an affair.

Narratives of Midlife Sex

My client Doug told me this lament:

I can go a month without sex. It's really not a big deal. I know men who are single who go a year or more without sex. They may be lonely or horny, but it's not a disaster. And when I know there's a good reason for us not to have sex—like she's sick, or the kids are sick, or we're staying somewhere in the same room with the kids, or she's having her period—I can handle it. I miss it, but I can handle it.

But when we should be having sex and she doesn't want to, I start to go nuts. I can feel the tension rising. A few days is okay, a week I can handle, then by about day ten I start to feel lost, empty, deprived, and ultimately totally resentful!

How can she do this to me? It's not fair! She's a withholding bitch! If she knows how easy it is to make me feel better and more whole and she doesn't do it for me, she must be truly cruel!

So, it's not so much a desperate drive for sex. It all has to do with the meaning, I guess. Because when we could and should be having sex and we're not, I feel unloved, unattractive, uncared for, unalive, unvalued. And, at those times, I convince myself that only her touch and passion can restore me!

Sexual Expectations

How do your story lines about the meaning of sex change at midlife? Sometimes this shift is positive and evidence of maturity, and other times this shift represents a panicked, desperate attempt to hold on to something that you fear you are losing. Whereas sexuality for younger men might be dominated by needs for affirmation, adventure, and reassurance of masculinity, midlife male sexuality ideally shifts more to an expression of affection and connection. Sexual frequency may be down, but not satisfaction and pleasure. The mutual maturity of men and women at midlife often leads to a more genuine connection, more relaxed playfulness, and less emphasis on sexual performance. Some theorists say that true sexual intimacy cannot begin until age fifty.

This is true, at least, if you are experiencing a reasonably graceful transition into midlife, with reasonably graceful levels of acceptance of the aging process. But you may be struggling with this transition, desperately fighting it and panicked by the creeping signs of physical loss. And nothing is more likely to panic men than signs of sexual decline.

The research of Masters and Johnson (1970) clearly demonstrates that the susceptibility of the human male to the power of suggestion with regard to his sexual prowess is almost unbelievable. Tell a man that he is supposed to be having sex daily to match his peers, and he will feel like a failure when he misses a day. Tell him that once a week is typical for married couples, and he will likely feel fine about that. A man who experiences occasional erectile dysfunction will typically panic until he learns how statistically normal this phenomenon is. In fact, I have often seen this reframing process work stunningly when I congratulate a man for an occasional "inability to perform" by telling him, "Your body—or, more specifically, your penis—is being very smart! It is telling you that something is not right here. Maybe you are not feeling emotionally connected, or maybe you are stressed out in ways that you don't consciously realize. You deserve credit for insisting that sexuality not be isolated from the other factors in your life. That is the sign of a whole person."

Men especially need some basic education about what to expect as testosterone levels slowly begin to decline (approximately 1 percent per year) around age thirty-five or forty. You can expect erections to develop more slowly and to be a little less firm. There will be a longer recovery period after an orgasm. You may find that you need more direct stimulation to your penis to get a full erection. The urge to ejaculate may not be quite as intense. There may even be times when you lose your erection completely during sexual activity.

If you are prepared for these slow, subtle changes, and if you think of these as signs that you are a full-fledged member of a very large worldwide organization called the Midlife Men's Club, you may be able to handle these more gracefully.

Independent Sexual Center of Initiative

The independent center of initiative concept from self psychology helps us understand another central midlife narrative. For many of us, it is a revelation that our partner has her own reasons—which have nothing to do with us—for doing what she does, including saying yes or no to sex.

For example, Clark told me about an evening when his wife was clearly giving him signals that she was interested in a romantic evening after her eight-year-old son (his stepson) went to bed. Her son had been having trouble falling asleep, so she lay down in bed with him and eventually fell asleep. When Clark went in to get her, she was groggy and had lost her appetite for sex. Clark told me, "I couldn't believe she was not following through! I griped and pissed and moaned! She said to me, 'You cannot come between me and my son!' It felt like one more huge piece of evidence that she didn't really love me. I could just tell that she was holding this back from me just to get me."

Clark perceived his wife's behavior only in terms of what she could offer him. There was no room for her to be doing the right thing by helping her son; there was no room for her to be tired. Clark could only think about what had been "promised." In Clark's eyes, at that moment, she was allowed no independent center of initiative.

In trying to understand men who behave badly in response to an emotional injury, we must consider the man's feeling of being powerless, no matter how much it might appear that he is acting powerful. Here Clark felt as if his wife was unilaterally in charge of their sex life. He was feeling powerless—his wife (and his stepson's emotional needs) governed his sex life, and he felt like he was just following along.

Exercise: The Stories of Sex

Here is a broad range of emotional and psychological needs that people try to fulfill through sex. Some of these are healthy reasons to have sex; others do not belong anywhere near the bedroom. See if you can identify the needs that you bring into the bedroom and consider positive alternative ways of getting these needs met. The list of needs and the accompanying alternatives are not meant to be all-inclusive—see what needs and creative alternatives you can generate.

Remember that self-knowledge is power. The payoff here is truly sexual sex and a relationship less disrupted by unmet needs.

The Need	Possible Alternatives
To affirm self-worth	Let your partner know that you need to feel more valued and appreciated. Coach your kid's soccer team. Invite friends over for your world-famous barbecued ribs.
To mask anger	Tell your partner that you are feeling angry and that you need to talk.
To escape boredom	Learn to play the electric guitar.
To cope with depression or anxiety	See a shrink.
To avoid loneliness	Find nonsexual ways to spend quality time with your partner. Join a bowling league.

The Need	Possible Alternatives
To atone for misdeeds	Tell your partner you're sorry. Don't do it again. Ask her what she needs from you.
To express pity	Offer emotional support and friendship.
To express rebellion against social mores or restrictions	Start a grunge rock band. Pierce your nipple.
To avoid intimacy	Respect your own need for distance. If you want to get past this pattern, just talk and kiss (no sex!).
To experience passion	Learn to hang glide or surf. Start a new business venture.
To express and experience affection	Find twenty ways to express verbal, physical, and behavioral affection to your partner, and ask her if she can do some of the same for you.
To be touched	Touch your partner daily in nonsexual ways. Don't stop there—touch your kids, your friends, your sister (obviously only in ways that are not sexual and not unwelcome!).
To have truly sexual sex	As long as your partner is willing, go for it!

George and Maggie's Story

George was a forty-six-year-old university professor, married, with two girls in grade school. His wife had called to make the appointment for him to see me. He sat down in my office and got straight to the point. "I have addictive personality behaviors."

George proceeded to tell me of his history of smoking pot every day for twenty years, beginning in college and ending several years ago. He had some problems with episodic drinking: he would often have a couple of extra drinks at parties and get nasty with his family. He had tried to quit drinking twenty times, but always started again, despite his wife's passionate protests. He was a workaholic, staying at work late and bringing work home to avoid interacting with his family. "But," he informed me, "I am especially addicted to sex! I always want more. My wife and I fight about this all the time because I harass her and hound her and make her feel guilty whenever she turns me down. It's never enough—I know that, but I can't stop it."

George had an insatiable sexual appetite and unrealistic sexual expectations. He always wanted more: more adventurous sex, more frequent sex, more dangerous sex (sex with the kids asleep in the same room in hotels, or loud sex when he and Maggie were staying with family).

I asked George why he came to see me. "To try to please Maggie. I am hoping that someone can tell her that she tries to control me too much and that she should just give me more room to do the things I want. I love her so much, she means everything to me—but I also want to get my way!"

I asked George what happened recently that made her so insistent that he come in. "It's the lying, I guess. I told her I had stopped looking at porn on the Internet, but I really have been sneaking it for months. And whenever she became suspicious, I harangued her for not trusting me until she finally let up. She felt crazy, and I didn't really care. The lying was such a betrayal to her."

In another session, I brought Maggie and George together. Maggie confirmed the portrait of their sex life. "I feel so pressured by his demands for his sex. If we had sex two times a day, he'd want it three—and he would make me feel guilty about not wanting to!" She leaned forward in her chair and her voice dropped. "But the worst part is his anger. His moods. I just see him retreat from me whenever his needs are unmet. He pouts and withdraws and gets all dark. I'm depressed about having a husband who hates me!" Maggie continued, through tears, to try to describe what she was going through. "Now, when I think about having sex, I can't tell where my own needs start and my obligation ends. Am I doing this for me or for him or for us?"

In self psychology terms, George perceived Maggie primarily as a selfobject. Her role in his life was to provide something that would enhance his sense of self and well-being. And he was highly intolerant of her when she denied him this experience; he was unable to recognize her independent center of initiative. He could not see that she had needs of her own which did not always exactly coincide with his—and that this was not an adversarial move!

So when George felt emotionally depleted—which was a regular experience for him—he had no way of identifying what was wrong. He simply responded to the dysphoria by turning to something—anything—which provided some distraction or relief from the empty feelings inside. Pot, alcohol, porn, excessive work, and especially sex all offered him the hope of relief. These were his sirens calling. They promised so much, yet all turned out to be empty promises. And when they were denied to him, or when they failed to fulfill a need, he fell into a mood.

George came to develop a vivid description of his moods:

I don't really trust anybody. I know I will be betrayed. It just takes over. I get ugly and aggressive. I don't care about the effect I have on anybody. I lie to Maggie if I feel like it—I tell her she's totally paranoid for thinking that I have still been looking at porn. I make her feel crazy and I don't care! And in a dark sort of way, it feels so good. I feel so justified to feel so shitty because everyone's so nasty to me. I get dug in deep. It feels comfortable and familiar. And I get the chance to be nasty and sulky. I feel drugged. And I don't want to leave!

The moods, of course, led to behaviors which confirmed his bitter views: he would act like a jackass and drive Maggie away. Although he desperately needed Maggie emotionally and was very attached to her, he also deeply resented this hold that she had over him—or that he believed she had over him. He confused her ability to arouse him sexually with her intent to control him. Maggie was right, in a way: George did hate her. He hated her for having the ability to determine his sense of well-being. He hated his position of emotional dependence. He believed that Maggie was dangerous to him, and he forgot that the true dangers were the psychological events within his own head.

I define myself by how she views me. I've given her a lot of power—and that's why I have to be so secret. I'm afraid of her! I have a hard time with her depression. I feel responsible, then helpless, then defensive. Then I attack. And I'm afraid she will abandon me if I do not conform to what she wants.

It's like there's a collision between these two needs. One is that I desperately need Maggie, and I will do anything to stay in her good graces. The other is my defiance: "You cannot make me do anything! You cannot control me! I will defy you! And I hate you for having so much power—that I have given you—over me!"

I get into this mood where I say to myself, "Why is it that she gets to call the shots? Why do I have to wait for her to be in the mood? It would be so easy for her to make me so happy, but she just withholds it from me." Then I get hit with this wave of shame and remorse: "My god, I'm such a selfish person, what's wrong with me? What am I doing to her? Look at the example I'm setting for our girls about how relationships should be!"

When George slowly began to understand what his moods were really about, his marriage began to change. As with many complex psychological issues, George didn't actually have to change his behavior very profoundly to bring about this shift, although it never would have been possible without the foundation of his experience of emotional turmoil and his dawning receptivity to new narratives. George learned to identify the moods before he succumbed to them.

It sounds so simple, but of course in practice it's not. George learned to understand the cravings for alcohol, porn, and excessive work as signals of internal unrest. When he began to notice the creeping resentment toward Maggie for denying him the sex he felt he was entitled to, he learned to stop and remind himself, *I feel a mood coming on!*

George began to discover some new skills and new rewards. He tried to identify, find words for, and express feelings to Maggie rather than slinking off into a mood and insisting on staying there. It began to work for him. The old reinforcement of sulking and feeling royally justified in the dark, victimized feelings was slowly replaced by a new reinforcement: feeling lighter, eliciting a positive response from his wife, no longer seeing her as the enemy, and feeling a sense of mastery over this whole disturbing process.

"Things feel better. I'm talking to Maggie about my job stress rather than turning to my 'addictions' like porn, drinking, my sexual demands. I'm not withdrawing or demanding something from her. I know what I need to do to care for her better. When she is blue, I just need to stop and ask her if there's anything I can do, or if there's anything she wants to talk about." George began to see the connection between past and present. "I really don't trust anybody. People will let me down. Growing up, I never trusted my mother to be consistent. I could tell that she would never get it from my point of view. She always saw everything through her own needs." George assumed Maggie was the same way: self-absorbed, intent on meeting her own needs at the expense of his.

A very important moment in their treatment as a couple took place after Maggie turned to me, in pain and confusion, and asked, "Am I abnormal for being interested in sex less than three times a week, like he says I am?" I told her that normal didn't always apply when it came to sexuality, but that most couples at their life stage have sex about once a week or often less. She was shocked and relieved and empowered. The amazing thing was that this bright, educated woman with many close friendships had never heard this information before!

George was disappointed, because this gave him less leverage to get what he wanted. But he was also relieved. The gap between his expectations and his reality had just become narrower. This was a new narrative. With this new information about what was "normal," Maggie felt less guilty and more clear about holding her ground. George could relax his demands because he no longer interpreted Maggie's behavior as a sign that she was depriving him of something he was entitled to.

George and Maggie had some setbacks. One week they reported that George had erupted into a mood of victimization. He threatened Maggie, "If we are only going to have sex once a week, then our marriage will not work!"

George explained what had taken place within. "I especially needed sex this week as an affirmation. I needed some positive feedback. And we went off to this weekend retreat where all anybody ever does is have sex. And she didn't want to. I couldn't stand it. I felt so much like I was entitled to have this and she wouldn't come through."

George had succumbed, once again, to his own version of Smith's golden fantasy: *If only I can get laid, I will be okay! And I will not be able to bear it if this is denied!* To give up this fantasy completely was still too much for him. The only logical conclusion he could reach after giving up the fantasy would be that nothing—and no one—could rescue him from his moods. At times, that was still unbearable. So he continued, intermittently, to relapse.

Maggie described how she found herself withholding affection or appreciation of George, even when she felt encouraged by some of his changes. "I'm afraid to act positively or warmly toward him. I think he'll get fat, dumb, and happy. He only looks at himself and works on these things when we are in crisis. The day I am convinced that he will take over the job of monitoring himself is the day I can relax and welcome him back. Because I do love him. I'm just scared."

Over time, the relapses became less frequent, the lying and deception receded, and the temper tantrums got more manageable. I continued to call upon George to do what "real men" do: do the right thing for the relationship. The sexual politics changed remarkably. George simply stopped initiating sex. "I'm not sending resentful messages. Going to bed used to be miserable, and now that feeling is gone."

He told me that some words of mine from sessions past kept ringing in his ears: *If you give up the constant expectations, it will be a huge relief!* He never realized what a difference that could make. He thought that the only route to happiness was more sex. When he gave up this pursuit, he found a different kind of happiness.

Maggie told me, "The pressure's all gone. I'm not always afraid, not always feeling bad; he's not always angry."

George told me that my assignment to find a way to express to Maggie how much he appreciated her every day had a profound effect on him. "Giving up this pressure on her is the most generous act of all. This shows how much I really cherish her." He grinned. "I know this sounds ridiculous coming from me, but at this point in my life, it's actually better than sex."

Authenticity and Intimacy

When all is said and done, and when the upheaval of midlife has peaked and begun to clear, you can finally taste the sweetness of authenticity and intimacy. Authenticity and intimacy are intertwined as the central positive outcomes of the midlife transition.

How do you get to the point where you truly know yourself and genuinely connect with those close to you? For most men, the ticket to this world is through relationships. Often this is through a loving relationship with a woman who provides the catalyst for discovering a hidden, more loving, and more emotionally open self than you ever knew was possible. Will Hunting discovers this through his relationship with Skylar. For others, the turning point is your relationship with your kids, or caring for a sick or dying family member, or resolving the long-standing conflicts with the father who has haunted you all your life.

Or you may be one of the men who wakes up only as a result of the pain and suffering in your relationship. Sometimes it is impossible—or at least it seems impossible—for you to be turned around and opened up just by the good stuff that a relationship generates in you. You may only get it after you have said or done something to hurt someone. You may have to flee—or damage or destroy—a relationship with a woman in order to really *feel* what you have to lose, and to realize that you want exactly what you are fleeing, or what you have damaged or destroyed.

Authenticity

Nemiroff and Colarusso (1990) define authenticity as the capacity to accept what is genuine within the self and the outer world regardless of the narcissistic injury involved. Becoming free from the preoccupation with narcissistic injury is one of the liberating forces of the midlife transition. It means that you can stop pretending and posturing. You don't have to impress anyone anymore. If you don't have the most beautiful wife or the most talented kids, it doesn't matter anymore, because they are who they are and you love them. And you are who you are, and you are fundamentally okay. You can accept yourself as special but not unique.

Hard as it may be to believe, this gradual acceptance of the self as imperfect can actually provide relief.

There is something profoundly satisfying, especially at midlife, about being seen and known—not just by others, but by yourself. This experience is one of integrity, not necessarily the integrity of morals and upstanding behavior but rather the sense of integration. Your inside and outside match. Your values and behavior match.

Before I was married, I was engaged to another woman. After a series of reckless behaviors and betrayals, we finally called off the wedding. And I felt victimized by her. I felt like she had been angry at me and had acted this out in ways that were irresponsible and destructive. I was a wreck and in therapy. My therapist heard my tale of woe and told me, "You're the one who was angry. You sat there all the time with her, thinking you were being the good guy, yet all the time you acted superior, you were controlling, you were passive-aggressive. We know you are a good guy, but you treated her badly—and if you continue to pretend differently, you're a fool!"

I couldn't even muster the energy to be defensive or threaten him with a lawsuit for defamation of character. His words just rang true. And it took such a burden off my shoulders to be seen clearly and to see the truth about myself. I had, like most of us, been living in a world governed by an idealized self-image, and it lacked integrity. The slap in the face from my therapist woke me up. I was able to accept what was genuine within myself and the outer world in spite of the narcissistic injury involved. Although I wasn't quite at midlife at the time, this was a defining moment: as soon as I could perceive and accept this dark side, this hidden aggression, a new capacity for tenderness and generosity of spirit emerged. Go figure.

If you take the opportunity to see yourself honestly, you may find out that you are selfish or greedy or competitive or worse. Join the club. The conscious man needs to know this about himself so he can make truly informed decisions about himself and his relationships.

Intimacy

This midlife moment of the emergence of the self is centrally played out through your relationship with your intimate partner.

The image you have always carried of the idealized partner (a symbolic representation or mirror of your idealized self) is, when all goes well, replaced by the real partner. It is normal to feel a sense of conflict about this, because your real partner never quite matches your ideal. She ain't perfect—and neither are you.

But, if you are lucky and good and conscious, and you are successful at seeing your partner clearly and accepting her as she is, there is a pot of gold at the end of the rainbow. You now have a shot at real intimacy, which diminishes the narcissistic sting of aging. Remember what George said: "I really cherish her. I know this sounds ridiculous coming from me, but at this point in my life it's actually better than sex." When you learn to appreciate and value long-standing relationships, in contrast to the more youthful gratifications of the body and not-so-connected sex, you have discovered your adult self and taken a major developmental step of midlife. For couples who make it this far, marital satisfaction increases. Couples who survive the midlife transition are much more satisfied with their relationship than they were at earlier stages.

A client of mine in his late forties came in one day complaining again about the ways his marriage had deteriorated. His wife, whom he was still crazy about, just didn't offer him as much. She was less interested in sex. She didn't glow quite as much when she saw him as she used to. She didn't focus as much on the details in his life because she had more of her own life and because their kids filled her consciousness more. I had met this woman, and she was great. There were no major problems in their relationship, just his nagging feeling of disappointment and rejection, and his inevitable increasing irritability.

I decided it was time to lower the boom. I paused dramatically, looked him square in the eye, and said, "You've just got to see this clearly: your wife is not going to take care of all of these emotional needs now." I expected him to be crushed or defensive or angry. He was none of the above. His face brightened and he said to me, "You mean there will come a time when she will?"

I realized that he had zeroed in on my use of the word *now* and had clung to it in a desperate act of denial. I clarified: "Your wife is not going to take care of all of these emotional needs now, or ever."

He left the session crushed and pouting. He called me that night and left a message telling me how thoroughly depressed my statement had made him. My words, he said, had doomed him to a permanent state of feeling like there was something missing.

But when I saw him the next week, he was changed. He told me that he had woken up the next morning feeling so much lighter. He noticed a new wave of affection for his wife. He realized that he felt freer now, free from the expectation that she was supposed to take care of these feelings for him, and free from his disappointment that she didn't. He felt released from these expectations, and as Buddhists know, pain stems from the gap between expectations and reality. When the expectations genuinely change, the opportunity for freedom from pain appears. He was so relieved at not having to be frustrated by his wife again and again, and it allowed him to take in what she genuinely had to offer him. And it was pretty damn good.

5

Men's Brains

Everything I have been telling you about how men respond to emotionally provocative situations has been wrong. Actually, that's a little melodramatic, but some new research about brain functioning makes us consider some alternative explanations.

Our traditional view of how the brain responds to emotionally laden situations is that we pick up information from the world around us through our sensory apparatus, then this information is relayed to the *neocortex,* our advanced brain. Then we process, analyze, feel, and act. Most of the time, this is a pretty accurate description of the flow of traffic between stimulus and response.

However, recent research about the brain and nervous system shows that, in some situations, the impulses generated from a challenging situation bypass the neocortex completely and go straight to the *limbic system,* our primitive brain—home of the most intense and disinhibited impulses and responses; our psychological and physical survival system.

Many men who tell me their stories insist that there is no lag time whatsoever between a threatening event and their explosive response. This new wave of brain research tells us that this is not just rationalization or justification: these men may be right.

This makes it sound rather hopeless. Before we discuss ways in which it is not quite as hopeless as it sounds, let's review what we currently know about men's brains.

Emotional Hijacking by the Limbic System

Brain research throughout the past several decades has uncovered some of the mysteries of how impulsive and aggressive behavior is generated. *Magnetic resonance imaging* (MRI), *positron emission tomography* (PET), and *computerized axial tomography* (CAT) scans now give us a portrait of the human brain in different activities: working, playing, arguing, meditating, worrying, creating. Researchers have also identified individual neurons that fire as we observe the activities of others, helping us interpret their actions and feelings, and perhaps forming the neurophysiological basis for empathy.

Fight or Flight

The *amygdala,* a tiny almond-shaped structure in the primitive limbic system, is at the center of the brain's emotional life. The amygdala functions like a security alarm at your home. When it reads some event as violating the known rules of safe behavior, it goes nuts and sets off screeching sounds that put you in a zone where you can't really think straight. When this alarm is activated in your body, you enter a primitive mind space in which words, thoughts, and consciousness are barely available. Hormones rule. It is here that your most potent emotional reactions are stirred.

Situations that our brain perceives as emotional emergencies stimulate the signals to the amygdala. The amygdala scans the information for potential danger: *Is this threatening to me?* The amygdala is very dependent on associational patterns: if something about the current event is similar to an emotionally charged memory from the past, the limbic system is likely to be activated in full force.

So when your partner says or does something that telegraphs *She doesn't love me* or *She is disrespecting me* or *She might be leaving me,* signals are activated along a pathway that serves as an express route to the amygdala. Once you determine that a situation represents a threat, a state of national emergency is declared. Civil rights and liberties are suspended, and you round up the usual suspects. The amygdala lights up the entire brain and body before the neocortex ever gets into the act. The neocortex, home of all of your most advanced functions and cognitive capacities, is bypassed. In other words, your brain is emotionally hijacked by your limbic system. Once the moment passes, you have the sense of not knowing what the hell came over you.

This is an essential tool for survival, and there are some terrific reasons why this system has evolved. The trouble is that, especially when you are reacting so quickly and the demands of the moment seem so urgent, you may not realize that what was once the case is no longer so. Your emotional mind fails to recognize the distinction between current event and past traumatic event—it reacts to the present as though the present were the past.

In our modern age, we have developed (for better or worse) the capacity to perceive threat not only from the saber-toothed tiger outside of our cave or the suspicious-looking guy in the parking lot. We also react to symbolic threats to our self-esteem. We are threatened by being dissed. If someone cuts us off in traffic or gives us a look when we're angling for a parking space, the same surge of brain chemicals can be stimulated. The chemicals released, known as *catecholamines*, give us a rush of energy and prepare us for action. Although it only lasts a few minutes, this surge is potentially volatile, and to defuse it you must discharge the tension or cognitively reappraise the situation (*Oh, that was my son crawling into bed with us who just kicked me in the head, not a threatening intruder—and he didn't mean to hurt me!*).

In the lingo of self psychology, this state of disorganization and suspension of judgment is known as *fragmentation,* which is at the opposite end of the psychological spectrum from self-cohesion. Psychologist Ross Greene (1998), in his work with "inflexible-explosive" children, refers to these states as "meltdowns." The hallmark of the fragmentation, meltdown, or emotional-hijacking state is that all bets are off when it comes to decision making. All that matters is dealing with the immediate, desperate emotional state. Good values, good judgment, and projection of future consequences fade into the background as the limbic system dominates. At a certain level of excited, aggressive arousal, you may become totally unforgiving; only revenge and retaliation for the perceived injustice matter. Zillman's research (1979) indicates that this level of brain and nervous system excitation even creates a mania-like sense of grandiosity, power, and invulnerability that makes aggressive behavior more likely.

Have you ever tried to negotiate with someone who is drunk or tweaking on speed? In fact, intoxicated people have been shown to lose a fundamental interpersonal skill: the ability to recognize cues that the other person is not interested in continuing the fight (Leonard 1989). This applies to drunk guys in bars and couples who are arguing about taking out the trash. It's like trying to reason with a hungry three-year-old who has missed his nap. Your only hope is to wait until the physiological imbalance has passed and Dr. Jekyll returns. So it is with emotional hijacking.

Origins of the Hypervigilant Brain

Neuroscientists are hard at work trying to understand how people learn to cope with distress. As with most psychological conditions and processes, some of the patterns are surely inborn—the luck of the draw. But emerging research about early parent-child attachment patterns sheds some more light on interpersonal factors that create specific brain structures and patterns, setting some of us up to be *hypervigilant:* quicker to mistrust and quicker to experience alarm (Siegel 2002).

Imagine this scene between infant and parent: The baby cries out in distress or frustration. Mommy hears the cry and responds. She picks up her little baby and rocks him, strokes him, whispers soothing sounds in his ear—any of the thousand things that an attuned parent offers to a child in need. And, not always but more often than not, the baby quiets. In the same way, parents help their children learn to respond to other emotional states. The baby is over-stimulated at bedtime, and the father helps to calm him down. The baby is delighted by the visual thrills of the mobile, and the mother smiles and laughs along with him.

More important than the immediate resolution to the crisis of the hour is the lesson the child learns from this interaction. This parent-child "collaboration" is crucial (Siegel 2002). With the help of the outside resource, the synapses in his *orbitofrontal cortex* (the region that integrates cognitive and emotional processes) grow. Like the mirroring selfobject relationship, this happens thousands of times, over and over, in the tiny yet crucial interchanges between parent and child, and the growing child develops a fundamental security and a fundamental skill: *I know how to get through crummy feelings!* At first, the child needs the alliance with his parent in order to achieve this feeling of security, but as the child grows up, he becomes more able to cope independently.

It is through this process that you have learned the basic skills of emotional intelligence: dealing with frustration, with anxiety, with sadness, and with joy. You have developed emotional resilience, fundamental confidence that you have resources—without and eventually within—for managing the disturbing moments, and confident that ruptures in relationships typically lead to reconnections afterward. None of us is ever free of fears of abandonment, and some of us are less free than others. This is actually manifested in discernible deficits in the growth of synapses in the orbitofrontal cortex (Siegel 2002). And if you have missed out on these fundamental collaborations, you are swimming upstream. You are less likely to be able to manage emotional states, to calm yourself, to deal with perceived threats or abandonment, or to tolerate lots of excitement.

For our discussion here about men's relationships, the ultimate cost of these deficits lies in the pattern of emotional unintelligence in relationships. If you have deficits in the brain circuitry for processing emotional cues, you will find it very difficult to make sense of interpersonal signals. You may experience the I-just-don't-get-where-she's-coming-from syndrome with some frequency. The result is disconnection, and disconnection and misreading are central reasons for mishandling relationships. This understanding of how we learn—or fail to learn—to cope with emotions, while not an excuse for destructive behavior in a relationship, gives us even more of a clue about the origins of good men behaving badly.

Emotional Flooding

As a man, you face three key challenges that can deeply affect your closest personal relationships.

- You may have trouble identifying, labeling, and expressing your emotions.

- Your nervous system is easily flooded and overwhelmed by uncomfortable feelings.

- You are inclined to take immediate action to get away from bad situations or to try to make them go away.

Normative Male Alexithymia

In Greek, *lexis* means "word" and *thymos* means "emotion." Combined with the prefix *a-,* meaning "not" or "without," the lexicon of psychiatry has generated the word *alexithymia.* Alexithymia literally means "lacking the words for emotions." Alexithymics just seem different; they are Spock-like aliens living on a planet with other people who are very affected by feelings.

In severe clinical cases of alexithymia, the individual is crippled by this handicap; he or she is unable to consciously know, and certainly unable to communicate, anything about his or her internal states. Trying to understand the impact of this reminds me of the experiment my tenth grade social studies teacher conducted with the class to help us understand the significance of stages of evolution. We were required to spend an entire school day with our thumbs taped to our palms. Without access to our opposable thumbs, we were awakened to the enormous impact that these opposable thumbs had on turning apes into humans. But who knew how big a deal this really was until we experienced it "firsthand"?

Likewise, most of us can't really grasp what an essential component of being human this is: the ability to translate our internal world into consciousness and communication. Without it, we lack something that makes us quintessentially human.

Ron Levant (1998) has coined the term *normative male alexithymia* to describe a widespread phenomenon in our culture. While it may not reach a level of clinically significant proportions like bona fide alexithymia, it still captures a "condition" that plagues men in relationships. Good men behaving badly often are poster children for normative male alexithymia.

This term refers to the pattern of boys who grow up to be men who are unaware of their emotions and even of their own bodily sensations. They rely only on their cognitive descriptions, analyses, and opinions. Because of this gap in self-awareness, these men are prevented from using the simplest and most effective method for dealing with complex feelings and difficult moods: identifying, thinking about, and expressing feelings. These are skills in emotional intelligence that women, for the most part, simply do better. This explains why women sometimes feel like they just can't get through to men.

We don't know for sure how much of this difference is attributable to gender-specific brain characteristics. Sifneos (1991) suggests that there is a disconnection between the two centers we have discussed, the neocortex and the limbic system. The feeling centers operating in the limbic system are still firing, but they are not sending the signals to the neocortex in an intelligible way. Or the signals may be getting through, but the verbal coding centers in the neocortex fail to function optimally, or even adequately. Think of it as an emotional learning disability.

We do know that boys learn early on that the male role involves keeping feelings inside and sucking it up. And this affects brain development. Even at the age of two, girls refer to feelings more frequently than boys do. Mothers use more words about emotions when they speak to their young daughters than they do with their sons (Dunn, Breatherton, and Munn 1987). Studies show that fathers use a wider range of language that expresses emotions with their daughters than with their sons—and their teasing is more aggressive with their sons than with their daughters (Gleason and Grief 1983). In fact, as boys grow older, they show less expression on their faces and their mothers find it more and more difficult to read the feeling behind the face (Buck 1977). After about age four or five, boys are held less than girls. Boys who are attached to their mothers are treated with a certain disapproval in a way that girls attached to their fathers are not. And girls, with their superior verbal abilities in childhood, talk and talk and talk about their feelings with their cohorts.

Levant summarizes this developmental process for boys:

Normative alexithymia is a predicable result of the male gender socialization process. Specifically, it is a result of boys being socialized to restrict the expression of their vulnerable and caring/connection emotions and to be emotionally stoic. This socialization process includes both the creation of skill deficits (by not teaching boys emotional skills nor allowing them to have experiences that would facilitate their leaning these skills) and trauma (including prohibitions against boys' natural emotional expressivity, and punishment, often in the form of making the boy feel deeply ashamed of himself for violating these prohibitions). (1998, 41–42)

Levant refers to the male socialization process as "trauma that is so normative that we do not think of it as trauma at all" (1998, 37). Many boys are left with no alternative but to shut down emotionally, implode with internal pressure, act out, or escape. Although we may feel we have no alternative, we do in fact have the ability to transcend this cultural, psychological, and neurochemical programming.

I remember a conflict that arose in a couple I saw several years ago. Lewis was a good man who struggled with his moods. He would feel bad inside and, frustrated by his inability to understand what was happening to him and certainly frustrated with his inability to express it to his wife, would take it out on her. He would withdraw. He would get quietly critical. He would get that look that told her and the kids to stay away from the bear. Finally, on an extended work assignment, he had an affair, which offered him a sense of vitality and excitement that he was missing in his regular life. The affair was exposed—he unconsciously set himself up to be caught— and the couple entered my office in the postaffair crisis.

In addition to all the other work that was needed to repair the damage of the affair, we focused on Lewis's normative male alexithymia. Frequently, when Lewis was feeling worried or hurt or depressed, his wife, Christine, would read the mood and ask him what was wrong. His standard reply? *I feel tired.* Finally she got sick of it and told him she couldn't stand hearing that anymore. Christine told me that she had outlawed the sentence *I feel tired* in their household. Christine was not being controlling—she was just being a leader in changing this relationship.

To his credit, Lewis did not immediately become defensive, nor did he use this as further proof that Christine was a controlling bitch. He allowed her to influence him. With the help of her intervention and our couples sessions, Lewis began to find labels for his feelings. I introduced him to some new vocabulary words so that he could talk like this:

- *I'm feeling burdened by the kids—I just end up feeling like I get no time for myself.*

- *I can't get these worries about work out of my head, and I need some time alone.*

- *I feel so frustrated trying to get Danny to listen to me—I never could talk back to my father the way we let him talk back to me!*

The complex process of listening to your inner signals, finding a label for the experience, and then expressing it respectfully reminds me of learning to shoot free throws. It's not really that hard to do. Some people are born with a special ability to do it well, but you can learn to do it pretty well with enough practice and commitment to the task.

The problem is not that true alexithymics or even normative male alexithymics don't really feel anything. It's that they lack skills for knowing what their feelings are, and they are especially unable to put these feelings into words.

And, because the first step toward making connections with others is recognizing and identifying with feelings, this alexithymic pattern cripples relationships. If you are confused about your own feelings, you are even more clueless when other people try to express feelings to you. This fundamental deficit in emotional intelligence leads to a fundamental deficit in relationship capability.

Emotional Overload

One of the physiological curses of being a guy is the susceptibility to experiencing emotional overload more quickly and more intensely than women do. Gottman's studies (1994) carefully examined the behavioral, emotional, and psychophysiological reactions of both men and women as they discussed difficult subjects in their relationship. This research showed that men consistently became more physiologically aroused during these discussions than their female partners did. Even in what most if us would consider to be mild areas of relationship conflict, men were more likely to become flooded with emotional agitation than women were. Specifically, men were much more likely to react to criticism from their partners with this level of arousal. At a neurochemical level, men secreted more adrenaline into the bloodstream, and it took less provocation (as measured by a team of observers) to get there. Even worse, the recovery period—the time it took them to return to their baseline levels of arousal—was longer for men than for women.

Steven Stosny (2001) illustrates what happens to men (or women, for that matter) in the face of emotional flooding by comparing a parent's reaction to a screaming baby to the destructive outbursts that result from emotional overload in adult relationships. Adults are physiologically mobilized by the distress cry of an infant. Your own nervous system reacts so intensely that you must either go to the aid of the child or get out of earshot; it is nearly impossible just to sit still and listen. As the cries get more intense, and as your sense of powerlessness likewise gets more intense, the internal distress signals skyrocket.

Under the best of circumstances, a very adaptive system shifts into gear. The baby is distressed, the parent becomes alarmed and activated, the parent offers soothing, the baby responds, and all is well. In fact, the baby learns one more time that distress is transitory, that help is available, and that the world is ultimately a safe and loving place. And the parent feels pretty successful.

However, as every parent knows, when you can't get the job done and the child is inconsolable, the distress alarm in both the parent and child intensifies. The available resources rapidly dwindle. Any parent in this situation is at risk for desperately turning to whatever it takes to turn off the alarm relentlessly screaming in his or her ears and inside his or her nervous system. Stosny compares this to hearing an alarm clock blaring when you are half asleep, unsuccessfully trying to turn it off, and becoming so enraged that you just hurl it at the wall to shut the damn thing up.

This is not unlike the experience of many men who get so frustrated with the complaints and criticism of their wives and girlfriends that they say, *I'll do anything to make her shut up!*

Perhaps you are one of the men who are afraid that emotional overload will make you feel powerless over your own reactions. So you emotionally withdraw. Or you stonewall. Or you belittle your partner when she tries to bring up difficult topics, desperately trying to keep away from subjects that will flood you.

When you immediately try to give advice or problem solve in response to your partner's concerns, you are subtly trying to "manage" the emotional input. When you tell her that this is not a good time to talk, you are communicating your self-knowledge about your potential for emotional overload and resultant destructive behavior. This is not necessarily dysfunctional; in fact, it is often very respectful of the relationship. But it is dysfunctional when you employ it consistently, and you use it to avoid the tough stuff that relationships require of you, and when the net result is that your partner feels like you are never really there for her. Or when she ends up feeling that she has to dance very carefully around your tender ego and delicate sense of self.

The fear of being overwhelmed by the suffering of another is one of the greatest inhibitors of compassionate and empathic responses. This leads many of us men, with our struggles to deal with emotional arousal and pain, to avoid people who might bring us down. Even worse, sometimes we distance ourselves further by generating contempt and anger for those who suffer: *You just brought this on yourself* or *Quit wallowing in your own self-pity.* Some of us just stay out of relationships altogether.

Real's I-don't-want-to-talk-about-it syndrome (1997), from an emotional flooding perspective, can be understood as a behavioral strategy for a nervous system that is simply overloaded. What may appear to be emotional coldness or power and control tactics in a relationship can also be viewed as a nervous system screaming out *No more!* But this does not excuse you. Remember that self-knowledge is power, and knowing how your brain is wired and how your nervous system works merely puts you in a better position to do something about it.

The catecholamines that are released provide the immediate surge, but all kinds of stress—especially relationship stress—create a more general adrenal and cortical stimulation that keeps you at a state of readiness, like a military on alert. When you're in this state, it doesn't take much more to put you over the top. Zillmann's research (1979) illuminates the waves of anger that can build on one another. Remember the teacher in chapter 3, who came home to a child who didn't listen to his orders to clean up her toys: *I let these second grade kids run all over me all day long, but I'll be damned if I'll let that happen in my own home!* His reaction to his daughter was amplified by the fact that he felt ineffective in his work. Each frustration or threat triggers hormonal arousal, which subsides only slowly. And if another threat comes relatively soon after the first, the wave peaks higher. And if another comes, the next wave is higher still. Add another wave, and you suddenly have complete emotional hijacking by the limbic system and another opportunity for a good man to look back at how he reacted and say, *That's not the man I want to be!*

Men Taking Action

As a man, you have probably been raised to take action. When something feels wrong, you are most likely to feel an urge to do something, often something bold and decisive, to correct the wrong. These skills are indispensable to you, and they serve society quite well in many situations.

However, this programming often screws you up in relationships. The combination of normative male alexithymia and a heightened sensitivity to emotional overload often creates a scenario in which something feels seriously wrong and you don't know quite what it is. When you add to this mix a lifelong inclination to take action, you have a prescription for getting into a bad mood and feeling propelled into action that is often destructive or counterproductive. We all need a dose of distress tolerance. Sometimes it is really okay to feel hurt or worried or frustrated or even powerless. These emotions are not pretty, but they are human, and if you cannot tolerate them, you are more likely to behave desperately, use poor judgment, and fail to anticipate consequences.

I once worked with a nineteen-year-old man who had put together a rock band. They had been rehearsing for months, and they started to feel really good about the sound they had created. They got a gig performing at a local party, printed up posters, and told all their friends to show up. They were ready for their big break. Then reality set in. "We went up on stage at this party. And I could tell right away that nobody liked us. Nobody was listening, and we didn't sound very good. I couldn't believe it. I was in shock. We had worked so hard for this, and I thought we were so hot. When we got offstage, the room was spinning. Reality felt like it was ten feet away. Everything was off."

In this foul mood, having suffered a devastating broken mirror experience, he proceeded to start drinking. He drove over to his girlfriend's house. She was babysitting some neighbor kids. He got loud and obnoxious and insisted that they have sex. The relationship never quite recovered from this stupidity.

Missing for this young man was the capacity to tolerate distress and take responsibility for feeling bad. All he needed to do was call his girlfriend and tell her that he was really bummed out; explain how lousy he felt; recognize that she was on his side and that sometimes mirrors break and we all feel bad. Instead, he fell victim to all three of the factors which often set the stage for good guys to behave badly: he didn't know how to make sense of his feelings, he became emotionally overloaded, and he could only think of bold action plans to try to make the bad feelings go away. He was not successful.

Getting Off on Anger

Another way of explaining why some men (and women, too) engage in relentless patterns of angry outbursts is that these outbursts offer something very rewarding at a brain chemical level.

Addiction to Magic Chemicals

First of all, your brain secretes *norepinephrine* when you are provoked. Norepinephrine produces an analgesic effect. The experience of being provoked—and the sympathetic nervous system arousal that follows—can accomplish the same very rewarding painkilling result as alcohol.

To make the cocktail even more potent, your brain also secretes the amphetamine-like hormone *epinephrine.* This allows you to experience a surge of energy throughout your body. This accounts for the adrenaline rush that so many people report during a sudden attack of anger.

Expressions of anger may offer you a sense of being in control or of letting someone else know how much they have hurt, offended, betrayed, or disappointed you. Stosny (2001) describes the function of anger as relieving self-doubt, feelings of powerlessness, and diminished sense of self. If this shoe fits, it means that you are trying to cope with internal distress (covert depression) through external regulation of experience, like controlling or bullying others. These are psychological functions, with psychological rewards and reinforcements.

Current brain research offers another explanation of how and why you engage in this pattern: your body and brain may be getting off on it! What we now know, more clearly than ever before, is that anger can make you feel powerful—not just psychologically but neurochemically. It is a magic potion that can lift you out of pain, self-doubt, and depression.

No wonder you feel like your anger is out of control: it ends up controlling you. The arousal in response to provocation and the resulting discharge of tension operates like an addiction, not fundamentally different from the more typical addictions (Van der Kolk 1987).

Seeking the High

People who are drawn to angry outbursts and other temper explosions often have an understimulated nervous system. People with truly psychopathic personalities typically exhibit less physiological response to stimuli, including less sweating and fewer skin changes, than the rest of us. In psychopaths, outbursts of anger may actually provide the rush of energy that jolts the brain to more normal functioning. While you are unlikely to be a psychopath, some elements of this pattern may be evident for you.

Have you ever gone out looking for a fight? Perhaps you have experienced this walking into a bar or a party. Perhaps you arrive home and walk in the door agitated and restless; you see your wife or kids and Mr. Hyde emerges. You desperately search for something to be pissed off about. There's always something. And when you find the excuse you are looking for, you blow up. You feel self-righteous, and you have a convenient excuse for the angst within. You are addicted to anger because it lifts you out of depression and gives you the jolt of energy you crave. It is your cocaine. And it always seems like it is justified and someone else's fault.

You can't afford to take responsibility for your anger, because then you (as a good man behaving badly) could not continue to indulge in this pattern. Your anger would not be the least bit socially acceptable, even to yourself.

Rosenbaum, Geffner, and Benjamin (1997) have highlighted the interactive effects of arousal factors (stress) and threshold factors (factors which propel you from the higher level of neocortex operations to more primitive limbic system reactions). With the potent combination of these two factors, you are very likely to retreat into behaviors which are old, familiar, and probably not very positive. These are *high habit strength* behaviors, which means that it takes either a very conscious man or some pretty powerful medications to interrupt the chain leading to them.

The Biopsychosocial Model

Here's how this works. You experience stress. Your marriage is in trouble, you have financial problems, your kids are having trouble in school, the traffic is nasty. From these experiences, depending on your personal narratives or the time of the month, you may start to feel like a loser. When your wife complains about not being able to pay some of the bills on time this month, she becomes a broken mirror reflecting back a loser image of yourself. Maybe you compare yourself to your wife. You observe her acting more comfortable in social situations or achieving success in her career, and all you can see is that there's something wrong with you.

As the internal arousal increases and you experience more and more frustration and unhappiness, you come closer and closer to a threshold level. You are at risk of becoming a good man behaving badly.

Not everyone gets there at the same rate or in the same circumstances, but if you are truly honest with yourself, you will recognize that you go there sometimes. How frequently, quickly, and intensely you go there is crucial.

Some people are just blessed with a better tolerance for stress and agitation, a genetically determined difference in temperament. It is the difference between having a short fuse and being patient or tolerant. From a brain chemistry point of view, if you are more the patient type, your neocortical inhibitory processes are more effective and dominant, meaning that the higher thinking centers of your brain will kick in and direct you toward good behavior. *Disinhibitors* lead you toward the limbic pathway, setting you up for bad behavior. Drugs and alcohol are temporary brain disinhibitors. It does not take a neuroscientist to recognize that drugs and alcohol serve as disinhibitors for relationship aggression and generally loosen up your control and impair your judgment. While this may seem to have a positive effect, like helping you unwind and be a little more fun at a party, for many men this disinhibiting effect leads to anger, sarcasm, insensitivity, inappropriate sexual behavior, and DUIs—all destructive relationship behaviors that can be generated by otherwise fundamentally good people.

Fogel and Stone (1992) suggest that head injuries, especially to frontotemporal areas, can seriously erode inhibitory controls. If you have suffered such an injury, you have an increased risk for some impairment to one of the most crucial higher-level neocortical functions: the ability to develop complex plans. Furthermore, injuries to other areas of the brain can affect your ability to figure out the meaning of an interpersonal event or your ability to read cues and develop an appropriate response. If you have a history of head injury *and* you use alcohol or drugs, you are especially likely to have trouble with the neocortical function of your brain.

None of these factors is guaranteed to lead to destructive or dysfunctional behaviors in your relationships. Some men manage to drink or snort coke and still stay out of trouble. Not all people with head injuries automatically lose their temper more easily than the rest of us. And some men who have a shorter fuse by temperament still have learned to get a grip. All of these are just risk factors: they increase the likelihood of behaving badly in relationships (and elsewhere), but they do not determine behavior. You are human, after all, and you have the ability to rise above what your limbic system seems to demand of you.

Cognitive Disinhibitors

You can't undo the effects of a head injury, but you can choose to limit drugs and alcohol and you can certainly challenge your self-talk. Cognitive disinhibitors play an enormously significant role in shaping relationship behavior.

In chapter 2, I discussed the "secret, silent decision" that Gottman identifies as a crucial variable governing the future success of intimate partner relationships. If you think the worst of your partner, your arousal is much more likely to be activated more frequently and more intensely.

Once your arousal is high, your self-talk becomes one of the most important factors in determining whether you cross over the threshold or stay just on this side of it. If your girlfriend is late— again—and you tell yourself, *I hate waiting like this, but it's not really personal. That's just the way she is,* you are more likely to stay below threshold than if your self-talk is *What a bitch! She is always disrespecting me!*

Reggie, a client of mine who ran a successful Mexican restaurant, described what he would do when his *What a bitch!* tape was activated—in his case, by his wife's lack of interest in having sex as frequently as he was interested. He started convincing himself that his own retaliatory passive-aggressive behaviors were really legitimate under these circumstances. It was almost like he was of two selves: the neocortical Dr. Jekyll, who respected his wife and lived his life with higher values, and the limbic Mr. Hyde, who did whatever the hell he pleased. "Here I was, hoarding all these porn videos, in the house with my wife and my little girl, and masturbating in bed with my wife, telling myself that it was secret but knowing somewhere that she probably knew I was doing it. It's almost like I wasn't thinking! I was not being respectful, this did not reflect my real values. What was I thinking?"

The *What a bitch!* self-talk serves as a classic brain disinhibitor. It feeds arousal and lowers the threshold for emotional hijacking by the limbic system by allowing us to feel justified in our retaliatory behavior. Thus is born an otherwise good man behaving badly—a man who tells us afterward, painfully and poignantly, *That's not the man I want to be!*

Studies by Carpenter and Halberstadt (2000) of the factors that put parents at risk for blowing up at their kids have identified the same patterns: what you think can either help you maintain neocortical dominance or can disinhibit your amygdala responses to reveal your worst self. For example, if you have repeatedly told your daughter to clean up her dishes, and you find them one more time scattered in the den, you are likely to start thinking *I can't believe this! This is so disrespectful, and she is so lazy!* And once that chain gets started, you feel quite justified in blowing up at her. Or your son mumbles and looks away when you speak to him—except this time he is doing it in public and you start thinking, *That kid's behavior looks so weak! And it makes me look bad that he can't relate better! This is really embarrassing!* Again, when that train leaves the station, the inhibitor brakes are more likely to be released, and you are more likely to do or say something that will be humiliating to him, instead of just quietly working with him on this or letting it go altogether.

Exercise: Cognitive Disinhibitors

This exercise lists eight types of situations that are especially likely to trigger cognitive disinhibitors, drawn from research by Meichenbaum (2001). In other words, in these situations you may be more at risk of thinking the worst, getting into a mood, and overreacting with criticism or hostility. Look at these categories and corresponding examples, then write down your own list of hot buttons, including an example from each category that might set you off.

Hot-Button Category

1. interruption of planned activities

2. implications of noncompliance

3. concern about possible injury or harm to self or others

4. expectations violated (breaking your rules)

5. history repeats itself

6. personal overload

7. personal pet peeve

8. embarrassment

Examples

1. We were just sitting down to dinner, and my wife takes a damn phone call from her sister!

2. If my daughter doesn't learn how to clean up better, she will always be a selfish slob! This is really serious!

3. I can't believe she drove the kids doubled up in seat belts! That is so dangerous!

4. Doesn't she understand that we are always supposed to be together on Friday night? How could she even think about making other plans?

5. See, I've told her a thousand times to leave the keys where I can find them, and she never listens to me!

6. I am so stressed out trying to pay these bills. Doesn't anyone care what I'm going through?

7. Everyone knows I don't like people talking and interrupting when I'm watching my TV shows, and they do it anyway!

8. God, when she laughs real loud like that, I can just tell people are turned off!

High Habit Strength Behaviors: The Default Mode

When you have become stressed and aroused, and when a disinhibitor like self-talk, drugs or alcohol, a short fuse, or a history of head injury has catapulted you beyond the threshold of neocortical governance—well, you are probably in deep trouble. Not doomed, but definitely in deep trouble. You are likely to retreat to some older and more primitive behavior which once worked as a psychological survival strategy when you felt desperate or threatened.

At these moments, after you and your brain have crossed the threshold from neocortical monitoring to limbic system rule, you tend to seek behaviors that help you escape (Baumeister 1991). Think of a bulimic teenage girl, painfully preoccupied with herself and the way she looks to others, going on a binge to escape the unbearable self-image. During a binge, meaningful thought is abandoned for a narrow focus on immediate sensations; the troubled self disappears from awareness as she becomes preoccupied with one cookie after another. Likewise imagine the depressed and withdrawn teenage boy, quietly cutting on his arms with a switchblade. Self-mutilators use pain to reduce the self to the body and to shrink the world to the immediate surroundings.

When you cross the threshold, your brain will summon up ways that your father handled these moments or how you desperately dealt with these overwhelming states on the playground, on the streets, or in your first marriage. You may simply shut down emotionally. You may become defensive and aggressive. You may insist on escaping through drugs or alcohol. You may be more "cleverly" aggressive, becoming passive-aggressive or sarcastic. But it is almost certain that you will not be at your best; in fact, you may be at your very, very worst.

Strategies for the Male Brain

It is quite ironic that all of this sophisticated and groundbreaking research delving into the complex world of the human brain leads us to strategies that are so simple. This reminds me of how years of medical research into cures for the common cold finally concluded that chicken soup was a pretty damn good treatment.

When you are charged up, you need to be able to recognize clearly what is happening to you. You need to find alternative behaviors to help you cool down. And you need to have readily available a new narrative, complete with instant self-talk alternatives, to plug in to detoxify the situation.

And, certainly, no list of strategies for the brain would be complete without a strong endorsement of the judicious use of medication. Many men who struggle with aggression, normative male alexithymia, emotional withdrawal, moodiness, self-centeredness, and anxiety stand to reap significant benefit from modern psychiatric medication. Particularly when the breakdowns in brain chemistry have been reinforced by habit, any intervention that breaks the chain is valuable. Many of the men whom I have described throughout this book have used various forms of medication at various times to accelerate their learning curve for new skills and behaviors. The medication will not do the work for you, but it may make it easier to access your God-given resources more effectively.

Self-Awareness: Antihijacking Tactics

Self-awareness not only expands your pool of information from which to make intelligent decisions, it also (we now know) changes your brain neurochemistry in measurable, observable ways. Increased electrical activity in the neocortex is stimulated by self-observational behaviors—and this increase (with the corresponding decrease in limbic system activity) is exactly the prescription for crisis management.

Self-awareness becomes the basic building block for all other emotional abilities. The ability to stop and observe what you are feeling has an effect something like the impact of an observer at the quantum level in physics, altering what is being observed. Just by stopping and observing your own experiences, you activate higher-level neocortex responses.

Perhaps you have developed refined skills at numbing your body to all the red flags of an emotional hijacking *(What are you talking about? I'm not tense!)* and, as a result, have trouble knowing what you are feeling at all. As we know, this normative male alexithymia can set the stage for destructive relationship behaviors. After we review all the different models and research, the practical advice boils down to the same thing: stand back and observe your own behavior, thus activating the neocortex rather than the limbic system. Simply becoming aware of your internal state activates your prefrontal lobes, actually changing your brain chemistry and helping you make better choices. This pathway of emotional self-awareness is the centerpiece of one of the most important indicators of emotional intelligence: being able to shake off a bad mood.

Distraction and Cooling Down

Research (Tice and Baumeister 1993) and common sense are unified in recognizing the value of distraction as a way to allow the brain and nervous system to shift gears when someone is dangerously upset. (Remember that "dangerously upset" is relative. For some men it may mean that violence is possible, while for others it may simply mean that they are at risk of making a sarcastic comment. The intensity and potential damage may be different, but we are dealing with the same basic pathway). In fact, in managing any mood (including depression, anxiety, and anger), distraction emerges as a most potent mind-altering device (Zillman 1993).

However, just thinking it over is not always the ticket. Many men who feel provoked and experience anger use "reflection time" simply as an opportunity to stew. If you are in this category, you may actually use this time to plan out more powerful retaliatory strategies (Sapolsky, Stocking, and Zillman 1977). And you may not even want to be distracted from the self-righteous anger that, in some ways, feels so good. The same is true with depression: if you are depressed and try to take a break to think things over, you are more than likely to use the time to ruminate about things that depress you rather than focus on something that is positive or at least neutral and distracting. Studies by Wenzlaff (1993) show that nondepressed people are able to let go of disturbing thoughts over time, while depressed people actually become more and more obsessed with the bad events, even as they are further in time from when it happened.

I used to be quite critical of people who distracted themselves when they were upset. I thought this was a form of escapism and an indication that the person was not able or willing to deal with tough emotional issues. I realize now that this was stupid. If distraction helps you cool down so that you do not say or do something destructive to the people you care the most about, or if it helps pull you out of a depressed mood, then it is a brilliant and creative use of your resources. Obviously, if you consistently employ distraction and never come around to face the meaningful issues in your relationship, you will have problems; but in moderation, the capacity to employ creative distraction is a gift and a sign of emotional intelligence.

A woman I used to know who suffered from serious depressive episodes kept an old, tattered copy of *Auntie Mame* always available no matter where she was. She and her mother had watched the movie and howled together when she was growing up, and rereading sections of the book never failed to crack her up and lift her spirits. She was under no illusion that this novel would solve her life problems, but this distraction brought her out of the lowest regions of her moods. For her, *Auntie Mame* served as the ultimate selfobject—better than Prozac.

When employing distraction (which some people do naturally, others need to do less of, and still others need to learn how to do better), the basic advice is to engage in pleasant, absorbing, and comparatively unexciting activities that do not stimulate more anger, depression, or anxiety.

Exercise: Creative Distractions

Below are some distraction techniques and the pros and cons of each. Think about which distractions you use already, and which ones you might be able to add to your repertoire. You may come up with others that are not on this list.

Absorbing mental activities. TV, movies, listening to music, reading, video games

Pros and cons. You feel better because you can't remember exactly why you felt sad or upset. Be careful about retreating excessively to passive activities like TV or video games.

Mood-lifting distractions. Watching funny movies, reading an inspiring book, watching sports (as long as your team is winning), reading *Auntie Mame*

Pros and cons. The best distractions are not just neutral, but actually lift you—but you can't always count on these to be available.

Exercise. Walking, running, working out, team sports

Pros and cons. This is one of the best sources of distraction because it is so physical and because it stimulates endorphins, but be careful of ruminating while working out, and avoid anger-stimulating activity like using a punching bag or playing an aggressive basketball game.

Relaxation techniques. Meditation, self-hypnosis, visualization, yoga

Pros and cons. Excellent for cooling down physiologically from anger or anxiety. Not as helpful for depression.

Personal pleasures. Massage, Jacuzzi, favorite foods, listening to music, sex, drinking or drugs, buying something

Pros and cons. Anything that activates pleasure can come in very handy—except if it leads to negative consequences (as can drinking, drugs, overeating, or spending money). Also, beware of sex as antidepressant—your partner may not be signing up for this contract.

Accomplishments. Cleaning your garage, balancing your checkbook, writing a thank-you note, taking care of some phone calls, finally getting the clock right on your VCR

Pros and cons. This activates a feeling of competence and distracts you from the unhappiness or powerlessness that you were experiencing.

Helping others. Playing with your kids, volunteering your time, tutoring, coaching your kid's sports team

Pros and cons. Helping others reinforces your feeling of being needed and valuable, and also absorbs you in a task separate from ruminating.

Using Brain Talk to Reframe

Perhaps the most profound strategy that you have to calm your agitated neurochemistry and to access more rational and constructive responses lies in your capacity to think about situations differently. I have been interchangeably labeling this process as *reframing, thinking differently, changing self-talk, developing a new narrative, telling a different story,* and *revising cognitions.* They are all the same. Keep in mind the words of psychologist Ross Greene: "Your interpretation will guide your intervention" (1998, 14).

Stories about the World around You

We know that the amygdala-dominated response is a reaction to perceived threat. This operates very clearly when the perceived threat is physical. Imagine that you hear a sound in the middle of the night. You sit upright in your bed. You look over and see that your wife is still in bed with you and still breathing. Then you hear it again. Then you see a shadowy movement near the window. Your heart starts racing, your muscles tense, your senses go on red alert. You reach for the baseball bat under your bed and poise, ready to strike. You hold your breath.

And then you hear a new sound: *Meow.* And once your brain integrates this new information, that somehow your cat has made her way into your bedroom and gotten tangled up in the curtains, your sympathetic nervous system arousal slowly decreases. Very slowly, much more slowly than it increased. You breathe again, and suddenly you notice how jittery your hands are and how sweaty your palms are. You don't bother to wake up your wife, although a moment ago you were about to attack the terrible threat you perceived to her and your kids.

From the moment you heard the first sound, nothing changed in this scenario except your understanding of what was causing the noise.

This same process is vital to the relaxation of tension in the emotional arena of your relationships. Only when you no longer feel threatened by your partner—by her perceived attack on your self-esteem or her perceived abandonment of you—will your amygdala shut off its internal alarm system. When this happens, you resume neocortical dominance, and you can respond to her with your more typical grace, compassion, nondefensiveness, and rationality. These responses lead to intimacy, while your threat-based responses sabotage intimacy.

So when your partner starts to act "controlling" (*You are spending way too much time with your friends on the weekend—I need you to spend more time with me)*, it can help you to reframe this as a behavioral expression that she fears losing connection with you. And when you act defensive in response to her complaints about you and she is so frustrated because she can't seem to get through, it would make sense for her to remember that you are perceiving her complaints as an unbearable threat to your positive feeling about yourself. Your brains are getting in the way, and the capacity that you each have to be both intelligent and generous with each other can make or break the relationship.

We also know that prayer and religious faith—if you truly believe—can help you make sense of complex and mysterious life situations. They offer you a framework to understand the problems you are facing and help you put things in perspective. The world feels more organized and meaningful when you can truly and sincerely attribute negative events to God's will. A Christian man going through intense marital difficulties once told me, "I am a God-fearing man, and the devil is trying to turn me away from my faith— this is a test for me to see how good a man I can be!" If you are able to activate this narrative, you can cool down from the state that could have been generated by *She's such a bitch!* Ultimately, whatever helps reduce your arousal and improve your emotional intelligence without causing new problems is a godsend.

Stories about Yourself and Your Biochemistry

If you develop a narrative about yourself that is informed by the understanding of neurochemistry, you are in a more powerful position in several ways. First of all, you simply have more information about yourself—and, as we know, self-knowledge is power. Second, you now are operating with a more compassionate view of yourself, a view quite compatible with our theme of good men behaving badly. You now know how powerful a force emotional hijacking by the limbic system can be. So, when you catch yourself reacting from that state of mind—when you hear yourself saying, *That's not the man I want to be!*—you can remind yourself that you are reckoning with powerful human forces that are universal.

This does not take you off the hook, because we are all 100 percent responsible for our own behavior no matter what. But compassionately observing your behavior allows you to shift to a neocortical response and choose better behavior. It also helps diminish the shame factor. While a little bit of shame is valuable as an alarm system, a lot of shame usually leads to nothing but worse behavior.

The story you tell yourself about who you are and why you do what you do is crucial and, for the most part, pliable. Knowing about the power of disinhibitors allows you to describe yourself as a man who has good values and good intentions and a vulnerable brain and nervous system that require extra anticipation.

This narrative is a definite improvement over *I just can't control myself* or *If I treated her that way, she must have deserved it.*

6

Odysseus, Relational Heroism, and Imaginary Crimes

Despite the cultural pressure to stay emotionally hidden or react strongly to perceived injuries to your sense of self, you probably know of remarkable exceptions. Exceptions in others and exceptions in yourself. Every day, men are heroes—not only in the conventional sense of rescuing people from burning buildings or making tough decisions in the workplace, but also by behaving in relationships in ways that are profoundly counterintuitive. For many men, good relationship behavior requires a tremendous act of will, and choosing the counterintuitive behavior is truly heroic.

To help you understand this concept of heroism, let me introduce the term *relational hero* from Terrence Real's 1997 book, *I Don't Want to Talk About It*. Real defines relational heroism this way:

> Relational heroism occurs when every muscle and nerve in one's body pulls one toward reenacting one's usual dysfunctional pattern, but through sheer force or discipline or grace, one lifts oneself off the well-worn track toward behaviors that are more vulnerable, more cherishing, more mature. Just as the boyhood trauma that sets up depression occurs not in one dramatic incident, but in transactions repeated thousands of times, so, too, recovery is comprised of countless small victories. (277)

Odysseus the Hero

I find it very valuable to use the story of Odysseus as a parable about personal maturity and relational heroism. Not the whole story, of course, for reasons of time management, but one particular episode from Odysseus's long journey homeward after fighting the Trojan War. After his success as a warrior in the *Iliad*, Odysseus spends ten years making his odyssey navigating his ship through troubled waters, enduring hardship and adventure. In this classic Greek tale of man's search for self-discovery, Homer's *Odyssey*, each challenge makes Odysseus stronger and wiser, fostering his development as an evolved and mature man. He is forced to develop as a psychological hero after his many years as a physical hero in the Trojan War.

Odysseus and his men encounter the sorceress Circe, a female creature with enticing and evil powers. She has the power to cast a spell over any man. She welcomes Odysseus's men and offers them wild pleasures, then turns them into swine. However, she takes a liking to Odysseus and spends a year frolicking with him on her island. When they finally realize that it is time for him to resume his journey, she offers him a gift. This is a gift of knowledge that will save the lives of Odysseus and his men. She warns him of the next island that he will encounter, the island of the Sirens.

Like Circe, the Sirens are capable of enticing men. The sound of the Sirens' music is so alluring to men that they can never resist heading toward the source. The Sirens, however, with bodies of birds and heads of women, tear apart any men who succumb to the sounds. Odysseus and his men would be prime candidates to succumb to the Sirens, except that Circe has warned Odysseus. As they approach the island of the Sirens, he orders all of his men to plug their ears with beeswax so they cannot hear the sounds. Odysseus, however, the ambitious seeker, wants it all. He insists on hearing the Sirens himself, so he does not put wax in his own ears, but he demands that his crew tie him to the mast of the ship so that he cannot yield to the seduction. He cautions his men not to release him under any circumstances, no matter how desperately he pleads, cries, or threatens. Thus prepared, Odysseus and his men continue successfully on their epic journey. His men note his writhing attempts to become free (although they cannot hear his words) but, following orders, continue to row until they are out of range of the Sirens. In despair, the Sirens kill themselves—illustrating that if you do not succumb to destructive temptations, they wither away.

The moral of the story is this: If you are aware of what temptations or struggles lie ahead, you can transform them, or at least meet them head-on. If you have no context or understanding, then you are doomed to simply react. Be a hero, like Odysseus. Get conscious. Prepare yourself for situations that you know may seduce you into destructive behaviors, and come up with a plan to handle them differently. If you know that hearing your kids arguing makes you start criticizing your wife, come up with a plan to prepare for this so you do not go there. Be a hero, man!

Acts of Relational Heroism

Remember Rick from chapter 3, who passed on the legacy of emotional cruelty to his son? Rick was the man who kept hearing the mantra *Nobody ever brought me fucking lunch when I was a kid!* whenever his son needed something from him.

Rick's past gripped him and insisted that he withhold from his son. He couldn't bear to offer Stephen more than he himself had received. In fact, offering more to Stephen would only serve to highlight the pain that Rick had endured; keeping the legacy going allowed Rick to pretend that he himself had not actually suffered much.

But when Rick's wife asked him to bring lunch to Stephen, Rick found a way to go counterintuitive. In making that decision, Rick entered the Hall of Fame for relational heroes. And there was nothing earth-shattering or dramatic about his actions. No newspaper would ever report it and no real Hall of Fame would ever take note. Rick simply brought Stephen lunch. And he did it with a positive attitude. Stephen looked at him, shocked and pleased, and gave Rick a look of appreciation he did not quickly forget. Rick told me, "After I did it, I felt really good about it!"

Rick had grabbed himself by the collar, thrown himself against the wall, and told himself that there was something bigger at stake and that he had better avoid just slipping into his default behavior. He sucked it up and became a hero. His son noticed, although few others would. The payoff for Rick was that the new behavior actually felt good and made him feel proud of being a different kind of man. As a footnote, Rick told me that he had been sick recently. Stephen, very uncharacteristically, fixed him a bowl of soup and took care of him. Rick told me, "In the back of my mind, I wondered if he was treating me generously because he remembered the time I brought him lunch, and maybe a few other nice things!"

Another story from chapter 3, of Luke confronting his father, also moved me to tears and qualified for Hall of Fame consideration. I watched Luke, usually so composed and slick, crying, snot running from his nose, yelling "Fuck you!" at his father, revealing long-repressed emotions—and his father taking it. And not only taking it, but obviously moved by it and even encouraging it. Even when he did not have the right responses (he would give advice, he would slip into platitudes), Luke's dad was open to this feedback about what his son needed from him. I did not know who was the greater relational hero, Luke or his dad! They were co-MVPs. When Luke's dad, in response to what must have felt like bitter condemnations and resentments, started talking about what a son of a bitch his own father had been, and how he had tried (with moderate success) to offer Luke something different, I did not hear a man trying to escape responsibility, but rather trying to take it. He wanted Luke to be able to tell him these things, which he never would have been able to say to his own dad. I think he wanted to model for Luke how a stand-up guy can take the truth and learn from it. When the dust had settled, I told them both, "If this trend continues, with each generation trying to be even more evolved than the one before, Luke's son is going to be one hell of a man!"

In one of my men's groups, Brantin described another one of those Hall of Fame moments that the casual observer might not notice. He and his wife had separated after months of tension and discord. By mutual consent, she had taken their six-year-old daughter with her to stay with her family in another state for a couple of months. She and Brantin decided they were ready to give the relationship another try.

When his wife and daughter arrived back in town on a Greyhound bus, Brantin met them at the station. His little girl came running up to him, yelling "Daddy, Daddy, Daddy!" with the kind of gusto that only little kids can generate. He swept her into his arms and hugged her tight, then turned to his wife, who was walking more slowly toward him, to embrace her. She turned away and said she was hurt because she should have been the one he hugged first.

Brantin's self-talk? To put it as he told me, *What a bitch! What am I supposed to do, not hug my own daughter? I can't believe this shit!* But instead of retaliating or pouting, he chose to react differently this time. He stayed calm. He told his wife that he was sorry, that he didn't mean to hurt her feelings, and that he was really glad to see her. He reassured her that he really loved her, it was just that their little girl came running up first. "C'mon, baby, you know I love you, and I'm really happy to see you!"

She paused for a second, then smiled and said okay. She reached out for him, and it was over. He had passed a test. Maybe she shouldn't have tested him like that, but that's the reality of it. Sometimes your wife or girlfriend, like you, will be insecure and will do something to check out whether or not you really care. You can either dig in your heels and tell yourself that you're not going to put up with it, or you can try and find some way to soothe her. Brantin found a way, and it brought out the best in both of them. He was a hero.

Preston, another man I worked with, was in the midst of a very rocky period in his marriage when the future was very much in doubt. He began talking to his wife about a vacation he was hoping they could take almost a year later. She looked at him and said, half-joking and half-serious, "Well, you're assuming a lot, aren't you?" Preston's commentary about his own reaction was this:

> *Sharice made that crack about how I was assuming too much, and I just shut down, like I always do. I felt so hurt. Same old stuff. But it didn't take me too long before I turned to her and told her that her comment had really hurt me, and I asked her, sort of nicely, why she had said it. And we actually had a conversation about the whole thing.*
>
> *I guess that's sort of the relational hero thing we've been talking about, isn't it? I guess I'm doing pretty well.*

Rob, the main character in Nick Hornby's 1995 novel, *High Fidelity,* is another man who becomes a relational hero. He has a long history of failed relationships and a long history of selfish, neurotic, immature behaviors that contribute to these failures. He makes a practice of preparing compilation tapes of carefully selected songs for each woman he is interested in, but his tragic flaw is that he selects songs based on his own very snobbish criteria of what the woman should be listening to. He always misses the mark, because he is never able to see her as she really is, only as he wants her to be.

Finally, after more and more errors and grief, he matures and has a breakthrough. About the love of his life, Laura, he says, "I start to compile in my head a compilation tape for her, something that's full of stuff she's heard of, and full of stuff she'd play. Tonight, for the first time ever, I can sort of see how it's done" (323). The task is so simple, yet it took him years to prepare for. And again, the actual behavior is not bold and dramatic to the outside observer, but bold and dramatic nevertheless.

Exercise: Daily Appreciation

Expressing appreciation is one way to test the waters of relational heroism. No twenty-four-hour period should go by without you telling your partner or kids something that you really appreciate about them. It can be something rather trivial, like *You really helped me out when you made those phone calls for me;* something major, like

You are such a great mom! I love watching how you handle things with the kids; or something in between, like *Hey, I really appreciate that you left me alone for a while tonight when I was in a bad mood. I really need that sometimes.*

Expressing yourself this way is a habit like any other. Couples who are in a good groove with each other just do this naturally. If things are not going well with you and your partner, or if there are ongoing tensions with you and your kids, you may have gotten out of the habit. Starting it up again may feel a little awkward and insincere at first, but it won't for long if you find things to say that you genuinely feel.

In your notebook or journal, prepare a chart for each day with a column for each family member. At the end of the day, check the spaces for the daily appreciations you have offered. If there are holes in your chart, make an effort to fill them the next day.

A tip: It is almost always helpful to tell your partner that you are doing this exercise. She is more likely to genuinely appreciate your intentions than she is to discount the appreciations because they are "just an exercise."

And one more tip: Just because your kids act like they don't care or don't even notice, don't be an idiot—they do!

When She Notices

Although it probably shouldn't matter so much, although your motivation for change should come from within, although you should not require quid pro quo for being a relational hero—it still feels good when your partner notices. We need our mirrors.

Jason, another man I saw after his marriage had unraveled almost beyond repair, began to see the ways in which he was always a little bit controlling, a little bit selfish, a little bit entitled.

Heather didn't ever want to drive the boat when I was skiing, probably because I was always telling her to do it differently. . . . I used to have this way of half-heartedly offering to make us sandwiches, then she would say that she could do it, and I would say, "Oh, okay, sure, great." And we both knew that I wasn't really offering, and I was just looking out for myself. I felt like I was entitled to get this.

But one day Jason came in and told me one of those relational hero stories, where the guy discovers that the new way of doing things carries with it rewards that he did not know were possible. Jason had received a coupon for a trip to Cabo San Lucas as a bonus at his job, and he and his wife had planned to celebrate his birthday there together. But now they were separated and very gingerly trying to make the relationship work.

> *When I finally got back to Heather and told her that she could have the coupon for the trip to Cabo, I told her how hard it was for me because I had always associated that coupon with my birthday, and I couldn't bear to give it up because it would mean that we weren't celebrating my birthday together. But after I thought about it, I still wanted her to have it. She broke out in a big smile, and I felt the warmest response I had felt from her in a long time. "That's exactly what I am looking for from you." And I knew she meant that I was telling her, honestly and vulnerably, what I was feeling and not trying to pressure her or control her. I guess I was "relating."*

It is important here to spend a moment reflecting on the quid pro quo issue. When relationships are flowing normally and respectfully, there is an inevitable and perfectly healthy quid pro quo system in place: *I'm fine with him playing poker Friday night with his buddies—I know the guy works hard, and he's really good about letting me have time to be with my friends when I ask.* Or *Of course I'll drive her to work today when her car's in the shop—I know she'd do the same for me, no questions asked!*

But the rules change when one of you has repeatedly wronged the other, when one of you has come home drunk and been nasty, or when one of you has consistently kept secrets that betrayed the trust in the relationship. Quid pro quo no longer applies. Now you are called upon to change simply because it is the right thing to do, and if your partner comes around to appreciate that, it's a wonderful bonus. But you never want to communicate the message that she should be really grateful that you're not drinking to excess anymore or that you are no longer yelling at her in front of her family.

Almost Heroic

Here's another story of a man who walked right up to the precipice of being a relational hero. This man, however, knew what he should do to be the hero, but could not bring himself to do it. In Wally Lamb's 1998 novel *I Know This Much Is True*, Dominick and his wife have lost their three-week-old baby. "Sometimes at supper or up in bed, Dessa would try to talk about her feelings. Talk about Angela. Not at first. Later. Three or four months afterward. 'Uh-huh,' I'd say. 'Uh-huh.' She'd want me to open up, too. 'What good would it do?' I told her once. 'We'll talk and cry and talk some more, and then she'll still be dead.' I stood up and walked out of the room—got the fuck out of there before my fucking head exploded" (215).

In self psychology, one of the central forces that generates a solid internal structure is the twinship selfobject. We all experience a drive to find others who are like us. This connection offers us self-cohesion through an identification with others, a sense of being like others. Dominick could not bring himself to pull out of his emotional shell and just be a normal human enduring an extremely painful experience with someone he deeply loved. He could not engage in the twinship experience that Dessa so desperately needed and that he could have used to pull himself out of the emotionally dulled pit that he had fallen into.

Dominick describes another scene of almost being a hero:

> Sometimes I'd wake up in the middle of the night and hear Dessa in the baby's room, sobbing. One night I heard her talking to Angela—murmuring baby talk down the hall. I sat up and listened to it, telling myself that only a complete and total son of a bitch wouldn't get out of bed, go down there and hold her, comfort her. But I just couldn't do it. Couldn't quite make my feet hit the floor, no matter what basic human decency was ordering me to do. So I sat there and listened to her, like she was a ghost of what we'd had and lost, the ghost of our life the way we'd planned it out. I've wondered a million times since then if we could have salvaged things at that point—if I'd just gotten out of bed and gone to her that night I heard her talking to the baby. (216)

The most tragic theme in this scene is that Dominick was neither ignorant nor out of touch—he just couldn't bring himself to make contact with Dessa, because that would have accessed too much of his own pain. He even knew that he was behaving like a "complete and total son of a bitch." Dominick did not make it to the Hall of Fame, although everything he learned from these bad moments led him to heroic acts later on.

In Jonathan Larson's 1996 Broadway hit musical, *Rent*, Roger is a young musician who is HIV-positive. He is emotionally burned out from the suicide of the love of his life, who discovered that she had passed on the virus to him. He is withdrawing from everyone in his life, bitterly waiting to die, when he meets Mimi, who sparks an unexpected wave of love and passion in him. He feels himself drawing closer to her, but he cannot bring himself to tell her his story. He cannot tell her that he has the virus, and the virus is a metaphor for all of his life story—his previous drug habit, his broken heart—that he cannot bring himself to reveal.

Roger is like so many men in emotional pain who have been trained (or perhaps even genetically hardwired) to hold it all in. His pain, and our frustration in watching him, pulsates through the story. It looks so simple from the outside: *Just do it! Just say what you are feeling! It's so simple, and so much will change.*

Roger suffers from what Terrence Real (1997) would call "covert male depression," or what Jungian psychologist John Sanford (1980) calls a "male mood." This mood takes over, like a dark cloud, sinking you into a state of gloom, indecisiveness, and projection of blame. You can become enveloped by a mood when your feelings get hurt or when you're having a feeling you can't understand or explain. If you find a way to express these feelings directly, the mood will likely dissipate and you and your partner will feel close instead of alienated.

Sanford uses the term *related anger* to describe the positive way of expressing difficult feelings in a relationship. He advises men to engage in an honest expression of genuine feeling, to relate. He cautions that if a man expresses anger without communicating his feelings or establishing a connection, he will do harm by creating a bad atmosphere. He will act hurt and perceive himself as being deeply and unfairly injured. On the other hand, if he expresses anger in a related way, he will clearly and respectfully tell his partner just what it is that is upsetting him. You and I both know, of course, that this does not always lead to happily ever after, but if you are a relationship hero, you are simply trying to increase the likelihood of a better outcome. And you at least can walk away knowing that you took care of your side of the street.

The dark mood of *Rent*'s Roger governed his ability to relate. The tragic part of his story is that the escape route out of the mood was so fundamentally simple, yet so difficult to activate.

The cure for the male mood is intimacy: expressing feelings directly in a related way. This requires recognizing the mood for what it is and making a determined effort not to take it out on others. Like Will from *Good Will Hunting* and Dominick from *I Know This Much Is True,* Roger eventually summons up the courage to do it, but not without pain and failure along the way.

Soft Underbellies

Even some men with the most gruff and hypermasculine exteriors are capable of extraordinary acts of tenderness and vulnerability. You may recognize this in yourself. This is the soft underbelly that many men long to express, and it is essential to recognize this tenderness and nurture its emergence whenever possible. Men who act cold and embittered with their partners often break down in tears when they recognize the pain they have caused their children. I am always stunned by the deafening hush in the room when a man realizes that he has not only been behaving badly toward his wife (which he can often justify) but has modeled this behavior for his kids—something he swore he would never do.

Some men have soft underbellies that are plainly visible; for others, even those who may at times act badly in relationships, these tender spots are buried deeper but still sometimes emerge.

If you want to get better at this life task of relationships, you have to identify, celebrate, learn from, and build upon these moments when your soft underbelly is exposed. The man you would like to be already exists, and it is your job to recognize this and build on what already exists. No lobotomies or major psychosurgery required!

One angry and emotionally guarded man, a man who had me pulling my hair out trying to figure out how to help him soften his relentless criticism and projection of blame onto his girlfriend, came in for an individual session with me. He hadn't been making much progress with couples counseling, and I decided to try asking him to come in alone. He came in with a single rose. A single rose as a gift to me. He told me about his rose garden and his green thumb for red roses. "It's the only place where I really feel at peace and the only thing I do that I know is good." I wondered who had died and come back in his body. "And I wanted you to know how much our work together has meant to me, so I wanted you to have this."

The true gift, for me, was that I was now more able to see, and feel, this man's soft underbelly. I saw some way to reach him, saw the humanity beneath the layers of embitterment and defenses. And I also began to understand what his girlfriend saw in him. She didn't stay with him just because she had low self-esteem or because she was overly dependent on him; there was something to love about him.

In Wally Lamb's *I Know This Much Is True,* Dominick describes an encounter with one of his longtime best friends, Leo. Leo is portrayed as a selfish, coarse, opportunistic sleazebag. Just as Dominick is about to leave after visiting Leo at work, Leo calls to him and tells him that he wants to be on the list of people allowed to visit Dominick's twin brother Thomas, who is schizophrenic and has just mutilated himself. Most people don't want anything to do with Thomas.

"Hey, Dominick!" he yelled. "Hold up!"

He came running toward me, that fancy suit of his fluttering in the breeze. He bent down to the window. "Hey, I was just thinking," he said. "You know that visitors' list you were telling me about? How many visitors did you say your brother gets?"

"Five."

"Well, tell him he can put me on it. If he wants to. I wouldn't mind going down there, seeing how he's doing. Saying hello. I mean, what the hell? 1969, you said? I go back a few years with Thomas, too."

I nodded—took in the gift he'd just given me. "I'll mention it to him," I said. "Thanks."

"No problem, man. Later."

See, that's the thing with Leo: he's sleazy and he's decent. He takes you by surprise. I drove away, one hand on the wheel, the other wiping the goddamned water out of my eyes. Leo, man. The guy's a trip. (1998, 195)

Even Tony Soprano has panic attacks, which reveals a soft underbelly if anything does. And even Leo the sleazebag has his moments.

In the 2001 movie *Life as a House*, a marriage is breaking up. Robin, now married to Peter, finds herself irresistibly drawn back to her ex-husband George. Peter comes across as shallow, self-centered, and attached to an unrealistic image of domestic life. As he senses his wife withdrawing from him, he eventually leaves her.

He shows up weeks later, facing kids who don't act like they have missed him very much and a wife who is elsewhere emotionally. He has grown a beard, and he looks softer and more vulnerable than before. The dialogue is simple but powerful. Robin says, "I hardly recognize you with a beard." Peter answers, "That was my plan ... to be hardly recognizable to you as me."

Exercise: Catch Yourself Doing Something Right

Most of us spend our time worrying about what is going wrong and what is missing. This seems to be unavoidable. Often, however, a different approach is needed to accelerate the self-discovery and change process. If you feel stuck and frustrated, it is very effective to embark on the project of catching yourself doing something right. This means noticing when you acted in a way you are proud of, when your best self seemed to emerge.

To do this, you will need to develop a clear picture of who you would like to be in the future. You already know how to be him! You already know how to be the mature man in your vision of yourself—it's just that you forget a lot, and you can't always remember how to find him. That's our job together: to help you get better at finding the good guy in there who already exists.

1. Visualize yourself at some future time (three months, six months, or a year from now) as a man who has moved forward. In this vision, many of the struggles and behavior patterns that you now face have faded from view, or at least have faded into the background.

2. Pay attention to a very specific piece of behavior—internal or external—that signals that you are different. For example, you know that you would like develop closer male friendships. You are looking for a specific clue that would confirm that your future self is doing this. In your vision of the future, if you could observe that your future self had at least one conversation in the past week with a male friend, speaking openly about your marriage, or your worries at work, or your struggles to be a better dad to your kids, then you have a clue.

3. Now make a list of several other clues that you have become the man you want to be. For example:

   • *I am spending more time at night playing with my kids, and it makes me feel more connected and valuable.*

   • *I worry less about what other people think. I am taking chances in my work that make me feel excited about what I am doing.*

   • *When I am in a bad mood, I stop and ask myself, "What am I missing right now?" rather than blaming my wife or anyone else.*

4. Bring yourself back to the present.

5. In your notebook or journal, write each of your specific clues at the top of a page. Each day, keep a running list of any moments when you catch yourself acting the way you have visualized your future self acting. Even if it's just for a moment, or if it's one small example, make a note of it.

6. Keep this list for several weeks, then add some new clues as you move forward.

7. Keep reminding yourself that you already know how to do many of these things. You already know how to be a

different and more fulfilled man. It's not that mysterious. You just need to act on the knowledge that you already have.

Imaginary Crimes

Sometimes unconscious guilt or shame is what leads good men to behave badly. According to *control-mastery theory*, children grow up believing that they have committed some crime against the family or that they are at risk for doing so (Weiss and Sampson 1986; Engel and Ferguson 1990). The perception of having committed these crimes leads them to feel shame. And shame, as we know, rarely leads to anything good. More often, shame generates rage, projection of blame, self-destructive behavior, and defensive reactions.

These crimes are truly imaginary, because most reasonable observers would say that it is not fair for the child to take on the burden of guilt. The child victim of sexual abuse at the hands of an adult may blame himself, saying, *I must have done something to seduce him* or even *I kind of got some pleasure from it, so it was just as much my fault.* In these examples, it is painfully obvious that the child has developed a narrative blaming himself, but we know this guilt is imaginary or fictional. In fact, it is absurd, but still very real to the child, and it may remain quite real even as the child matures and develops more life perspective.

If you believe that you have committed, or are in danger of committing, imaginary crimes, then you are an ideal candidate for relational heroism. Why? Because it takes such effort to go against the grain and relate to the most intimate and trusted people in ways that are emotionally risky and make you feel emotionally vulnerable.

Crimes of Survivorship and Success: Holding Back

You may feel guilty about imaginary crimes of survivorship and success when you think that something good that you have done has turned out to be hurtful to others, when you succeed where others have failed, or even when you survive where others have not.

Zack, a man in his late twenties committed to staying clean and sober, told me about his conversation with his father about drinking. "I have been trying to stop, because I have seen how much this has messed me up. I'm going to AA meetings. My father has tried this off and on but never stayed with it. He says, 'How long is this not-drinking thing going to last?' Like there's something wrong with it or it's kind of silly."

Zack is on the receiving end of some imaginary-crimes messages. His father sees Zack taking charge of his life by controlling his drinking. This serves as a broken mirror to the father, who is reminded that he himself has a problem but has not been successful with it.

So Zack's father has two choices. He can be thrilled with his son's success and even use him as inspiration. Or he can demean what his son is doing so that he won't have to acknowledge that there is something worthwhile in the task Zack is accomplishing.

The second choice is easier, and this is what he does.

Zack unconsciously learns that he can be loyal to his father and keep his father in a better emotional state if he does not surpass or outdo him. Zack may actually believe, at some level, that success with his own drinking patterns is a crime against his father. He doesn't want to be his father's broken mirror. It's not difficult to see how Zack's guilt over his imaginary crime could lead him to sabotage his own success.

In the 1980 movie *Ordinary People,* Conrad is the younger of two brothers in the "perfect" American family: white, upper middle class, country clubs, ritzy Chicago suburb. Perfect until the two boys are out on a boat on the lake and get caught in a storm, and Conrad's older brother drowns. Conrad, plagued with guilt about having survived when his brother died, deteriorates into depression and ultimately attempts suicide.

Conrad's belief in his imaginary crime of surviving, compounded by the subtle message from his emotionally cold mother that he has failed to replace his brother, makes it impossible for him to succeed. His grades drop, his mood plummets, he quits the swim team. And, most importantly for our discussion here, he becomes entangled in relationships where he is obsessed with protecting others from having bad things happen to them. And, when he is offered a genuine positive opportunity by a girl who likes him, he is paralyzed with guilt and doubt. Like Will Hunting, Conrad hurts her with his emotional withdrawal and never really explains why.

Zack and Conrad struggle with guilt about becoming successful. They fear that they do not deserve their success or that their success will prove harmful to someone they love and care about. The crimes are imaginary. And these imaginary crimes haunt their relationships.

Crimes of Separation: Being Different

You believe you are guilty of imaginary crimes of separation when you come to believe that your own independent choices will do irreparable harm to your parent or someone else who is important to you. In the 2002 movie *My Big Fat Greek Wedding*, Toula is a woman in her twenties who cannot bear to separate from her tight-knit Greek American family. Her family makes many attempts to match her with nice young Greek men, and when she finally falls in love with a young man of the wrong ethnicity, her family goes ballistic. Toula struggles with the seemingly irreconcilable conflict between her heart's desire and her family's values. This family (which could just as easily be Italian, Jewish, Mexican, or Chinese) has defined a set of crimes which we, the audience, perceive as nothing but imaginary. But she experiences them as crimes because they cause undeniable pain to the people she loves and respects. She must be committing a crime if these people are hurt.

Alex, a man in his early twenties, had recently been traumatized by a nasty relationship breakup when he came to see me. His girlfriend had become fed up with his emotional clinginess. He was never able to stand up to her, despite her frequent emotional mistreatment of him. Alex never felt like he had the right to confront her. He told me, "I can't be happy unless my partner's happy. I burden myself with her unhappiness."

Where does a young man learn to think like this? He explained it to me:

> When I was ten, my parents divorced, and (probably like a lot of other kids) I told myself that this was my fault: There must be something about me that caused this—if only I were a better kid!
>
> More recently, my mother has often complained bitterly about all the sacrifices she has made for me. "I'm doing all this for you! And you have never really succeeded like you could have. And now I have to deal with you being depressed. Do you know how much extra pressure this puts on me?"

What kind of mother would say that to her kid? Of course, at one level, there is emotional truth here. If your child has problems, it makes your life more difficult. But most parents are able to make a distinction between a child who willfully makes their lives more difficult and one who is plagued with some sort of personal burden (physical, intellectual, or emotional) which impacts both the child and the parent. Alex's mother lost sight of Alex's independent center of initiative, and could see only how his problems were affecting her.

This sets the stage for Alex to accuse himself of the imaginary crime of hurting someone he loves. *I can't be happy unless my partner's happy.* Alex could not be more assertive and could not develop a healthy separation. He believed it would be profoundly disloyal to abandon someone in their unhappiness or to cause them even more. Defying this belief system is an act of relational heroism.

Lane had developed a script about his imaginary crime that had stayed with him for twenty years and counting. "I feel plagued with guilt that the last words I spoke to my father when I was seven years old, the night he was hit by that car and killed, were *Good night.* Why didn't I tell him that I loved him? Why didn't I tell him how much he meant to me? I let him down, and I keep doing that to people all my life."

Imaginary Crimes and Relationships

Imagined crimes actually indicate fundamentally positive qualities in a person: loyalty, sensitivity, concern about the welfare of another, the capacity for guilt and remorse. It is not these qualities that sabotage relationships, but rather the distortions that emerge from these qualities.

Eric, a young man who was in treatment with me off and on for several years, offers us a dramatic and poignant example of how guilt about imaginary crimes can lead to destructive behavior.

Eric grew up in a family that was, to say the least, dysfunctional. When he was in grade school, his mother became addicted to pain medication and alcohol, and deteriorated into a chronic state of substance abuse, irritability, depression, and irresponsibility.

> *She lied, cheated, stole to get her pain pills. Then she would burn herself with cigarettes because she was so out of it. She still does it. She wrecked her car. Everything in that household was so stressful, and she got so hostile. I was always ashamed—I had to hide this from my friends. It's really like I had to be the parent to my mother. When I was fifteen, I would drive her around to different doctors to get her different prescriptions. She would give me money to buy pot if I would do it for her. Then I would steal her pills from her and sell them back to her, and she didn't even know it. It was so sick.*

When Eric was about eleven, he started drinking daily, later progressing to almost every street drug I could imagine—and a few I couldn't. He was arrested (by his count) at least ten times, for vandalism, drug dealing, hit-and-run, robbery, battery, assault. He was in and out of residential treatment centers and juvenile hall.

Eric first came to see me when he was seventeen, after he had hit rock bottom and became clean and sober through 12-step \programs. He was in a very stormy, off-and-on relationship (never violent, but emotionally exhausting for both) with a girl named Danielle, whom he loved passionately but could not get along with well enough to make it work. Danielle was working without a green card, having recently moved to the U.S. from Mexico to flee an abusive father at home.

Eric finally broke up with Danielle. She was devastated, he moved on—until he got some news about six months later. He came in and told me the story.

> *You know I broke up with Danielle months ago. And I've been screwing around with a couple of different girls at this point. But I still couldn't get her out of my head. A friend of mine told me that he had heard Danielle was dancing again in strip clubs because she was so broke. I went nuts. I stormed over to her place and I started fucking screaming at her, "I'm gonna turn you in to immigration if I ever find out you are dancing again! You're gonna have to go back to your father and everything he has done to you!" I wasn't really gonna do it, but I felt like it.*
>
> *I know I totally lost it. When I get like this, I feel hopeless. Label me suicidal. Nothing mattered.*
>
> *How can your life be so small that you would kill yourself over that?*

Eric is another on my very long list of good men behaving badly. He is a classic example of how imaginary crimes can propel someone to destructive relationship behavior. When Eric lived with his mother, he desperately tried to rescue her from her psychological abyss. He tried to cheer her up. He tried to hide her pain pills. He tried to get her more pills to make her happy. He tried to yell at her to force her to become a real mom.

Eric's imaginary crime was that he failed to rescue his mother, and he did all he could to escape the pain of having failed her. But somewhere inside, not quite within the reach of consciousness, he had made a decision that he would never let someone down like this again. So when he heard that Danielle was on what sounded like a downhill path (strip dancing), he absolutely could not bear it. It was not jealousy. It was not control or possessiveness. It was actually a deep and tortured concern.

Danielle's dancing was Eric's broken mirror, reflecting back to him a person guilty of unbearable imaginary crimes. This time—stupidly, irrationally, destructively—he was determined to do something to rescue the person he loved.

To Eric's credit, he began to get it. He developed more of a capacity for consciousness and reflection. He knew the story of Odysseus, and Eric learned to prepare himself for situations likely to seduce him into destructive or self-destructive behavior.

Now, several years later, although Eric is more self-aware, the same emotional challenges continue. He still finds it very difficult to be around a woman in pain, and he has a hard time being empathic. Why? Because it arouses too much despair and powerlessness in himself. He struggles to not get critical, impatient, controlling. "Now when I see my girlfriend really upset, I want to *do* something. When I grew up and I was in pain, I kept it all to myself. Seeing her in pain makes me very uncomfortable and very powerless. I want to make her okay, and I get mad at her when I can't. But I'm a lot more on top of it than I ever was before."

Like Odysseus, Eric knows he cannot avoid passing by the island of the Sirens. But at least he can anticipate this event and plug up his ears or tie himself to the mast until he knows it is safe for him to be released. So can you.

How Relational Heroes Let Go of Imaginary Crimes

The process of releasing yourself from imaginary crimes involves several steps—and ultimately requires you to perform an act of relational heroism. The first step is for you to call the crime what it is: imaginary. While this is easier said than done, no healing or release is possible otherwise. The next step is to develop a new narrative that explains the event without identifying yourself as the imagined criminal. It is usually not enough, however, to just tell yourself *It's not my fault.* You have to find a new narrative that is genuinely credible.

The new narrative is not always obvious, and it often involves implicating someone else for the crime. The someone else may be a person whom you have been determined to protect for years. If you were emotionally or physically abused by your father, it is quite likely that you resolved the cognitive dissonance of being abused by someone you loved by convincing yourself either that you deserved it or that it was ultimately good for you. And if you believe this, you are that much more likely to behave the same way toward your own kids. A new narrative might require you to recognize that your father acted like a son of a bitch. And how can you love, admire, respect, and identify with a son of a bitch?

The experience of shame as a boy often sets the stage for you to become an emotionally cold man, like Will Hunting. It's a way for you to defend yourself against the potential pain of vulnerability: you can't take the risk of being humiliated or rejected when someone finds out more about you, so you get cold and rejecting yourself. There is a logic to this, but it is a relationship-killer. Furthermore, if you humiliate and reject others, you model this for your children, who may grow up to repeat the pattern of shame-inducing behavior for still another generation.

How did Will of *Good Will Hunting* choose a path of release from his imaginary crimes and shame?

First, he is in crisis. For the first time, he really has something at stake emotionally that could cause him pain if he screwed it up or passed it up.

Second, his psychiatrist dramatically tells him that all this stuff in Will's case file, all the documentation of his history of abuse and neglect, is not Will's fault. He repeats this mantra, *It's not your fault*, until finally Will breaks down, sobbing, and embraces his shrink. Will is tremendously relieved to be able to accept this new narrative: someone else was at fault.

Third, Will is released from his imaginary crimes by his buddy Chuckie. Chuckie challenges Will by telling him that he has something that few others have and that he is just plain afraid to cash in on it. He tells Will that it would be an insult to Chuckie and the rest of his buddies if Will is still in the same neighborhood, doing the same manual labor, in twenty years. And then Chuckie really rattles Will's cage. He tells Will that his favorite part of his day is when he knocks on Will's door to pick him up for work—in these ten seconds, he lets himself imagine that Will is gone. Will just wouldn't be there. He would have moved on. And that would be the ultimate act of loyalty and respect for Chuckie—not sticking around and hanging out with his old buddies, growing old together.

There is probably not a more powerful reframing, guy-talk style, than calling your best friend a wimp for not leaving the 'hood, going after the girl, and starting a new life.

The final courageous act takes place later. When all this sinks in for Will, it is still up to him—completely up to him—to make a move based on this new information, a move that still carries enormous risk. Not everyone could do it, but he does. He heads out to California to be with Skylar (he hopes), and his plaque in the Hall of Fame for Relational Heroes is inscribed.

And our friend Conrad from *Ordinary People* is released when he, too, after the crisis of losing a friend to suicide, confronts his imaginary crime of surviving when his brother drowned, and rewrites the old narrative. His psychiatrist challenges him by asking what was the one wrong thing he did. What was his imaginary crime? Conrad blurts out, "I held on!" And then comes the new narrative: *Did you ever think that maybe he just wasn't strong enough?*

Again, the breakthrough in self-talk is necessary but not sufficient. Like all potential relational heroes, Conrad is still faced with the challenge of conducting his relationship business differently. And that he does, as he insists on talking to his parents honestly about their feelings and behavior as well as his. As it turns out, his father can handle it and his mother can't. His mother treats Conrad like he *is* a criminal, making him feel worse. But that's the risk you take when you act with integrity: there are no guarantees, and in the end you've just got to take care of your side of the street.

7

Guy Talk

The language that you use in talking to yourself about being a man in relationships must respect the cultural limitations—and the cultural strengths—of being male. As a guy, you are less likely than that other gender to be particularly comfortable expressing emotions that make you feel—or appear to be—weak, dependent, unsure, threatened, or emotionally needy. Our culture rewards men for being strong, independent, and confident. Emotions, vulnerability, and uncertainty are generally considered more acceptable in women.

The history of psychotherapy and couples counseling—and the mind-boggling industry of self-help books—have taught us that the whole field is more user-friendly to women than to men. Certainly, the language is more compatible with women's way of thinking than it is with men's.

What are we therapists usually asking you to do? We insist that you "share your feelings." We insist that you "process." We honor your "vulnerability." We teach you to communicate openly, to work as a team, to honor interdependency, and to allow change to happen organically. We ask you to listen (sometimes for a long time) without taking action or problem solving.

There are certainly many men who share these values and are quite capable of doing these things. But perhaps you are one of the men who feel that this is "girl stuff." Perhaps you are reading this book and working on your relationship problems only because some woman in your life is unhappy or has insisted you do so. In trying to master relationships and foster healthy communication, you may feel alienated, inept, and impatient.

I am going to try and explain why this is the case. And I am going to give you a lot of different ways to think about emotions, vulnerability, change, and communication so that they make more sense and seem more compatible with being male.

Emotional Unintelligence

Because of the gender training course you were enrolled in, you are likely to have some particular roadblocks as you try to deal with the complexities of your inner emotional life and relationships. Many men—despite being very successful in many different areas of life— still have holes in their emotional development and their ability to express key elements of their inner world through language. Some men function in a way that can only be described as emotionally unintelligent, desperately trying to manage relationships and trying to fend off the discomfort of male depression.

One roadblock is the one I discussed in chapter 5: normative male alexithymia, or difficulty in identifying and talking about vulnerable and caring emotions. This is one of the primary contributors to emotional unintelligence. You can't know much about who you are and you can't figure out what is happening during relationship conflicts if you can't identify your feelings in the first place.

And even among men who at least have the capacity for identifying and expressing internal states, many are reluctant to acknowledge problems that may exist. It connotes weakness and dependency and everything unmasculine. John Wayne and other stoic men are the cultural icons for this aversion.

Humorist Dave Barry captures this experience in the following conversation between male patient and doctor:

Doctor: So what seems to be the problem?

Patient: Well, the main thing is, I keep coughing up blood. Plus I have these open sores all over my body. Also I have really severe chest pains and double vision, and from time to time these little worms burrow out of my skin.

Doctor: It's just a sprain.

Patient: That's what I thought. (1995, 149)

This dialogue is a joke and a caricature, but it is funny because it contains an element of truth. And stoicism relates to another roadblock, which is difficulty in asking for help. Pollack (1995) refers to this trait as "defensive autonomy." You may be determined to maintain your self-sufficiency and find it intolerable to be perceived (or to perceive yourself) as dependent on anyone. Perhaps you are like the stereotypical man who has a hard time asking for directions, resists the idea of going to a therapist to help straighten out his life, and even finds it hard to tell his partner that he is worried or doubting himself. This pattern strikes right at the core of masculine identity issues: *I cannot afford to look like I am not in control of things in my life!*

When I was in my thirties, I developed serious back pain and (as was in vogue at that time) was prescribed complete bed rest for weeks on end. My wife had to cook my meals, help me up to go to the bathroom, bring me whatever I had forgotten to ask her for the first time. I was in guy hell. The pain was the least of it; the dependency was the killer. I couldn't stand needing her so much, and I was sure that it was only a matter of time before she became disgusted by my weakness and dependency. So, contrary to the principles of relational heroism, I never talked about this with her or anyone else—I just acted it out. Her helping me was like a broken mirror reminding me of my inadequate state, and I acted nastier and nastier to her. My friends noticed but didn't have the heart to tell me until later. Not only was I unaware of how I was treating her, I was clueless even about how I was feeling.

This brings us to the next roadblock: anxiety about revealing too much of your needs to someone else and placing yourself in a position of potential vulnerability. Perhaps you carry around fears about being known too well or getting too close to someone who could—and very well might, in your narratives—reject you, abandon you, judge you, or control you. So you keep your mouth—and often your heart—shut. Remember Will Hunting, who emotionally and physically exploded at Skylar because she wanted to advance the relationship further and know him even more intimately? It activated shame for him, or, more precisely, fear of shame, and he became a good man behaving badly.

Speaking the Language of Men

In order to become a good man behaving well, you need to frame your goals in language that does not challenge your fundamental definitions of male identity. In fact, you need to think about these changes in thinking, feeling, and acting in terms of what is best about masculinity.

Male Metaphors

If I tell you how important it is that you display more emotional vulnerability, you might roll your eyes and harden your defenses. You may reluctantly comply to keep your wife happy if she insists, but you won't quite buy in.

However, if I tell you that it is time for you to live up to your responsibilities and become a relational hero, I am talking to you in language that allows you to embrace the new behavior and perceive it as being within the definition of masculinity. Terrence Real challenges men by telling them, when they act belittling or cold with their wife or kids, that they are choosing to comply with the training that they received from their own father. He tells them that they are, in effect, announcing the following: "I am giving myself license to act abusively just like my dad. I know this is going to really hurt you kids, but I don't really care. Indulging my anger is more important to me, right now, than you are. . . . Dad, this one's for you!" (1997, 240)

There is nothing manipulative about reframing behavior this way. It just sets up the problem—and the challenge—in men's language. You might respond to this kind of message about repeating your own father's behavior with a wave of shame (*I can't believe I'm being just like him!*) followed by a firm-jawed determination to be your own kind of man.

Carey told me about his thoughts after he would go off on his kids or his wife. "That's not the type of man I am! I'm a nurturing man and a caring man and I know what the right thing to do is! I hug my son and tell him I love him—a lot! It's weird—in some ways I do things just the opposite from what my father did, and in other ways I end up exactly the same. I don't understand that."

You may find it helpful to think in the language of power and control. If you're familiar with the theory of abusive, male-dominated relationships, you will recognize these as the central evil in the most pathological stories. So who, writing a book on helping men in relationships, would want to encourage men to take power and control? Actually, it makes sense to recognize that you are attracted to feeling powerful and being in control—and know that you can use these impulses for relationship good rather than relationship evil. I call it power over yourself and control over yourself. Here are some questions to ask yourself that may help you reframe "power" and "control":

Do you want your girlfriend's frustrating habits to control your temper?

Do you want some other driver on the road to have the power to determine how you act in front of your kids?

Do you want to give your teacher the satisfaction of knowing that she was right about you, that you have a really bad attitude?

When you think about your capacity to "take charge of your life" or "be the captain of your own ship," you are engaging archetypal male metaphors. This paints the track or path ahead—fraught with anxiety and unpredictability—as a classical male journey. A journey not unlike that of Odysseus, who was not allowed by the gods to return home to Ithaca until he had spent his ten years on the open seas learning cleverness, compassion, and humility. The companion stories of the *Iliad* and the *Odyssey* represent two different and essential chapters of the male journey. The *Iliad* is the story of a man fighting the demons outside of himself, and the *Odyssey* is the story of a man fighting the demons within. If you can frame the skills of humility, compassion, self-awareness, and acknowledging the need for help as a classical male journey, you are more likely to embrace them. The tasks themselves become more male-friendly.

Real Men

Jackson Katz, one of the pioneers in the modern American men's movement, challenges men to redefine their notions of what a real man is. He has developed training programs designed specifically for male bastions of society: the military, college fraternities, and high school and college sports teams. His programs are aimed at consciousness-raising regarding gender-based violence. But unlike other similar programs, his model targets not the perpetrators but the bystanders, the collective of reasonably good guys who determine the zeitgeist of male culture, attitudes, and behaviors. He challenges the bystanders and male leadership figures (such as quarterbacks on football teams) to not tolerate offensive and unacceptable behaviors in their peers. If they hear guys bragging about screwing a girl who was hopelessly drunk at the frat party, for example, he challenges them to imagine what this would be like if the girl were their sister, or cousin, or girlfriend, and to imagine how they would react to other men who knew about it and said or did nothing.

Katz's programs are brilliant in their creative co-opting of male-friendly language. His *MVP Playbook* (MVP Project, 1994) is full of gender relationship vignettes like "Illegal Use of Hands," "Piling On," and "Pass Interference." Each "play" depicts an act of mild to severe offensive behavior committed by men against women, and challenges men to examine their own beliefs and to rise to the occasion.

Talking to Other Men

You can use male language not only to frame your own goals in a way that feels comfortable but also to connect with other men.

In a 1999 article in the *American Psychological Association Monitor*, Freiberg and Sleek tell the story of Texas psychologist Gary Brooks, who was conducting group counseling sessions with men. And, as is often the case in men's discussions, football was the topic that came up. Of course, in Texas, football means the Dallas Cowboys. The men in this group were talking about star running back Emmitt Smith, who was being described at the time as washed-up (although he managed to go on and gain thousands and thousands more yards through his brilliant career). But the group members focused on their appreciation of Smith the man and his determination to stay on the playing field as long as possible.

Brooks recalls that the group members began talking about issues of physical strength and about the vulnerability of aging. They ended up getting to a crucial question and a crucial fear in the lives of most men: What happens when you're no longer able to do what you could once do? Does that mean you're a failure?

If you want to take a chance and talk to other men not only about blitz packages and screen passes but also about the vulnerability of aging, there are plenty of opportunities to do it. If those men turned Emmitt Smith's rushing average into that kind of discussion, you can too. Take a chance. Some of the men in your life will probably be grateful.

Exercise: Reframing Your Goals in Male Language

You can talk about relationship issues in the language of numbers, engineering, business, sports, art, the military, or the Bible.

Pick at least three goals that you have developed for how you would like to handle or think about your relationships differently. On a separate sheet of paper or in your notebook, write instructions to yourself about these goals in language that you can relate to as a guy. Here are some examples:

Nobody's perfect. If your wife is not perfect, join the club. All of us can reasonably figure that our partner can be around 80 percent of what we are looking for. If it's above that, count your blessings, and if it's below, the match may not be the right one. Do the math.

It makes sense to diversify your portfolio by having multiple people you can turn to to talk about emotional stuff. You are in better shape if you can talk with friends, not just your wife. That way, if one market sector crashes, you still have assets elsewhere.

Remember the 1973 Oakland A's, who never got along but still won the World Series? Keep this in mind when you are managing child custody and parenting decisions with your estranged or divorced wife.

It is normal and tolerable to make mistakes in your relationships with your loved ones: Tony Gwynn was the greatest pure hitter of our generation, and he made an out two out of every three times!

It makes sense to practice skills for handling your reactions in emotional situations. Why? Think of Jerry Rice running the same route hundreds of times, so that under game conditions, with a defensive back barreling down on him, he still knows exactly what he needs to do.

Developing Action Plans for Complex Tasks

Another male-friendly way of thinking about the complex tasks of deepening and improving your closest relationships is to take these tasks and break them down into recognizable and easily achievable components. Even the complex skill of empathy—one of the surest signs of emotional intelligence—can be learned, even by men who claim to be clueless in this department. How? By breaking the task down into small steps. Empathy, this rather mysterious skill that seems to rely on some inner intuitive sense, becomes something real, unmysterious, even fascinating. Each component becomes known, then reassembled. Thinking of a new skill as a simple engineering task increases your likelihood of taking it on and gaining success.

Exercise: A Man's Guide to Empathy in Seven Easy Steps

While there is no substitute for the "natural" empathic skills that some people (men or women) are blessed with, you can do pretty well in developing this capacity by breaking it down into components and following these steps. Step 4, *active listening*, is a skill unto itself, so we'll break that step down into even smaller steps.

1. Stop and pay attention. Mentally focus your attention on your partner.

2. Listen carefully to what she is trying to tell you. Pay attention to her story.

3. Shut up. Don't try to defend yourself or problem solve.

4. Use *active listening.*

Active listening is a communication technique that encourages the other person to continue speaking. It also enables you to be certain you understand what the other person is saying. It's a way of checking it out. It's called active listening because you not only listen but also actively let the other person know that you have really heard her.

Active listening involves *paraphrasing.*

Paraphrasing is stating in your own words what you think the other person is feeling, based on what she says.

> *You sound really (feeling) about (situation) .*

> *You must really feel (feeling) .*

> *What I hear you saying is _____ .*

Active listening also involves *clarifying.*

Clarifying involves asking questions to get more information.

Clarifying helps you hear more specifics about the situation and feelings.

Clarifying also lets the other person know you are interested in what she is saying.

> *So, tell me what happened that got you so upset.*

> *How did you feel when that happened?*

Active listening often involves *personalizing.*

Personalizing involves offering a personal example of feeling the same thing or being in the same situation.

> *I think I know what you mean. I've been there too.*

> *I felt the same way when I lost my job. I think everyone does.*

Personalizing helps the other person feel less alone, and it implies that someone else has experienced this and recovered from it.

Personalizing can be harmful if you talk *too* much about yourself and stal the spotlight from the person who needs it.

You think that was bad? Listen to what happened to me!

5. Shut up again.

6. Listen some more.

7. Offer aedvice or problem solving only if invited.

Multimedia Approaches

Another way for you to develop the ability to identify, label, and express emotions is by watching and learning from movies. Many therapists and counselors assign men homework of watching certain movies to help them observe how other men feel and react in similar situations. In my work with men, I often recommend *Good Will Hunting* for shame issues, *The Great Santini* or *Life as a House* for father-son relations, *Affliction* for men who mismanage relationships, *Carnal Knowledge* for men who shut themselves off emotionally, *Parenthood* for men who look to their kids to determine their own self-worth, and *Ordinary People* and *Good Will Hunting* for imaginary crimes issues. For additional suggestions, refer to Hesley and Hesley's 2001 book, *Rent Two Films and Let's Talk in the Morning: Using Popular Movies in Psychotherapy.*

The Importance of Hope

For good men behaving badly, or good men who say, *That's not the man I want to be,* or simply good men who are feeling emotionally isolated or shut down, one of the key missing pieces is the experience of hope. Hope is the cornerstone of your healing process. If you are locked in emotional shutdown, you can become supremely discouraged, even despairing. Discouragement can lead to dark moods, which can generate escapist behavior, emotional withdrawal, or aggression and hostility directed at the perceived source of the discouragement—usually the people closest to you.

Encouraging Yourself

If you are discouraged, you need to experience hope. One way you can do this is by finding a way to identify with the good-man-behaving-badly narrative.

Chris was a young man who had been engaged in a pattern of escalating arguments with his wife after their child was born. He dearly loved his three-month-old son, but he could not handle the deterioration of his life as a new father. His wife, who had once offered him so much more attention, was now in a bad mood much of the time.

One time, as he turned on his wife again for some perceived crime (I think it was her excessive complaining), Chris became so angry that he started screaming at her and slamming doors until pictures crashed down off the wall. His wife (and, we can guess, his baby) was terrified. A neighbor called the police, and Child Protective Services eventually investigated and put him on probationary status so that Chris could not be alone with his child for several months. He had never exploded like this before (or since).

As Chris was telling the details of this incident after a couple of months of group treatment—without passion, without a flicker of remorse—I interrupted him and said, slowly and meaningfully, "Chris, I know you, and I know you are not the type of person who wishes harm on your baby or on your wife. So you must have felt so desperate, like there was such an awful feeling inside of you that you just had to get rid of it somehow, to make you do something that goes so much against your basic values. I know that what you did is not the real you!"

He looked down and started crying. "It's true," he said. Chris's ability to see himself as a good man behaving badly melted his defensiveness and allowed him to highlight the positive values he carried within. This did not take him off the hook. But thinking of himself in this way redoubled his commitment to change.

The Importance of Labels

In chapter 2, I related the story of Namir and his wife Ellen, who had separated after Namir went off verbally on her when she rejected his sexual overtures in the shower. He had insulted her body, told her that no one else would ever want her, and that she should feel lucky and grateful that he was so interested in her.

Namir had pulled stunts like this before, but this really went over the top. Ellen told him she couldn't stand this abuse anymore and insisted that he move out.

After weeks of pleading from Namir, Ellen agreed to come in for a couples session with me to see if there was any hope for this relationship. They told their story. I talked to Namir about good men behaving badly. They both knew that he was both a good man and clearly behaving badly. He told me he would do anything it took to deal with his depression that led to his destructive behavior. I felt hopeful. I was encouraged that Namir was experiencing a healthy dose of shame that was motivating him to change.

I made an appointment to see Namir individually. He asked me if there was anything he could read that could help him get started on all these changes he needed to make. I wrote down the name of a book, *The Verbally Abusive Relationship,* on the back of his appointment card. As he was leaving and thanking me profusely for agreeing to see him and offering him some light at the end of the tunnel, he glanced at the card.

"Verbally abusive! Verbally abusive! I'm not abusive! What do you take me for? I don't abuse my wife! Is that what you think of me? Abusive! I love my wife! I am a good man! I'm not an abuser!" This diatribe continued into the reception area where his wife was waiting for him, and out to the street. As they left, his wife gave me one more look that said, *You see what it's like?*

I never saw Namir again. He never showed up for his appointment and never answered my calls or my letter.

Again, I learned a lesson. Although I certainly wanted Namir to take responsibility for his destructive behavior in his marriage, I especially wanted him to take a legitimate shot at changing it. Labels are important to people. The label I inadvertently pushed on him served as a broken mirror reflecting an unbearably shameful picture of himself, which paralyzed his potential for genuine change.

If you read this and think that I am advocating letting anyone (men, women, or children) off the hook for their destructive relationship behavior, you are wrong. It's just that Namir couldn't reconcile his self-image as a responsible and decent male with the label *abusive,* as would be true for most men. This was a violation of the principles of "guy talk." Namir didn't stick around long enough to embrace the good-men-behaving-badly narrative that would have allowed him to maintain some self-respect and helped loosen the noose of shame. Chris, in the previous example, did—and you can too.

Reframing Familiar Language

Another way to change the way you think and talk about relationships is to redefine old terms in new ways, focusing on the positive aspects.

Machismo: Invoking New Definitions of Manhood

The idea of machismo is a great candidate for this type of reframing. The common use of this term implies a caricature of masculine traits. Men characterized as dominated by machismo are controlling, threatening, aggressive, entitled, and defensive.

But, even in the machismo culture in Mexico, there exist definitions of manhood that also imply the very best of being a man: demonstrating personal integrity, displaying honorable behavior, providing a positive example. In other words, acting as a relational hero. A macho man is the head of the household, but also listens to, respects, and protects women. A recent study of Mexican men in relationship counseling programs found that interviewees unanimously declared the importance of their nuclear family (Welland 1999). Most of them reported being concerned about their children's education. Their main concern was to be responsible men, both by providing for the family economically and by protecting their partner and children from outside harm. These values constitute the core of the positive male gender role for Mexicans. This positive identity centers around the role of protector and provider and displaying stoic strength in the midst of adversity.

Many of the men in Welland's study recognized that they had cheated themselves and their families by buying into the negative version of machismo, and many of them attributed the unraveling of their relationships to the blind worship of machismo more than any other factor. One man described his remorse at how he had treated his wife. "I thought that this was the way to show her that I was a man. . . . But . . . I didn't realize, everything I did, everything was wrong. No one ever taught me, I never saw a good example of how to treat a woman. If I had seen it, I would have done it, but I never did" (189).

What does this mean for you? It just gives you another example of how powerful your language and self-talk can be. The men in these studies were driven to be "real men," but by their own description, the qualities that they thought defined a "real man" were warped by their narrow cultural definition: in this case, machismo. The problem is not that you, or they, are committed to male values or to developing a male identity. There is so much to be celebrated about masculinity. The challenge is in learning how to frame acts of tenderness as relational heroism, controlling knee-jerk reactions as a task worthy of Odysseus, or treating women with more sensitivity and respect as the highest evolution of masculinity.

In other words, if you are a man strongly identified with culture-specific values about masculinity, you are more likely to be open to new relationship behavior if it makes sense to you as just a new way of defining what you have always valued. Anyone who tries to tell you that all your values are wrong or sexist or immature is likely to run into a brick wall.

Courage: Invoking New Definitions of Heroism

Courage is another central idea about masculinity that can be framed differently. The word *courage* comes from the Latin root word *cor*, meaning "heart" or "soul." So an act of courage does not necessarily mean some act of physical risk, but rather an act that is truly from the heart—where the heart, or what truly is right, dictates the behavior.

We need to get away from the idea that courage is behavior reserved for Odysseus, Martin Luther King Jr., and firefighters in the World Trade Center. If these are the only definitions of courage, then few of us will ever be able to measure up and recognize the courageous or heroic traits within ourselves. The reality is that we are all performing—or have the potential to perform—courageous acts every day, in many situations, in ways that may only get noticed by a few people closest to us, or perhaps not even noticed by anyone else at all. Every man—every day—has the chance to be a relational hero.

Accountability, Exceptions, and Disinhibitors

Another way in which personal narrative makes a difference— another way in which reframing your thoughts in "guy talk" can help you—lies in the way you explain the reasons you said or did something destructive. Here, I am making the assumption that we men who are not psychopaths embrace fundamentally similar social values: *Don't hit women. Do not say or do something abusive to children. Be honest. Take responsibility for what you do. Do not cheat. Be fair in how you handle things with other people. Be loyal to the people you care about. Try to model positive behavior for your kids.* Add to this list other key commandments and basic social agreements.

However—and here is where personal narrative fits in—we all make exceptions to these values under certain circumstances. We tell ourselves that under these circumstances, in this situation, with this justification, it is all right to violate the values.

- *She kept nagging me and I had to do something!*

- *I wasn't gonna let that kid show me up in public!*

- *It was finally my turn to let them all know how I felt!*

- *I have had a really hard day, and I am entitled!*

- *I can't win with her, so I'll just withdraw from her and see how she likes that!*

Think carefully about these. It is crucial for you to identify how you have justified your exceptions. The point is not to generate excuses for self-indulgent or destructive behavior, nor is the point to nail you for being some sort of relationship criminal. Instead, you want to reinforce your identity as a good guy who takes responsibility for his behavior: *I am a good guy with good values, and sometimes I convince myself that it is okay to act badly. I've got to watch out for those times when I justify my exceptions!*

One man I worked with described it like this: "Sometimes I just get so frustrated, I must tell myself that it's okay to treat the people I love in a nasty way. Like I tell myself, *She just won't listen to me!* or *She cares about the people at church more than she does about me!* So then it's okay—in my own head—to yell at her or embarrass her in front of our kids. To force her to hear me. What bullshit!"

If you know how you justify your exceptions, you will be in a better position to avoid the danger of destructive behavior—like Odysseus anticipating the Sirens.

Exercise: Justifications

Most likely, you, like all of us, have behaved in the following ways even with (perhaps especially with) the people you love the most:

- getting sarcastic

- withdrawing emotionally

- yelling and put-downs

- not following through on commitments

- betraying secrets

- breaking relationship ground rules

- demanding your own way

But it is unlikely that these behaviors reflect your values. How is this possible?

You found a way to justify it in your own mind at that particular moment. Even afterward, you may insist that it was okay rather than simply saying, *I blew it. I behaved badly, and it's nobody's fault but my own.*

Here are some typical justifications. On a separate sheet of paper or in your journal, note any that you have used and write in the specific self-talk that went with the justification. Then see if you can come up with a few more that aren't on this list.

No big deal. *I wasn't really that mean; all I did was tell my son something he knows is true!*

I didn't mean to. *I didn't mean to yell at her and scare her—I just wanted her to understand!*

I couldn't help it. *I was drunk—what can I say?* or *I just flipped out; I didn't even know what I was doing.*

I had to take care of myself. *It was my turn to let her know what I've been going through!*

It's her fault. *If she hadn't nagged me,* or *If she hadn't spent too much money,* or *If she just was more interested sexually . . .*

I had to teach her a lesson. *Of course I went out and had an affair—it was the only way to get her to pay better attention to me!*

It was for her own good. *I had to embarrass her in front of her friends—she was acting so crazy, I had to get her to stop.*

Disinhibitors

Remember the discussion in chapter 5 about brain disinhibitors? Justifications—and the self-talk that goes with them—serve as disinhibitors of judgment and behavior. Alcohol and drugs likewise function as disinhibitors. So does peer pressure. So do fatigue and stress. So does relentless nagging. So, certainly, can sexual arousal. A real man is able to identify his personal disinhibitors and try to anticipate and prepare for them—like Odysseus and the Sirens. Odysseus didn't say, *Oh, well, these Sirens are just too much for me and my men to handle. We can't stop ourselves.* Instead, he knew of his own human vulnerability. He knew that even though he had many heroic and mature qualities, he was just as vulnerable as all the rest of us. His true heroism lay in recognizing this and taking responsibility, doing what he could to avert acting badly or stupidly.

And you may find it helpful to identify yourself as a good man who, when affected by certain disinhibitors, sometimes acts badly in relationships.

We're All in This Together: Twinship and Self-Disclosure

Last but not least, "guy talk" is about men talking to men. This is a key step in the process of developing your resources and feeling more hope.

Guys Talking to Guys

The problem is not only that many men rely excessively on the woman in their life for emotional support or as a catalyst for emotional access. It is also that so many men have never developed any kind of diversified portfolio for alternative sources of support, which can offer you the opportunity to be a more full-fledged and emotionally mature adult man.

Here's an illustration of what is missing: A subtle but powerful moment in *Good Will Hunting* (1997) takes place in a conversation between Will and his best buddy, Chuckie. A week previously, Will has gone through a traumatic breakup with the love of his life, Skylar.

In casual conversation, Chuckie asks Will how things are going with "your lady." Will tells him flatly that she's gone. Neither man shows any emotion. After a few grunts and monosyllabic responses from Will, Chuckie uncovers the information that Skylar has taken off to medical school in California—a week ago!

Chuckie sips from his can of beer, raises his eyebrows a little, and responds: "That sucks."

The shock in this dialogue comes from what is not there. How is it possible that this young man could be going though so much emotional turmoil without his best friend—a friend who actually cares—even having a clue? Will loves Chuckie, and they would do anything for each other. Although Will has been experimenting recently with letting his emotional guard down with a woman (with mixed success, as we know!) and with a male therapist, he has not yet learned to turn to one of his peers. This is an opportunity lost.

An important aspect of guy talk is what Brooks (1998) refers to as "participative self-disclosure," which generates self-cohesion based on the twinship experience. *Participative self-disclosure* is the fancy psychological term for talking about yourself with other people and exchanging meaningful information.

When you discover that you can get real with other people besides the woman in your life, you find hope. Especially when these other relationships include conversations with other men—conversations which take place at a deeper level than typical locker room banter.

Skills Development

When you talk to other men about how to deal with relationship issues, sometimes the most positive impact is simply that you pick up a few pointers. This is plain old skills development. Some men learn the most profound lessons about dealing with the unhappiness or anger of women by watching other men and listening to their stories. Hearing how other men respond to women can help you understand this rather delicate process of maintaining a relationship.

The danger, of course, is in listening to the wrong men. In many conversations among men, there is the tendency to sink to the lowest common denominator and enter a world where you trash women, where women are the adversary, and where you identify yourself as a member of the Male Victims Society. It is tempting to relate to other men by focusing on women's relationship flaws at the expense of your own and at the expense of the strengths of the woman in your life. Don't feel singled out here—women tend to do the same thing when talking about men, as any viewer of *Sex and the City* will attest.

The Power of Twinship

Even more powerful than the exchange of pointers is the profound benefit of simple twinship. When you find that you can actually have a conversation with other men about your doubts, about your frustrations, about experiences growing up that have always been tinged with shame, you usually experience (after perhaps some initial panic) enormous relief: *You mean I'm not the only one?* The discovery of commonality inspires hope in ways that personal analysis or introspection can only begin to touch. There is nothing more likely to generate the hopefulness of the good-man-behaving-badly narrative than the discovery of this twinship experience.

One of my clients was a highly respected and acclaimed university professor who had spent many therapy sessions in my office dealing with his intense frustration and despair about what he considered the failure of his academic department. He had always carried a passionate vision of what this department could offer, and he suffered every day with the gap between what he had envisioned and the reality of what was.

He often felt like a loser because he had been unable to fulfill his vision. In his own narrative, he had fallen short, and the ongoing dysfunctional politics served as a broken mirror for him.

So, one day, I went to get him in the waiting room of my office for his appointment. We were in the process of remodeling our office, and there were three different color samples painted on the wall. He made some jokes about which ones he liked and why he liked them; then, as we entered my office, he asked me which one I would be choosing.

I looked at him and paused dramatically. I told him that I was hardly the one who would be doing the choosing:

> *Don't you get it? There are four of us here with equal power, all quite headstrong and opinionated. We've been working on these decisions for five months. You think I'm going to decide this? You know, it is so humbling to watch us and other groups of psychologists, with all our so-called communication skills and empathic abilities, squabble and jockey for power in group decisions. It's like being a parent; I speak all across the country advising professionals and parents about dealing with difficult teenagers, and then I fumble so badly with my own. It is so humbling!*

He looked at me for a moment and then said, "It is such a relief to hear you say these things!" And he told me later that he remembered this rather uneventful moment more than the hundreds of profound things I had tried to pass on to him.

Another client of mine described his terror at the prospect of calling off his imminent wedding to a woman who, he finally realized, was not right for him to marry. He reported his feelings of failure and shame, especially as he found himself acting colder and colder to her, hoping that she would break up with him.

I proceeded to tell him the story of my own called-off wedding. And I told him how meaningful it was to me that, months later, my father reshaped this event forever in my personal narrative by telling me that he didn't think he would have had the courage to do what I did.

To my client, I offered no solution, only a twinship story about shame.

A big smile spread across his face. "That's why I keep coming to see you. You tell me about yourself, and you help me feel like we're all in this together. That's something I can really take home with me. I guess I'm not the only one!"

That's exactly the feeling that can mean so much. Moments like these can help you experience relief from your emotional isolation and develop a broader range of language for your internal experiences. And it makes it easier to believe in yourself and to make sense of your own—male—experience. If you carry a narrative that you are a good man sometimes behaving badly, then you are a member of a very large club. And you have a much better chance at coming through in relationships than the man who is paralyzed, defensive, and feeling hopeless because of his shame.

8

What Women Can Do

If you are a woman who has read this far in this book, you have probably developed many of your own ideas about how to get through to the good man who is your husband or boyfriend, or perhaps your son or brother or friend. This chapter aims to help you spot men who are not good men behaving badly but actually bad men behaving badly. You need to know the warning signs to recognize men who are dangerous relationship partners, men who are not motivated to become—or not capable of becoming—relational heroes.

If you are in a relationship with a good man who sometimes falls into patterns of bad behavior, this chapter will show you how to get better and better at helping to bring out this good man. It is not your responsibility to do this (women have felt far too responsible for men's emotional well-being for far too long), but it is in everybody's best interest for you to set the stage for his best behaviors to emerge.

Finally, if you are the mother of sons or someday will be, you will find the latest research and guidelines about how to raise boys who are most likely to develop into good men. No book on men would be complete without this perspective.

Bad Men Behaving Badly

Although the central theme of this book involves a humanistic and compassionate perspective on male struggles and behavior, it would be naive to insist that all men deserve this much slack. Some men are psychopaths, meaning that they are truly evil: their behavior is motivated strictly by personal gratification. These men are incapable—or barely capable—of genuine remorse or consideration of others. Some men behaving badly are just plain bad.

Psychopathy

Hare (1993) identifies two main components that define the psychopath. The first is the personality factor: psychopaths are selfish, callous, and remorseless. Psychopaths use people. The fundamental psychological problem here is one of underattachment: psychopaths are capable of profoundly hurtful and exploitative behavior because they simply don't care enough to behave differently. The typical factors that inhibit most of us from hurting others with our words or behaviors are glaringly absent in these people. While superficial charm and acts of apparent generosity are quite common, they mean little. These patterns of behavior dry up quickly when these people are denied, frustrated, or bored. They crave stimulation, and it does not matter whether the source of this stimulation is prosocial (sex with a loving and loved partner, watching a football game, achieving success at a job) or antisocial (plucking the wings off butterflies, forcing sex on an unwilling partner, playing mind games). The lust for stimulation is limited only by the possibility of getting in trouble—and in many cases, even the fear of punishment does not make a difference.

The second factor in psychopathy is a pattern of chronically unstable, antisocial, and deviant behavior: gang membership, jail time, coercive sexual behavior, serial domestic violence relationships. Not all of these patterns actually manifest in criminal behavior, because many psychopaths are too clever to get caught or to be exposed. Think of the sleaziest politician or corporate executive, or even the husband who systematically presents a positive front to the community but emotionally tortures and controls his wife or kids. Researchers do not technically label these guys as psychopaths, but they are at least psychopathically inclined.

Gottman, Jacobson, and colleagues (1995) conducted research on marital interactions that provides a fascinating glimpse into the psychophysiological world of the psychopathic male. In the University of Washington's "Love Lab," researchers hooked up married couples to measures of heart rate, respiration, and galvanic skin response (the way electrical resistance of the skin changes following stimulation) and observed the couples through one-way mirrors and hidden microphones. The couples were instructed to begin a conversation about a particularly volatile subject like parenting, financial management, sex, or in-laws. And the research team just watched what happened. Personally, I find it hard to believe that research subjects in this setting would let their hair down—I know I would be on my best behavior. But members of the research team have told me that it is surprisingly easy to launch the tense marital conversations and that the subjects are quick to ignore the cameras, electrodes, and microphones.

Once the arguments were underway, most subjects (both men and women) showed the expected increase in psychophysiological response: heart rate went up, breathing quickened, muscles tensed, galvanic skin response became more aroused.

However, among a certain minority of male subjects, the psychophysiological responses went the opposite of the expected direction. As the behaviorally observable tension and conflict increased, these subjects showed a *decrease* in all of these measures. The researchers found that approximately 20 percent of severe domestic violence offenders responded this way. These men actually became calmer, quieter, and more focused during these conflicts. Gottman and his colleagues called this subgroup "cobras" because of the cobra's capacity to become quite still and focused on its victim just prior to launching the fatal attack.

These are the men to be extremely wary of. These are the men who actually thrive on hostility, because they know that they are in their own element. Conflict is stimulating, and this is an arena in which they excel. While most of us get flustered and erratic in these situations, these men are at peak efficiency. And—most dangerously—they look composed and contained, cool as a cucumber. Although these researchers never specifically identified the cobras as psychopaths, the profiles are the same. Beware the charm and exterior calmness and control. These guys are scary.

Exercise: Recognizing Dangerous Men

Below is a list of behaviors and traits to be wary of in a relationship partner. Look at this list and, on a separate sheet of paper, note any of these traits you (or others) observe in your partner. The more items or even question marks you have, the more likely that you will not be seeing the good-man behavior that you are hoping for in your partner.

displays unpredictable moods

does something scary, then says he was just kidding

has a history of violence in relationships

blames you when things go wrong

gets bored and restless easily

plays mind games

abuses substances

has a pattern of affairs or deception

acts possessive and controlling (including engaging in stalking behaviors)

threatens to hurt you, himself, or others

has a history of criminal behavior

lies chronically

Substance Abuse

It's important to note that the good man within the alcoholic or drug abuser is not likely to emerge until he is no longer abusing these substances. This man might wake up the next morning lamenting *That's not the man I want to be!* But as long as he is likely to drink or use drugs again, he is likely to engage in the same bad behavior under the influence, and it is going to be very difficult for him to follow through on changing his behavior. A good man who is using may resemble a psychopath.

Distinguishing Behavior from Personality

There is never a legitimate excuse for relationship violence. But not all relationships are permanently destroyed by such violations of the relationship contract. In addition to the values and tolerance level of the victim of these behaviors, there is another key variable that often determines whether or not a relationship can (or should) weather such a damaging storm.

Contemporary research about male domestic violence (Holtzworth-Munroe et al. 2000) tells us that the same act of aggression (such as a slap or a shove or grabbing the phone out of someone's hands) can have very different contexts and can represent very different motivations. Men who commit acts of violence toward their partners fall into three clusters of personality patterns. *Generally violent aggressors* are antisocial power and control freaks who often have psychopathic personality traits. *Emotionally dysphoric/borderline* men are emotionally unstable and prone to intense bouts of depression, jealousy, insecurity, and anger. The third category is *family only*, men who respond to the frustrations of everyday relationship life by losing their temper in destructive and sometimes abusive ways: a misguided, cathartic response.

If you are in a relationship with a man who has become abusive, threatening, or violent, you would be well-advised to get out fast. But if you are wondering whether or not there is hope for resurrecting a relationship with a man who seems like a good man most of the time, you must recognize what kind of man he is. The men who compose the family-only category are much more likely to experience genuine remorse, to care about what other people think of them, to want to learn skills for managing their temper and their relationships more effectively, and to truly want to understand you and your feelings. Always proceed with caution in these situations, but there is hope.

Bringing Out the Best in Good Men

Gottman's studies of successful couples (1999) show that positive communication is based on old-fashioned good manners more than anything else. These couples talk respectfully to each other. They are affectionate. Even when they are trying to bring up something potentially provocative, they find a way to do so with some grace and gentleness. They believe in each other, and they can tolerate irritating behavior in each other because they fundamentally love and respect each other. And, particularly for men, they choose to accept influence from their partner rather than perceive the partner as being controlling. Each wants to make the other person happy, if possible, and if this can be done without unacceptable sacrifice.

Let's look at a less-than-positive dialogue that might take place when things are going wrong.

Sondra: (with a bit of an attitude) Instead of just watching TV, can you help me pick up some of this stuff around the house?

Sondra does not intend to sound very critical of her partner, but he could certainly interpret her request that way.

Phillip: (privately resentful) Okay.

Phillip says to himself, *I work fifty hours a week and she has all sorts of time to go to the gym, have lunch with her friends—and still the house is a fucking mess! But I won't get on her about that because she takes care of Kyle all day and I understand she is balancing her life the best way she can.* Phillip complies, but he cops an attitude. His body language communicates resentment; he is feeling defensive and attacked. He pouts for hours. Instead of trying to chalk this up to Sondra's bad mood, Phillip takes it very personally. Sondra is a powerful mirror for him, and he is unbearably sensitive to how she perceives him. Sondra finally asks him what's wrong, and he explodes.

Phillip: I never bug you about the house or how you spend your day! But frankly, the house is a fucking mess! I want you to tell me when you need something from me, but you didn't have to have such an attitude!

Sondra responds to his escalation without trying to soothe and clarify. She counterattacks.

Sondra: When can I ever tell you anything? Am I never supposed to ask you anything? Nothing is ever good enough for you! You always take everything so damn personally!

And they are off to the races, harassing each other through a cycle of attacks and counterattacks. Phillip has trapped himself with the toxic self-talk of *It's not fair! It's not fair for her to hassle me about cleaning up! And it's not fair for her to talk to me like that! If I did that, she'd be on me for a week!* When both parties feel treated unfairly, disrespected, or betrayed, we have a conflict that can cycle forever.

What do successful couples do? Successful couples reframe. They change the self-talk, and they behave as if they trust and respect each other. One partner will soften, and the cycle of defensiveness is interrupted.

It actually doesn't take that much for the conversation to go differently—if both partners feel fundamentally charitable toward each other and have a few basic skills in their hip pocket.

Softened Start-Ups

Throughout this book I have been trying to illuminate for men the process of mirroring that governs much of their emotional well-being in relationships. I have recommended that they use this knowledge to understand their own behavior better—and ultimately to place less pressure on the key people in their lives, like you, to bear the burden of this mirroring.

In particular, men have a crucial responsibility to keep their defensiveness in check. They can interrupt the whole nasty sequence of bad behavior by generating a more compassionate narrative to explain the situation, not taking the (perceived) criticism quite so personally, and recognizing their partner's independent center of initiative (that is, your partner should recognize that you have your own valid reasons for doing what you do and that these reasons may have nothing to do with him). I have repeatedly implored good men to keep in mind that it's not all about them.

That is the man's challenge, and the men who get better and better at this are relational heroes. That's what this book is mostly about.

But you can help, too. You can contribute to the health of your relationship, and to the likelihood of drawing out the good man rather than the good man behaving badly, by perfecting the art of what Gottman (1999) has described as the "softened start-up." Softened start-ups fall into the category of old-fashioned good manners. The harsh start-up sounds like *Why am I the only one who ever does any cleaning up around here?* It may seem true at the moment, but it is an exaggeration of the truth, it does not honor the positive qualities of your partner, and it is usually communicated in a hostile tone of voice. Some men, who are blessed with patience or tact or who avoid conflict or who are simply having a very good day, can accept the harsh start-up and deflect it. More typically, they respond defensively and prepare to retaliate. The harsh start-up communicates your distress but does nothing to contribute to the atmosphere of generosity and mutual respect that you ultimately want in your relationship.

The softened start-up sounds more like *I am really feeling overwhelmed with how messy the house is—can we spend some time tonight working on this together?* Isn't that how you would like to be addressed? Although many men need a shove sometimes, most men do best if they feel fundamentally respected and appreciated. Then they are much more likely to feel generous.

The softened start-up is concise. It may register a complaint, but without much blame or accusation. It comes with a softened tone of voice and nonconfrontational body language. It usually starts out with something positive, includes a message of *We're in this together* and *I care about you*, and is more descriptive than judgmental. To put it most simply, it is polite, and your partner may—on good days, at good moments—actually experience it as a gift.

Many women engage in the practice of mind reading. When applied sensitively and with insight, this is a precious skill of emotional intelligence.

She: I got the feeling that it was really upsetting for you when Justin acted so cold to you in front of his friends.

He: Yeah, he acts like such a smart-ass when his friends are around. It makes me feel like shit.

She: That's hard for me, too.

He: I guess that's life as a parent, huh?

This conversation can be extremely productive, because she has drawn him out with the feeling probe. Also note the use of twinship in this exchange. He has not felt threatened by her approach. Contrast it with this approach to mind reading:

She: What the hell's wrong with you? You always turn on Justin whenever your feelings get just a little bit hurt! You've been so sensitive ever since you got that bad performance review at work. It's not fair to take it out on him.

He: I don't always do that! You don't know what you're talking about! This has nothing to do with my job! Just shut the hell up!

Mind reading backfires when the other person feels attacked and responds defensively. You may be able to observe how your partner is feeling, but be careful about assuming that you know why. And, even if you are exactly on target, your start-up goes a long way toward determining the outcome.

Remember the power of your mirroring. You may resent it, and your power may be undesired and burdensome, but it is a reality. If you fundamentally love and respect the guy, you take the whole package. I give the same advice to men.

Keeping the Train on the Right Track

Successful couples have a remarkable capacity to generate soothing, nonthreatening responses that keep the relationship on the right track. It never fails to surprise me and delight me to hear some new way that a couple stays connected that I would never have dreamed of. The best techniques are invented by real couples, not self-help authors.

Gottman (1999) suggests that successful couples manage to express appreciation, soften complaints, respond nondefensively, back down, and use humor. Successful partners of all ages, at all stages of relationships, communicate that they like and accept each other. Through their words, body language, tone of voice, and subtle behaviors, they communicate a fundamental message of acceptance: *Please don't worry—I really like you and I really love you.* Once that basic message is established, they can afford to move on to the issue at hand: *I don't like this specific behavior and I'd like you to change it!* For the most part, the partner can handle this because it is not perceived as a fundamental threat. The limbic system is not activated; the fundamental sense of appreciation serves as an antithreat device.

Communication Strategies

Good communication strategies apply just as much to men as they do to women. There are hundreds of books and articles that teach sound principles for positive communication. Following are nine of my favorite strategies. In addition to applying some of these, try looking at what the two of you already do that works.

Joining Together

Marie was feeling frustrated and irritated that the house was messy and the hall closet was totally disorganized. Cory had said he would clean the closet. She started to snap at him; he got defensive. Then she stopped herself. She softened. She said to him, "I have an idea. Let's start working on this together. I'll go through these things, and you tell me what you think we can throw out." It worked, because they became engaged in the project together. And Marie resisted the temptation to turn this into an I'm-getting-screwed narrative; instead, it became a we're-in-this-together twinship story.

Ignoring the Negative

One day a client of mine called home to say hello to his wife. He began the conversation with the very confrontational gambit "Hi!" Her response, bitter and tense, was "Don't you 'Hi!' me!" Her tone was not the least bit humorous.

What were his options for reacting to this?

1. Tell himself that this is one more example of how emotionally unstable his wife is—and emotionally withdraw from her.

2. Tell himself that he doesn't need this crap, that she doesn't understand anything about what his needs are, that he was just trying to be friendly—and complain that she should be a hell of a lot nicer to him.

3. Take a deep breath and remember that this is not typical for her and that she must be having a very bad day—then ask

her what's wrong, as if she has said, *I'm in a terrible mood—just leave me alone!*

The correct answer is 3. When your partner's behavior is completely over the top, your best bet is to just let it go by and instead react compassionately to the feelings underneath the behavior.

Using Self-Deprecating Humor

Johnny and his wife, Takeesha, were driving with their kids to a family gathering at a place they had never been before. It was really important to Takeesha that they not be late, and she had told Johnny this several times. He was driving and she was trying to give him directions, but they were getting more and more lost. She wanted to stop for directions, but he thought he could figure it out himself, and they became later and later. They started snapping at each other. He blamed her for not giving him the right directions; she blamed him for not listening to what she told him and for being a bullheaded guy who refused to ask for help.

When they finally arrived at the party, late and apologetic, the kids were fighting and the tension between Johnny and Takeesha was thick. When someone asked them what happened, they glared at each other. Then Johnny got a sheepish grin on his face and stepped up to the plate. "It was just me having too much testosterone and not asking for directions. Next time I'll listen to my wife." Takeesha looked at him, and then they both laughed, and the day was rescued.

Using Physical Affection

Darren and his girlfriend, Michelle, were arguing about how he had treated her in front of her family. Darren was acting very defensive because he felt stupid and exposed. Although he did not say so, he felt worried that Michelle had really lost respect for him, and this was unbearable to him. Michelle sensed this. She reached over and stroked his arm, and his defensiveness melted. Her touch communicated that of course she still loved him, which allowed him to let his guard down and really listen to what she had to say.

I have heard some couples describe a similar sequence at the end of an evening of arguing. They go to bed with icy feelings in the room, backs turned to each other (despite what their mothers told them about never going to bed angry). Then one of them takes a chance, turns around, and snuggles up in the spoon position—no passionate sex required. The tension dissolves as the receiving partner gets the message *It's okay, I still love you, we're going to be all right.*

Ganging Up on Somebody Else

Michelle came home from work complaining about how much of a mess the house was. She was on a rampage, going off on both Darren and the kids for not cleaning up enough. Then she told Darren, "I can't believe I have to come home to this on top of getting hassled all day by my supervisor!" Darren seized the opportunity and said, "What color were her fingernails today? Are they still that purple color that goes with her hair?" Michelle laughed. They were launched on a trash-the-supervisor session, which helped break the mood and join them together. This is one situation in which gossip and cattiness come in very handy.

My kids like to pull this one on me. Both of them are in bad moods, and they start hassling each other. I have one goal and one goal only: for all hostile action to yield to an immediate cease-fire. So I launch into some psychobabble, trying to find out what started it all and reminding them that all it takes is for one of them to not react and this whole thing will die down. And then they turn on me!

She: Dad always has the lamest little words of wisdom! I can't believe he thinks that's going to work on us!

He: Can you believe any of his clients ever put up with that? It's so stupid!

The subject has changed. They join forces. I pretend to be miffed, but I am secretly grinning. I have thrown myself on the grenade and the battle has ended. Pretty soon they will forgive me for my "ineptitude" and we will get back to some sort of equilibrium.

Allowing Space

When your partner is upset and haranguing you, sometimes the most effective strategy is a very old-fashioned one: just back off and give him some space. Many couples have mastered the art of stepping aside and waiting for the storm to pass. This does not qualify as a problem-solving technique, nor does it qualify as a path toward exploring the deeper feelings and issues that triggered the conflict in the first place. But many successful couples do it, and you can't argue with success.

The younger couples whom I have worked with often balk at this strategy, objecting that this is just sweeping things under the rug. Couples who have been around awhile smile in recognition. They know that successful relationships value "selective blindness" to irritations as much as they address the occasional important issues that cannot be ignored.

Distraction

The same could be said for distraction. Perhaps you have learned how to steer the subject away from the incendiary topic; again, many successful couples do this all the time. They pick their battles, because when tempers are starting to flare, there is usually very little to be gained and much at risk.

Staying in the Present

Another essential strategy used by many successful couples is keeping the argument specific and in the present: *It really bothered me that you didn't call this afternoon to tell me you were going to be late* rather than *You never think about anyone but yourself.*

Forfeiting the Last Word

Successful couples also have a remarkable capacity to not insist on getting the last word. When both of you insist on the last word, the last words go on infinitely. When one person manages to let the last-word opportunity go by, the game is usually over. Just leaving well enough alone is a key strategy in successful relationship damage control and is evidence of emotional intelligence.

Staying Empowered

If you have come of age since about 1968 and are reading books like this, you have been implored to maintain a sense of empowerment in your relationships with men. What you may not recognize is that for many men, women's steps toward empowerment are an enormous relief. I have actually heard men say *I didn't know how out of control my emotional needs and my controlling behavior were getting! I really needed her to stand up to me and put a stop to it.* Of course, this is not always the initial response, which sometimes looks more like a child's tantrum when the TV is turned off or he is told he can't have any more candy. But while some men never recover from a situation in which their needs are not getting met the way they had come to expect, plenty of others are better men for it and in fact appreciate and respect the woman's efforts in being an agent of change and growth. After the initial protest and narcissistic injury, many men feel relieved, centered, and grateful.

When a man is reluctant to embrace the ways in which his partner is becoming more assertive, independent, and empowered, I point out to him the illusory benefits of being involved with an unempowered woman: Unempowered women don't just act passive and mousy. They act passive-aggressive. They get sarcastic. They withdraw emotionally. They are often sexually uninterested. A relationship with an unempowered woman doesn't offer the richness of a relationship between equals.

Realistic Expectations

Perhaps you have been disappointed and resentful in your relationships with men, and perhaps you have come to expect disappointment in the future. I would never suggest that you ignore your personal history or forsake your own legitimate relationship expectations, but it makes sense to keep these realistic. The goal here is to actually increase the likelihood of his becoming the man that you want him to be.

Friendship Demands

If you expect your partner to reciprocate every emotional offering and to talk to you as your best girlfriend would, you may be setting yourself up for a major disappointment. You may have a set of expectations that your husband or boyfriend will never be able to meet. If your personal narrative says that these criteria are deal breakers, then the deal is likely to unravel.

Modern relationships are often burdened with expectations that far surpass those of previous generations. Many of us now expect our long-term relationships to provide compatibility, mutual respect, sexual passion, loyalty, deep emotional connection, mutual spiritual growth, and fun. We want to be best friends, best lovers, best parent teams.

You ask, *And there is something wrong with that?*

Of course not. These are terrific features of a relationship, and there are probably some partnerships that have it all or pretty damn close. But most relationships do not. These relationships live in the land called Good Enough. If what you get from your partner does not feel good enough, then you have three choices. Change the relationship. Change your expectations. Or get out, if you have thoroughly exhausted both of the first two without good enough success.

A woman's expectation that her partner will be her best friend often adds to the difficulty of developing the good enough relationship. I recently worked with a couple who represented one of the most dominant patterns of the male-female dynamics in our culture. Stacy was emotional, excitable, passionate, energetic. Gary was rational, logical, patient, reserved. With two young kids at home and an excellent relationship, Stacy came very close to pursuing an affair with a married man. When she confessed the details of what almost happened to Gary, she tried to explain what she felt was missing in their marriage. She leaned forward, looked him straight in the eye, and said, "I want you to tell me the essence of your soul!" Gary mumbled something about how he would try his best, but he told me later that he didn't have a clue what she was talking about.

In this marriage, the mutual project certainly required Gary to come out emotionally and offer more. But it also required Stacy to relax her expectations. She had grown up believing that real love and connection required drama, and when she did not get enough of that from Gary, she felt lost and unloved. But she found that she could deeply appreciate all that Gary did have to offer her (and there was plenty of that), mourn some of what she wished she had from him but didn't, and move on. She could get most of her needs for deeper conversations met elsewhere—as long as the "elsewheres" did not have an erotic component.

Appreciating Changes

For many women, a standard frustration in relationships is that he is not "something" enough. He doesn't show his feelings enough. He acts defensive whenever you try to give him any feedback. He doesn't express enough affection or appreciation. He acts bored when you try to talk about what's going on in your life. He heads off to the TV or his computer as soon as he gets home and doesn't spend enough quality time with the kids. He doesn't call you to let you know when he is going to be late.

So you put some heat on and insist that he offer more of the interpersonal qualities that you are looking for. Maybe you do this in some form of couples counseling or just in the everyday encounters at home. Maybe you insist that he read this book.

Then he starts to do some of the things you have asked for. This should be a cause for celebration and reward. But it is at this point in the sequence that many women find something wrong with the how and why of the changes the man is trying to make.

- *Yes, you've been showing more affection and appreciation lately, but it's just because the counselor told you to. You don't really mean it.*

- *I know you've been giving the kids baths more often, but you're not doing it right!*

- *You've been ignoring my feelings for so long that there's no way you can make up for it now.*

- *Of course you're doing it now, but that's only because I'm watching you so carefully. As soon as I take the pressure off, this will all go back to the way it used to be.*

If you respond to your partner's efforts like this, it is extremely unlikely that you will get what you want. It may be a challenge to keep encouraging your partner if his behavior still falls way short of what you are looking for, but the laws of behavioral psychology demand that you reward successive approximations. Although it is not your job to make sure your partner's ego is left unbruised, don't forget how much your opinion means to him. Most men turn to the women in their lives and see reflected back an image of themselves. This reflection has a profound impact on a man's self-image and the behavior that follows. If you forget how sensitive your partner is to messages that he is falling short, you run the risk of undermining the further emergence of the good man you love.

Reframing Masculinity and Guy Talk

Ultimately, it is not the responsibility of any woman to find exactly the right words to say to her boyfriend or husband so that he will not feel hurt, offended, or criticized. But, just to be practical, it is not exactly smart to ignore those concerns either. One thing that seems to set off many men is when their partner expects them to think, feel, express themselves, and behave like women do. This gets back to the idea of guy talk from the previous chapter. It is usually not very effective to tell a man that you need him to be more vulnerable or to process more. I am not saying that it never works; there are certainly many men who are very responsive to this request, stated in this language. The majority of men, however, respond better to requests or critiques that call upon their finest masculine qualities.

Exercise: Bringing Out the Best

Here are some examples of things a woman could say that would increase or decrease the likelihood of bringing out the best in her partner. The situations, feelings, and needs are all the same; the presentation is different. Go through these parallel lists and see which items sound familiar to you. On a separate sheet of paper, pick out one example of your communication to your partner each day for the next week. Put it in the proper category (*Bringing Out the Best* or *Shaming and Distancing*) and write down a parallel statement that would fall in the other category.

Bringing Out the Best

1. The kids really look up to you so much, and they need to see a man who is big enough to apologize! I know you can do this for them!

2. It would really mean a lot to me if you could fix some of these things.

3. It bothers me when you make fun of me in front of other people. I don't think you realize how disrespectful it sounds.

4. I really like it when you stick up for our son at those teacher conferences. Can you try to do that even more?

5. You deserve some time doing absolutely nothing over the weekend—but I need some more help from you, too. And I think our kids will pick up the cue if they see you helping out more.

6. I don't know if you realized this, but the way you talked to Mark was really harsh. It almost sounded like your father, and I know you don't want to sound like him!

7. I think it would be great if you spent more time getting together with some of your friends.

Shaming and Distancing

1. What kind of a loser are you?

2. Why aren't you the type of man who knows how to do things around the house?

3. What kind of a man would act like that?

4. My father would never have let that happen! Why can't you be more like him?

5. You just sit around all day in that big chair, watching football and NASCAR!

6. You're acting just like your father!

7. What's wrong with you? It's like I'm the only person you ever talk to anymore!

Sarcasm, especially when it addresses areas that a man will identify as assaults on his masculinity, goes nowhere fast. You may feel very justified, but you need to think of the big picture: *What can I do to help him be a better man?* Does it help you when he is sarcastic or puts you down, or do you just become more shamed, resentful, and defensive?

This does not mean that you are supposed to be unassertive or codependent. Most men need to be confronted about their relationship mistakes. But there are ways to send the message so it's much more likely to be received—and others that are almost sure to elicit defensive reactions. It is really not in your best interest to be in a relationship with a man who consistently feels bad about himself, especially if he perceives you as the broken mirror in his life. You may not ultimately be in control of his feelings about himself and his perception of you, but given what's at stake in making a relationship work, it is worth doing what you can to avoid being a mirror that always reflects a negative image.

Raising Good Boys, Raising Good Men

Perhaps you are raising boys or will raise boys in the future. Or perhaps you have grown sons, and you are trying to understand more about their experiences of growing up male and your own experiences in trying to reach them.

William Pollack's 1998 research on boys' psychological development suggests that the "mask of masculinity" emerges from two central parenting practices that pervade the family environment, consciously or unconsciously, of most of the homes in which boys are raised.

Using Shame to "Toughen Up" Boys

The first factor is the use of shame in the toughening-up process that boys undergo as they traverse the developmental stages of growing up male. Throughout this book I have described example after example of men who withhold from their sons or directly inflict emotional or physical abuse in the name of making a man out of him. Football coaches humiliate teenagers with the justification *He's got to learn how to take it.* Boys hear, in countless ways, the message that it is not acceptable for them to show weakness or worry, or even to care too much.

Boys are not allowed to step outside the box of what Pollack refers to as the "Boy Code." This code, written nowhere but understood everywhere, insists that boys be stoic, stable, independent. That they be bold, adventurous, and risk-taking. That they achieve status, dominance, and power. That they act like everything is under control. And, perhaps most crippling, that they do not reveal feelings or express themselves in such a way as to appear "feminine." Violations of any of the central precepts of the Boy Code often lead to ridicule and the experience of shame. And once shamed, boys are extremely unlikely to venture into the dangerous territory again. Most boys will incorporate these values not only as social and psychological survival mechanisms, but as truths about the way the world is and should be for other men and for their own sons a generation later.

My son is, at the time of this writing, twelve years old. One of the true joys in my life is watching the delight he experiences with his boy friends. He loves them. He lights up when he sees them and even when he's talking about them. He will come home and relate a goofy story or joke from one of his pals and he will get a dreamy look in his eyes, like this friend is just the coolest guy in the whole world. I watch and listen with envy, knowing how hard it is for boys and men to express so much delight with anyone except a lover. I want to enjoy it while it lasts—and maybe use it as a model for my own relationships—because before I know it, the way he relates now will seem shameful to him and (in the worst violation of the Boy Code) "gay."

Of course girls are sensitive to shame, but boys are mortified by it. And boys and men will do whatever it takes to avoid, escape, deny, and mask shame. This is perhaps the most central trigger for good men behaving badly, leading to impulsive actions, escapist behavior, aggression, projection of blame, emotional withdrawal, relationship avoidance, desperate acts of bravado—anything to turn off the damn spigot of shame.

Weaning Boys from Mother-Love

Fueled by generations of worry and the cautions of many practitioners in the field of family development, mothers have been afraid of keeping their sons too close to them. We encourage mothers to separate from their sons for fear of "sissifying" the growing boy. This is the second factor that contributes to Pollack's "mask of masculinity."

Terrence Real (1997) tells the story of a family he was seeing in treatment. The seven-year-old son was resting his head in his mother's lap—and the boy's father took the boy's hand and led him away. At first, the mother was confused by this, and then she asked her husband what he was doing. He informed her that the boy was now too old and that she must learn to let go of him. Agitated, this adult man leaned over into his wife's face and commanded her not to smother the boy.

This is a misguided prohibition. Of course there is potential damage in being an overbearing, micromanaging, controlling, emotionally dependent mother to a son. And certainly it is inappropriate (and potentially the worst thing in the entire world that could happen to a boy) for his mother to come up to him on the playground and give him a big kiss. But the same is true for being an overbearing or overinvolved father to a son. And the solution lies not in the opposite.

Your love, your mother-love, is vital to your son's emotional well-being. A mother's love can help a boy become more self-reliant and more adventurous. This connection provides an ongoing, life-long selfobject relationship that transcends your separation or even your death.

In Pat Conroy's novel *The Great Santini,* Ben Meecham turns eighteen in a household with a dynamic yet tyrannical father who can be described only as an emotional cripple. On the occasion of this special birthday, Ben's mother sends Ben a letter that captures the spirit of the mother-love that this tenderhearted man-in-progress needs as a rudder in a tough male world. It is a letter about learning lessons of love. The loving role that his mother plays in Ben's life literally saves him from being drawn into his father's cold world of bastardized masculinity. Ben's father, who desperately needs mirrors to reflect back to him a confirmation of his warped masculinity, has spent Ben's lifetime trying to lure him into becoming this mirror image of himself.

Ben's mother writes,

> My dear son, my dear Ben. My dear friend who becomes a man today. I wanted to write you a letter about being a man and what that means in the fullest sense. I wanted to tell you that gentleness is the quality I most admire in men. But then I remembered how gentle you were. So I decided to write something else.... I have had my regrets and many sadnesses, but I will never regret the night you were born. I thought I knew about love, and the boundaries of love, until I raised you these past eighteen years. I knew nothing about love. This has been your gift to me. Happy Birthday. Mama. (1976, 203)

Your son needs to hear the same kind of words from you. It will not "sissify" him to be praised for gentleness and to learn more about love.

Childhood and Emotional Intelligence

Recent research on attachment theory and interactions between mothers and babies now points to a pervasive pattern of mothers responding to their sons differently than to their daughters—unconsciously and even in the earliest days of the baby's life.

By age four to six, boys mask more of their emotional expression than girls do. Buck's research (1977) showed that mothers of boys that age were significantly less able to identify their sons' emotions than their daughters' emotions at the same age. The boys had found a way to hide their emotions. And if your own mother can't even read your emotional state, something is not right.

Some of this is attributable to the pattern of mothers working harder to not upset their sons' emotions (Malatesta et al. 1989). These same mothers apparently felt more confident about their daughters' emotional resiliency. Studies also show that both parents tend to talk more about emotions with their daughters than with their sons. Fivush (1989) found that mothers were much more likely to speak about the experience of emotions with girls, in contrast to the causes and consequences of emotions with their boys. This is not a conscious process, but its unconsciousness and its subtlety do not make it any less significant in shaping boys.

In chapter 5 I described the process in which parent and child join forces in helping the infant, child, or teen deal with distressing emotions. The parent soothes the infant, reassures the child, communicates respect for the self-doubting teen. When this happens regularly (not necessarily every time, of course) throughout the child's development, he learns emotional intelligence and emotional competence. If you fear the distress of the boy you are raising, or if you even accidentally or unconsciously contribute to limiting his development of emotional vocabulary, you are not collaborating. When you help him stay present with distressing emotions and lend your wisdom, love, and life experience to help him sort them out, you are offering a wonderful gift.

Practical Suggestions for Raising Good Boys, Good Men

Most of these tips—many of which are inspired by Pollack's interventions (1998) for counteracting the effects of the Boy Code—apply to daughters as much as to sons, and many of these suggestions are certainly useful to fathers as well as to mothers. Others are specific to mothers staying connected with and influencing their sons, respecting the central conflicts of growing up male.

Making Conversation

Take advantage of any opportunity to listen to your son, even if it is inconvenient. When your boy seeks reconnection, try your best to be there for him. Maybe he wants you to hang out with him as he's falling asleep, when his defenses are down. Even if you're dead tired or resentful that he has waited so long, try to find a way to seize this golden opportunity anyway.

When your son is hurting, don't hesitate to ask him whether he'd like to talk, but avoid shaming your boy if he refuses to talk with you. If he blows you off, no matter how hurt or frustrated you feel, do not say, *You're never going to get any help from me if you won't even tell me what's going on!* Boys often are not ready to talk right away or when you think they should. It may come later, and it is your job to pay attention to the signals and windows of opportunity.

Take a chance. When in doubt about what is going on with your son, guess: *I'm not sure about this, but I know your coach has really been on your case lately—are you feeling down because of that?* There are three possible outcomes, and two of them are good. The negative outcome is that your son will blow up at you, tell you you're totally clueless, and banish you from his room. But sometimes you will guess right, and this will stimulate the conversation. And, at other times, you will guess wrong—and in his disgust with how clueless you are, he will blurt out the real reason for his distress.

Be proactive about bringing up complicated subjects like sex, drugs, and teen suicide. He will eventually take his cue from you.

You may be surprised how effective the fifteen-minute-per-day technique is. Each day, set aside a fifteen-minute period in which you completely devote yourself to your son. Let him know when it is starting. You are not on the phone, you are not cleaning up, you do not have one eye on the computer or the TV. Even if no earth-shattering conversational breakthrough happens, you are still there, and he knows it. When fire lookouts in national forests stand guard in their towers, most of the time nothing happens. But they are ready for the very important moments when something does happen. Don't demand too much, don't withdraw. Just be waiting in the wings.

Boys are usually most comfortable with triangle conversations, with people making up two points of the triangle and an activity making up the third: watching TV together, listening to music together, taking driving trips so you're forced to talk and you can both stare at the road.

Get to know your son's friends. If nothing else, it will give you more to talk about with your son. Turn your house into the place where kids want to hang out.

Accepting and Encouraging Feelings

When your son does open up to you, listen empathically. Don't lecture or judge, just relate. Find a way to talk to your son that does not shame him. When a boy expresses vulnerable feelings, avoid teasing or taunting him. If he starts to tear up watching a sappy movie, say nothing about this, or maybe just touch him lightly on his shoulder—quietly, discreetly. If he expresses an opinion about something he has been thinking about, do whatever it takes to take it seriously, no matter how ridiculous you find it to be. More than anything else, you want to establish his home life as a sanctuary: a shame-free zone.

It is so tempting to find it "cute" when a boy first shows an interest in the opposite sex, and to engage in some playful teasing. An older brother or sister usually drools over the opportunity to make fun of the younger brother who shows this first tender interest. I remember one time when I was out in a shopping mall with my mother. I must have been about twelve or thirteen, and I could not take my eyes off the parade of cute girls that God had arranged to stimulate me. My mother noticed me looking at a girl we passed by, and she playfully said, "I saw you looking over there!" She was just playing with me, maybe even indirectly trying to open a conversation about the complexities of puberty. But I was horrified. I waited not even a second before I spat out, "That doesn't mean I like what I see!" I felt ashamed that my mother had seen my feelings and was teasing me about them. I had violated one of the laws of Boy Code: *Do not let anyone know what you are feeling inside.*

Help your son find a way of identifying and expressing feelings to defy normative male alexithymia. When he tells you about getting hassled by a teacher, find labels for his feelings besides just *pissed.* Try *embarrassed, misunderstood, disrespected.* However, when you are naming feelings, keep in mind how susceptible boys are to shame. Boys have a hard time accepting certain words. I have learned to stay away from words like *afraid* and *threatened* and *intimidated,* because I usually get a response like *Afraid? No way! What are you talking about?* It doesn't matter if you're right. *Worried* or *frustrated* are a little more palatable.

Tell him about your own experiences. Your son needs to experience twinship about feeling insecure, foolish, and incompetent. He will observe that you seem to have survived, and come to understand that these experiences do not last forever.

Messages about Being Male

Pollack (1998) suggests talking openly about the Boy Code. This will give your son a wider perspective on the complicated experience of being male. This will also give him a head start in thinking critically about the Boy Code.

In your adult relationships, look for men who are not just caricatures of masculinity. Choose men who treat you well and who share the cooking and cleaning. Don't let your partner refer to parenting as "helping out with the kids" or "babysitting." Do whatever you can to discourage the use of gender privilege (by either gender) in your relationships with men: *I'm the man, and I will decide how we spend our money* or *I'm the woman, and you should stop interfering with how I want to raise these kids.* In chapter 2, I told the story about the boy who heard his mother challenge her brother about his treatment of his wife. The boy, now a man, realized that "it is women who teach us to be men. They play a defining role in our development as men." Believe it.

This may violate your sense of privacy, but your son will listen closely if you tell him about the men you love and why you love them. The letter from Ben Meecham's mother in *The Great Santini*, celebrating gentleness in men, is a prime example. Introduce the concept of relational heroism to your son, so that he expands his concept of heroic male behavior to include acts of integrity, taking personal responsibility for his emotional life, treating his loved ones with respect, and offering others glimpses into his own emotional life even when he doesn't feel like it.

Love and Affection

Finally, don't hold back your love and affection—just be sensitive about kissing your son in front of his friends. Provide frequent affirmations. Let your son know all you appreciate about him. Not just the obvious achievements, but also the personality traits: *I love seeing you play with Maya—your tenderness for animals is such a wonderful thing!* This reminds me of a story I once heard from the mother of a son. She had learned, from reading all the best books, that the preferred way to help build true self-esteem in kids was to say, *Wow, you should feel really proud of yourself!* instead of *I feel so proud of you!* This is sound practice. Except that one day, when her son was fourteen, she said this to him and he looked at her, vulnerable and stricken, and said, "How come you never tell me that you're proud of me?" She explained her philosophy, reassured him of her pride in him—and was reminded that no advice about raising kids is always right.

No advice about raising kids—and no advice about intimate relationships—is always right. But even your imperfect role in nurturing emotional intelligence in your son's life is one of the greatest gifts you can offer him.

References

Annie Hall. 1977. Santa Monica, Calif.: MGM.

Banks, R. 1989. *Affliction*. New York: Harper & Row.

————. 1994. *Continental Drift*. New York: Harper & Row.

Barry, D. 1995. *Dave Barry's Complete Guide to Guys*. New York: Ballantine Books.

Baumeister, R. 1991. *Escaping the Self*. New York: Basic Books.

Becker, E. 1973. *The Denial of Death*. Glencoe, Ill.: Free Press.

Brooks, G. 1998. Group therapy for traditional men. In *New Psychotherapy for Men*, edited by W. Pollack and R. Levant. New York: John Wiley & Sons.

Buck, R. 1977. Non-verbal communication of affect in preschool children: Relationships with personality and skin conductance. *Journal of Personality and Social Psychology* 35(4):225–36.

Carnal Knowledge. 1971. Santa Monica, Calif.: MGM.

Carpenter, S., and A. Halberstadt. 2000. Mothers' reports of events causing anger differ across family relationships. *Social Development* 9:458–77.

Conroy, P. 1976. *The Great Santini*. New York: Bantam Books.

Dunn, J., L. Breatherton, and P. Munn. 1987. Conversations about feeling states between mothers and their children. *Developmental Psychology* 23:132–39.

Dutton, D. 1995. *The Batterer: A Psychological Profile*. New York: Basic Books.

————. 1998. *The Abusive Personality: Violence and Control in Intimate Relationships*. New York: Guilford Press.

Engel, L., and T. Ferguson. 1990. *Imaginary Crimes*. New York: Houghton Mifflin.

Erickson, E. 1950. *Childhood and Society*. New York: W. W. Norton.

Fivush, R. 1989. Exploring sex differences in the emotional content of mother-child talk about the past. *Sex Roles* 20:675–91.

Fogel, B., and A. Stone. 1992. Practical pathophysiology in neuropsychiatry: A clinical approach to depression and impulsive behavior in neurological patients. In *The American Psychiatric Textbook of Neuropsychiatry*, edited by S. C. Yudofsky and R. E. Hales. Washington, D.C.: American Psychiatric Press.

Freiberg, P., and S. Sleek. 1999. New techniques help men uncover their hidden emotions. *American Psychological Association Monitor* 30(3). www.apa.org/monitor/mar99/men.html.

Gleason, J., and E. Grief. 1983. Men's speech to young children. In *Language, Gender and Society*, edited by B. Thorne, C. Kramare, and N. Henley. London: Newbury House.

Goleman, D. 1995. *Emotional Intelligence*. New York: Bantam Books.

Good Will Hunting. 1997. Burbank, Calif.: Miramax.

Gottman, J. 1994. *Why Marriages Succeed and Fail*. New York: Simon & Schuster.

————. 1999. *The Marriage Clinic*. New York: W. W. Norton.

Gottman, J., J. Jacobson, R. Rushe, J. Shortt, J. Babcock, J. La Taillade, and J. Waltz. 1995. The relationship between heart rate activity, emotionally aggressive behavior, and general violence in batterers. *Journal of Family Psychology* 9:227–48.

Greene, R. 1998. *The Explosive Child: A New Approach for Understanding and Parenting Easily Frustrated, "Chronically Inflexible" Children*. New York: HarperCollins.

Hajcak, F., and P. Garwood. 1995. *Hidden Bedroom Partners*. Northvale, N.J.: Jason Aronson, Inc.

Hare, R. 1993. *Without Conscience*. New York: Pocket Books.

Hesley, J., and J. Hesley. 2001. *Rent Two Films and Let's Talk in the Morning: Using Popular Movies in Psychotherapy.* 2nd ed. New York: John Wiley & Sons.

Holtzworth-Munroe, A., and G. Hutchinson. 1993. Attributing negative intent to wife behavior: The attributions of maritally violent versus nonviolent men. *Journal of Abnormal Psychology* 102(2): 206–11.

Holtzworth-Munroe, A., J. Meehan, K. Herron, U. Rehman, and G. Stuart. 2000. Testing the Holtzworth-Munroe and Stuart (1994) Batterer Typology. *Journal of Consulting and Clinical Psychology* 68(6):1000–1019.

Hornby, N. 1995. *High Fidelity.* New York: Riverhead Books.

Jung, C. 1977. *C. G. Jung Speaking,* edited by W. McGuire and R. F. C. Hull. Princeton, N.J.: Princeton University Press.

Lamb, W. 1998. *I Know This Much Is True.* New York: Regan Books.

Larson, J. 1996. *Rent.* Glendale, Calif.: Dreamworks.

Leonard, K. 1989. The impact of explicit aggressive and explicit non-aggressive cues on aggression in intoxicated and sober males. *Personality and Social Psychology Bulletin* 15:390–400.

Levant, R. 1998. Desperately seeking language: Understanding, assessing, and treating normative male alexithymia. In *New Psychotherapy for Men,* edited by W. Pollack and R. Levant. New York: John Wiley & Sons.

Levinson, D. 1978. *The Seasons of a Man's Life.* New York: Ballantine Books.

Life as a House. 2001. Los Angeles, Calif.: New Line Home Video.

Linehan, M. 1993. *Skills Training Manual for Treating Borderline Personality Disorder.* New York: Guilford Press.

Malatesta, C., C. Culver, J. Tesman, and B. Shephard. 1989. The development of emotion expression during the first two years of life. *Monographs of the Society for Research in Child Development* 50(1 & 2): Serial No. 219.

Marlatt, G., and J. Gordon. 1985. *Relapse Prevention.* New York: Guilford Press.

Masters, W., and V. Johnson. 1970. *Human Sexual Inadequacy.* Boston: Little, Brown.

Meichenbaum, D. 2001. *Treatment of Individuals with Anger-Control Problems and Aggressive Behaviors: A Clinical Handbook.* Clearwater, Fla.: Institute Press.

Mirande, A. 2003. Presentation at *Domestic Violence 2000,* San Diego, Calif.

MVP Project. 1994. *The MVP Playbook.* Boston: Northeastern University's Center for the Study of Sport in Society.

My Big Fat Greek Wedding. 2002. Jericho, N.Y.: IFC Films.

Nemiroff, R., and C. Colarusso. 1990. *New Dimensions in Adult Development.* New York: Basic Books.

On the Waterfront. 1954. Burbank, Calif.: Columbia Tri-Star.

Ordinary People. 1980. Hollywood, Calif.: Paramount Studios.

Parenthood. 1990. Universal City, Calif.: MCA.

Pleck, J. 1980. Men's power with women, other men and society. In *The American Man,* edited by E. Pleck and J. Pleck. Englewood Cliffs, N.J.: Prentice-Hall.

Pollack, W. 1995. Treating the fallen hero: Empathic psychoanalytic psychotherapy designed for men. Paper presented at the annual convention of the American Psychological Association, Toronto, Canada.

———. 1998. *Real Boys.* New York: Henry Holt & Co.

Real, T. 1997. *I Don't Want to Talk About It: Overcoming the Secret Legacy of Male Depression.* New York: Fireside.

Rosenbaum, A., R. Geffner, and S. Benjamin. 1997. A biopsychosocial model for understanding relationship aggression. *Journal of Aggression, Maltreatment & Trauma* (1)1:57–79.

Sanford, J. 1980. *The Invisible Partners.* New York: Paulist Press.

Sanford, J., and G. Lough. 1988. *What Men Are Like.* New York: Paulist Press.

Sapolsky, B., S. Stocking, and D. Zillman. 1977. Immediate vs. delayed retaliation in male and female adults. *Psychological Reports* 40:197–98.

Saturday Night Fever. 1977. Hollywood, Calif.: Paramount.

Shapiro, S. 1995. *Talking with Patients: A Self Psychological View.* New York: Jason Aronson.

Siegel, D. 2002. *The Developing Mind: How Relationships and the Brain Interact to Shape Who We Are.* New York: Guilford Press.

Sifneos, P. 1991. Affect, emotional conflict, and deficit: An overview. *Psychotherapy and Psychosomatics* 56:116–22.

Silverman, L., F. Lachman, and R. Milich. 1982. *The Search for Oneness.* New York: International Universities Press.

Smith, S. 1977. The golden fantasy: A regressive reaction to separation anxiety. *International Journal of Psychoanalysis* 58(3):311–24.

The Sopranos. 2000. Episode 20, "D-Girl," aired February 27. HBO. Written by Todd A. Kessler.

Stosny, S. 2001. The compassion workshop for partner and child abusers. In *Batterer Intervention Programs: A Handbook for Clinicians, Practitioners, and Advocates,* edited by E. Aldarondo and F. Mederos. Kingston, N.J.: Civic Research Institute.

Tice, D., and R. Baumeister. 1993. Controlling anger: Self-induced emotion change. In *Handbook of Mental Control,* edited by D. Wegner and J. Pennebaker. Englewood Cliffs, N.J.: Prentice Hall.

Van der Kolk, B. 1987. *Psychological Trauma.* Washington, D.C.: American Psychiatric Press.

Weiss, J., and H. Sampson. 1986. *The Psychoanalytic Process.* New York: Guilford Press.

Welland, C. 1999. A qualitative analysis of cultural treatment components for mexican male perpetrators of partner abuse. Doctoral dissertation, California School of Professional Psychology, San Diego.

Wenzlaff, R. 1993. The mental control of depression. In *Handbook of Mental Control,* edited by D. Wegner and J. Pennebaker. Englewood Cliffs, N.J.: Prentice Hall.

White, M., and M. Weiner. 1986. *The Theory and Practice of Self Psychology.* New York: Brunner Mazel.

Zillman, D. 1979. *Hostility and Aggression.* Hillsdale, N.J.: Erlbaum.

———. 1993. Mental control of angry aggression. In *Handbook of Mental Control,* edited by D. Wegner and J. Pennebaker. Englewood Cliffs, N.J.: Prentice Hall.

David Wexler, Ph.D., is the founder and executive director of the Relationship Training Institute in San Diego, an organization designed to help relationships in conflict. You may contact him and find out more about him and his work at www.RTIprojects.com.

The California Psychological Association has honored Dr. Wexler with the Distinguished Contribution to Psychology award. He is also the author of several books, including Domestic Violence 2000 and The Adolescent Self.

Dr. Wexler lives in San Diego with his wife and two teenage children.

Some Other
New Harbinger Titles

The Power of Two Workbook, Item 3341 $19.95

Adult Children of Divorce, Item 3368 $14.95

Fifty Great Tips, Tricks, and Techniques to Connect with Your Teen, Item 3597 $10.95

Helping Your Child with OCD, Item 3325 $19.95

Helping Your Depressed Child, Item 3228 $14.95

The Couples's Guide to Love and Money, Item 3112 $18.95

50 Wonderful Ways to be a Single-Parent Family, Item 3082 $12.95

Caring for Your Grieving Child, Item 3066 $14.95

Helping Your Child Overcome an Eating Disorder, Item 3104 $16.95

Helping Your Angry Child, Item 3120 $17.95

The Stepparent's Survival Guide, Item 3058 $17.95

Drugs and Your Kid, Item 3015 $15.95

The Daughter-In-Law's Survival Guide, Item 2817 $12.95

Whose Life Is It Anyway?, Item 2892 $14.95

It Happened to Me, Item 2795 $17.95

Act it Out, Item 2906 $19.95

Parenting Your Older Adopted Child, Item 2841 $16.95

Boy Talk, Item 271X $14.95

Talking to Alzheimer's, Item 2701 $12.95

Helping a Child with Nonverbal Learning Disorder or Asperger's Syndrome, Item 2779 $14.95

The 50 Best Ways to Simplify Your Life, Item 2558 $11.95

When Anger Hurts Your Relationship, Item 2604 $13.95

Call **toll free, 1-800-748-6273,** or log on to our online bookstore at **www.newharbinger.com** to order. Have your Visa or Mastercard number ready. Or send a check for the titles you want to New Harbinger Publications, Inc., 5674 Shattuck Ave., Oakland, CA 94609. Include $4.50 for the first book and 75¢ for each additional book, to cover shipping and handling. (California residents please include appropriate sales tax.) Allow two to five weeks for delivery.

Prices subject to change without notice.